# Using
# Simply
# Accounting
## 2007

PRO & BASIC VERSIONS
BY SAGE

# M. Purbhoo

CUSTOM EDITION FOR
UNIVERSITY OF WINDSOR

Taken from:

*Using Simply Accounting® 2007 by Sage: Pro and Basic Versions*
by M. Purbhoo

D1310401

Cover Images: Courtesy of DigitalVision/Getty Images and Brand X Pictures.

Taken from:

*Using Simply Accounting® 2007 by Sage: Pro and Basic Versions*
by M. Purbhoo
Copyright © 2008 by Pearson Education Canada, Inc.
Published by Addison Wesley
Toronto, Ontario

This special edition published in cooperation with Pearson Custom Publishing.

Simply Accounting® is a registered trademark of Sage Accpac International, Inc. Screen shots from the Simply Accounting 2007 software are reprinted with the permission of Sage Accpac International, Inc.

Printed in Canada

10  9  8  7  6  5  4  3  2  1

ISBN 0-536-64763-1

2007280107

ED

Please visit our web site at *www.pearsoncustom.com*

PEARSON CUSTOM PUBLISHING
501 Boylston Street, Suite 900, Boston, MA 02116
A Pearson Education Company

# CONTENTS

**1  Getting Started:**
   **Introduction to Simply Accounting**  *2*
Objectives  *2*
Getting Started  *2*
   Data Files and Abbreviations  *2*
   The Simply Accounting Program  *4*
      Simply Accounting Program
         Components  *4*
   Backing Up Your Data Files  *4*
      Installing Your Data Files  *5*
      Copying Data Files on the Hard Disk  *6*
      Working with Other File Locations  *7*
      Removing Read-Only Attributes  *7*
   Starting Simply Accounting and Accessing
         Data Files  *8*
      Opening a Data File  *9*
      Simply Accounting Home Window  *11*
      Simply Accounting on the Windows
         Desktop  *12*
      Simply Accounting Module Window  *12*
   Simply Accounting Help Features  *13*
   Date Formats and Settings  *18*
   Saving and Backing Up Your Work  *20*
   Finishing a Session  *21*
   Creating New Folders  *21*

**16 Flabuless Fitness:**
   **Payroll & Inventory Setup**  *23*
Objectives  *23*
Introduction  *23*
Company Information  *24*
Instructions for Setup  *40*
Keystrokes for Setup  *41*
   Creating Company Files  *41*
   Preparing the System  *42*
      Changing the User Preference
         Settings  *42*
      Changing Company Defaults  *43*
   Preparing the General Ledger  *45*
      Creating New Accounts  *45*
      Defining Account Classes  *47*
   Entering Company Default Settings  *48*
      Setting Up Credit Cards  *48*
      Setting Up Sales Taxes  *48*
      Adding a Foreign Currency  *51*
      Updating Bank Account Settings  *53*
   Entering Ledger Default Settings  *55*
      General Ledger Settings  *55*

      Payables Ledger Settings  *56*
      Receivables Ledger Settings  *58*
      Payroll Ledger Settings  *60*
      Inventory & Services Ledger Settings  *66*
      Entering Users and Security
         Passwords  *68*
   Preparing the Subsidiary Ledgers  *68*
      Preparing the Payables Ledger  *68*
      Preparing the Receivables Ledger  *72*
      Preparing the Payroll Ledger  *74*
      Entering Job Categories  *82*
      Setting Up Payroll Remittances  *82*
      Preparing the Inventory Ledger  *83*
   Finishing the History  *89*
      Making a Backup of the Company
         Files  *90*
      Changing the History Status of Ledgers
         to Finished  *90*
   Exporting Reports  *91*
      Using Simply Files and Reports with
         Other Software  *92*
   Source Document Instructions  *93*
   Source Documents  *94*

**17 Stratford Country Inn:**
   **Comprehensive Practice**  *113*
Objectives  *113*
Company Information  *113*
Instructions  *119*
Source Documents  *119*

**Appendices**

**Appendix A:**  Installing Simply Accounting  *A-2*
**Appendix B:**  Windows Basics, Shortcuts &
         Terms  *A-11*
**Appendix C:**  Correcting Errors after Posting  *A-16*
**Appendix D:**  Working in Multi-User Mode  *A-26*

**Appendices on the Student CD-ROM**

**Appendix E:**  Review Questions and Cases  *A-29*
**Appendix F:**  Customizing Sales Invoices  *A-59*
**Appendix G:**  Setting Security and Passwords  *A-65*
**Appendix H:**  Integration with Other Software  *A-75*
**Appendix I:**  Online Banking  *A-89*
**Appendix J:**  Review of Basic Accounting  *A-95*

# Getting Started

## OBJECTIVES

*After completing this chapter, you should be able to*

- *access* the Simply Accounting program
- *access* the data files for a business
- *understand* Simply Accounting's help features
- *save* your work
- *back up* your data files
- *finish* your session
- *change* default date format settings

**NOTES**

The instructions in this chapter for starting the program and copying files refer to Windows XP procedures. If you are using a different version of Windows, please refer to Windows and Simply Accounting Help and manuals for assistance with these procedures.

**WARNING!**

You will be unable to open the data files with Simply 2007 Release A or earlier versions.

The Student CD-ROM with Data Files will be referred to as the Student CD-ROM throughout the text.

# GETTING STARTED

## Data Files and Abbreviations

The applications in this workbook were prepared using Windows XP and the Simply Accounting 2007 Pro and Basic (Release B) software packages produced by Sage Software. You will be unable to open the data files with Simply 2007 Release A or earlier versions. Later releases and versions of the software use later income tax tables and may have changes in screens or keystrokes. If you have a version other than 2007 Release B, you can install the Simply Accounting by Sage 2007 – Student Version (Release B) that comes with this text to work through the applications.

The instructions in this workbook have been written for a stand-alone PC, with a hard disk drive and a CD-ROM disk drive. Windows should be correctly installed on your hard drive. Your printers should be installed and accessible through the Windows program. Refer to Windows Help and manuals for assistance with these procedures.

This workbook reflects the author's approach to working with Simply Accounting. There are alternative approaches to setting up company accounts and to working with the software. Refer to Simply Accounting and Windows Help and manuals for further details.

**DATA APPLICATION FILES**

| Company | Folder\File Name | Chapter |
|---|---|---|
| Getting started | Start\start.sdb | 1 |
| Missoni Marbleworks | Missoni\missoni.sdb | 3 |
| Toss for Tots | Setup\Toss\toss.sdb | 4 |
| Chai Tea Room | Chai\chai.sdb | 5 |
| Air Care Services | Aircare\aircare.sdb | 6 |
| Dorfmann Design | Setup\Dorfmann\dorfmann.sdb | 7 |
| Helena's Academy | Helena\helena.sdb | 8 |
| Lime Light Laundry | Limelite\limelite.sdb | 9 |
| Adrienne Aesthetics | Adrienne\adrienne.sdb | 10 |
| Andersson Chiropractic Clinic | Anderson\anderson.sdb | 11 |
| Maple Leaf Rags | Maple\maple.sdb | 12 |
| Truman Tires | Truman\truman.sdb | 13 |
| Village Galleries | Village\village.sdb | 14 |
| Tesses Tresses | Tess\tess.sdb | 15 |
| Flabuless Fitness | Setup\Flab\flab-apr.sdb | 16 |
|  | Setup\Flab\flab-may.sdb | 16 |
|  | Setup\Flab\flab-jun.sdb | 16 |
| Stratford Country Inn | user setup | 17 |
| Flabuless Fitness (Pro version only) | Time\flab-time.sdb | 18 |
| Able & Associates Inc. (Pro version only) | Able\able.sdb | 19 |

The applications increase in complexity. Each one introduces new ledgers, setups or features as shown in the following chart.

**DATA APPLICATION**

| DATA APPLICATION | LEDGER USED | | | | | | OTHER |
|---|---|---|---|---|---|---|---|
|  | GL | AP | AR | PAY | INV | PROJ |  |
| Missoni Marbleworks | * |  |  |  |  |  |  |
| Toss for Tots | * |  |  |  |  |  | 2 |
| Chai Tea Room | * | * |  |  |  |  |  |
| Air Care Services | * | * | * |  |  |  | 3 |
| Dorfmann Design | * | * | * |  |  |  | 2, 3 |
| Helena's Academy | * | * | * | * |  |  |  |
| Lime Light Laundry | * | * | * | * |  |  | 2 |
| Adrienne Aesthetics | * | * | * | * | * |  | 3 |
| Andersson Chiropractic Clinic | * | * | * |  |  |  |  |
| Maple Leaf Rags | * | * | * |  |  |  | 3, 4, 7 |
| Truman Tires | * | * | * | * | * | * | 3, 7 |
| Village Galleries | * | * | * | * | * |  | 3, 5, 7 |
| Tesses Tresses | * | * | * |  | * |  | 6 |
| Flabuless Fitness (Chapter 16) | * | * | * | * | * |  | 2, 3, 4, 7 |
| Stratford Country Inn | * | * | * | * |  |  | 1, 3, 8 |
| Flabuless Fitness (Chapter 18) | * | * | * | * | * |  | PRO 1 |
| Able & Associates Inc. | * | * | * | * | * |  | PRO 2 |

**LEDGERS**

| | | | | | |
|---|---|---|---|---|---|
| GL | = General Ledger | | PAY | = Payroll | |
| AP | = Accounts Payable | | INV | = Inventory | |
| AR | = Accounts Receivable | | PROJ | = Project (Allocations or jobcosting) | |

Other:

1 All realistic source documents (most chapters have some realistic source documents)

2 Setup application with keystrokes    5 Budgeting    7 Foreign currency transactions
3 Credit cards    6 Account reconciliation    8 Setup application without keystrokes
4 Internet links

PRO 1 Time and Billing and Build from Bill of Materials    PRO 2 Departmental Accounting
    These additional features are available only in the Pro version.

**⚠ WARNING!**
    Before using your data files, you should make backup copies of all the files. Always work with this working backup copy, so that you can use the original to restore the files later if you have data errors. Refer to page 6 and your Windows manuals for complete instructions.

**📄 NOTES**
    The Stratford Country Inn file is not set up in advance for you. You must create that file on your own.
    The Student CD-ROM also includes a copy of the Skeleton template file for Chapter 4 and data files for bank reconciliation for Chapter 15, Case 6 for Chapter 16 in Appendix E, and online banking in Appendix I (Appendices E and I are also on the Student CD-ROM.)

# The Simply Accounting Program

Simply Accounting is an integrated accounting program with many features that are suitable for small- and medium-sized businesses. It includes several ledgers and journals that work together so that data entered in one part of the program will be linked and available in other parts of the program. Thus ledgers are automatically updated from journal entries, and reports always include the most recent transactions and ledger changes. A business can use one or more of the accounting modules: General, Payables, Receivables, Payroll, Inventory, Project and Time and Billing (Pro version). Only the features used are set up. Thus, if payroll is not used, there is no need to set up the Payroll module, and it can be hidden from view. A more complete description of the program and its features is presented in Chapter 16, pages 621–622.

## Simply Accounting Program Components

When you select the Typical Installation option, several components will be installed:

- **Simply Accounting Program**: the Simply Accounting software you will need to perform the accounting transactions for your company. It will be placed in the main Simply Accounting Pro 2007 folder under the Program Files folder or the folder location you selected.
- **Samples**: complete company records for both accrual-basis and cash-basis accounting methods for two sample companies — Universal Construction and Universal Crustacean Farm. They will be placed in a folder under Simply Accounting Pro 2007 called Samdata.
- **Templates**: predefined charts of accounts and settings for a large number of business types. These files will be stored in a folder under Simply Accounting Pro 2007 called Template. Two starter files with only charts of accounts also appear in this folder.

- **Crystal Reports Print Engine**, **Forms** and **Management Reports**: a variety of commonly used business forms and reports that you can customize to suit your own business needs as well as the program to access and print them. They will be placed in a folder under Simply Accounting Pro 2007 called Forms.
- **Customizable Forms** and **Customized Reports**: a variety of MS Office documents designed for integrated use with Simply Accounting. They will be placed in a Reports folder under Simply Accounting Pro 2007.
- **New Business Guide**: a number of checklists showing the steps to follow when setting up a new business, customized for a variety of business types in different provinces. This guide includes addresses and phone numbers as well as Web addresses that you can access for further information.
- **Manuals**: documentation that will help you learn how to use Simply Accounting.

# Backing Up Your Data Files

Before you begin the applications, you must copy the data files to your hard disk drive. You cannot work from the CD because Simply Accounting will not open read-only files, and all CD-ROM files are read-only files. Next, you should make a working backup copy of all the files. Keep the original for future use to begin again without returning to the CD. The following instructions will copy all the files to your hard disk drive, create the necessary new folders and remove the read-only file attributes or properties.

# Installing Your Data Files

The Student CD-ROM contains Basic and Pro versions of the data files and several supplementary files for the book. It also has programs that will automatically copy the data files to a new SimData folder on your hard drive (drive C:). If you want to use a different location for your data files, proceed to page 7.

   You must work with the correct version of the data set. You cannot open Pro version files with the Basic program. If you are working with Basic version, install the Basic data files. If you are working with Pro version (Student or regular), install the Pro data files.

> If you are using the **Basic version**, refer to sidebar notes for the differences between the Basic 2007 and Pro 2007 versions.
>
> **Insert**   the **Student CD-ROM** into your CD drive. The home window appears:

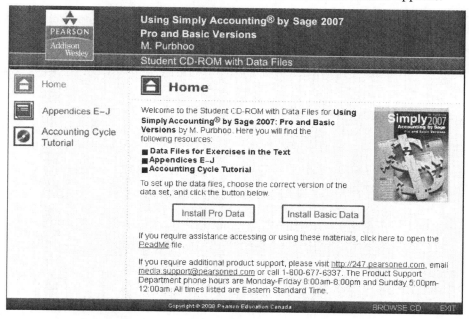

> **Click**   **Install Basic Data** (to copy the data set for Basic 2007), or
>
> **Click**   **Install Pro Data** (to copy the data for Pro 2007 and Student versions).

When all the files have been copied, you will see the following message:

> **Click**   **OK**. The data files have been copied to C:\SimData.

If the Student CD-ROM home window does not open automatically,

> **Choose**  the **Start menu** on the desktop and **click Run** to open the Run window.
>
> **Type**    d:\start.exe   (where D: is the drive letter for your CD drive.)
>
> **Click**   **OK**.

You can also view the supplementary files on the CD. You can save these files to your hard drive or print them if you want.

> **Click**   **Appendices E–J** and then **click** the **file** you want.
>
> **Close**   the **PDF file** when you have finished viewing or printing it.

**Click**   **Exit** to close the Student CD-ROM window.

All the data files for the book are now located in the new SimData folder in drive C:. You should now copy or back up the files to your working folder.

## Copying Data Files on the Hard Disk

To copy the data files to another folder on your hard disk, we will use the Windows Explorer program.

We will copy the data files from the SimData folder (created with the autoinstall feature) to the Data folder under Simply Accounting Pro 2007 in the Program Files folder, the default location for the program's installation.

**Click**   **Start** (on the desktop task bar).

**Choose**   (point to) **Programs**, then **choose Accessories** and **click Windows Explorer**.

**Click**   **My Computer** in the Folders list.

**Click**   **C:** to view the folders on the hard drive.

**Click**   **SimData**, the folder you just created, on the Folders side so that the contents — all the folders — appear on the Name side of the window. (Scroll down ⬇ if necessary to include SimData in the list of Folders.)

**Click**   **Able**, the first folder in the Contents list. Scroll down.

**Press**   (shift) and **click Village**, the last folder in the Contents list. Or, you can **choose** the **Edit menu** and **click Select All**. This will highlight all the folders in SimData as shown:

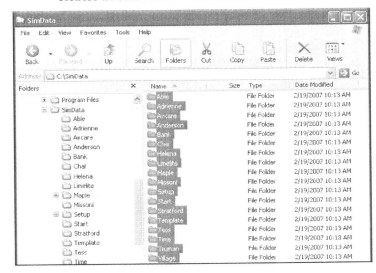

If you view the files and folders in icon form, your selections will look like this:

**Choose** the **Edit menu** and **click Copy** or **click** the **Copy tool** .

**Click**    to scroll up the Folders list to the Program Files folder in drive C:.

**Click**    the  **beside** the **folder** to see the folders under Program Files.

**Click**    the  **beside Simply Accounting Pro 2007** to list the folders under Simply Accounting Pro 2007. The Data folder should be visible.

**Click**    the **Data folder** so that it is open. The Contents or Name side of the Explorer window should be empty because the folder is empty.

You can choose a different destination folder for your data files if you want.

**Choose** the **Edit menu** and **click Paste** or **click** the **Paste tool** .

Your screen will show the files being copied. When the copying is complete, all the folders and files from SimData will be copied to the Data folder under Simply Accounting Pro 2007 that was created during installation. When you click the new  icon beside Data, you will see the data folders listed.

**Click**    to close Windows Explorer.

If you want to copy only the files for a single application, click the folder for the application you want (e.g., Missoni) under SimData to highlight it. Complete the copy as you would for the entire set of folders — use the copy command, open the destination folder and then paste the folder.

## Working with Other File Locations

You can copy the files to a different location by copying data folders from the CD just as you would copy other files to your hard disk drive. Choose the correct version of the data set (Basic or Pro) and always copy complete folders.

After copying the folders and files, you must remove the Read Only attribute from all the data files before you can open them with Simply Accounting. If you do not change the attribute or if you try to open the data file from the Student CD-ROM, you will receive an error message about access rights when you try to open the file:

**Click**    **OK** to return to the opening Welcome screen.

If you tried to open the files from the Student CD-ROM, copy the data to your hard disk drive and then remove the Read Only attributes if necessary.

## Removing Read-Only Attributes

File attributes must be changed for the files in one folder at a time. You must change the attributes for each data application individually because each application is in a separate folder. Changing the attributes of a folder does not change the attributes for the files inside the folder, but all files in an open folder can be changed at once.

You can change the file properties in Windows Explorer.

**Open**    **Windows Explorer** and **find** the **folder** that contains your **data set**.

**basic BASIC VERSION**
The first folder is Adrienne. Click this name instead of Able.

**NOTES**
Windows XP Pro removes the read-only attributes from files when you copy from a CD to your hard drive.

**NOTES**
The files remain selected while the Properties window is open.

**NOTES**
If you added a desktop shortcut when you installed the program, you can double click it to open the Simply Accounting program.

**NOTES**
If you used a different name for the program when you installed it, choose that name.

**Double click**   **Able**, the first data folder, to open it.

**Click**    the **first file** in the folder and **press** ⌐ctrl⌐ **+ A**, or **press** ⌐shift⌐ and **click** the **last file** in the folder to select all the Simply Accounting data files. Some data folders contain only two files; others may have more.

**Choose**  the **File menu** and **click Properties** or **right-click** (click the right mouse button) and **choose Properties** from the pop-up menu.

The Properties window for the files opens:

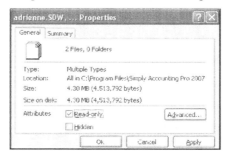

**Click**    **Read-Only** to remove the ✓. **Click OK**.

**Repeat**  this **procedure** for the remaining folders and files.

# Starting Simply Accounting and Accessing Data Files

From your Windows desktop,

**Click**    **Start** (on the task bar) so the pop-up menu appears.

**Point to**  **Programs**. Hold the mouse on Programs until the list of programs appears.

**Point to**  **Simply Accounting Pro 2007**. Hold the mouse on Simply Accounting until its cascading menu list of programs appears.

**Click**    **Simply Accounting Pro 2007**. You should follow the path illustrated in the Classic Windows view that follows:

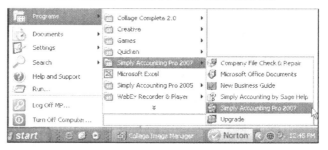

If you are using the Windows XP view,

**Click**    **Start**. **Point to All Programs** and then **point to Simply Accounting Pro 2007** as shown in the following screen:

You will open the registration screen the first time you use the program. Otherwise, you will see the Simply Accounting Select Company screen below.

If you have not yet registered the program refer to Appendix A, page A-7 in the text. Until you register and activate the program, you will be allowed to use the program only for a limited time.

## Opening a Data File

You will now see the Simply Accounting Select Company Welcome screen:

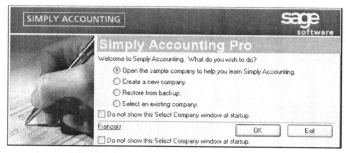

The opening window gives you several options: working with the sample company files, creating new company files, restoring backup files or working with existing data files. If you have worked with the program before, the option to Open The Last Company You Worked On appears last with the name of the file you used. If you use this option when you use the same data set for several work sessions, you will bypass the Open Company window (shown below).

**Click**    **Select An Existing Company**.

**Click**    **OK**.

The Simply Accounting Open Company window appears next. The most recently used file will be selected if you have previously used the program. Therefore, the File name you see on your screen may be different from the ones we show.

The next time you start the Simply Accounting program, the name of the file that you used most recently will be selected for you to accept or to change.

**Click**    the **Look In field list arrow** to see the folder path for the file selected:

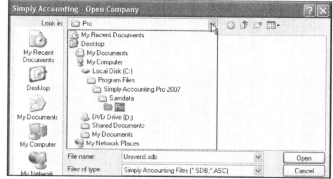

The path shown here is for the sample company, Universal, in Program Files\ Simply Accounting Pro 2007\Samdata\Pro in drive (C:). The following instructions will access data stored in the Simply Accounting Pro 2007\Data folder.

> If your starting point is different from the one shown here, click drive (C:) in the Look In field list. Then in the folders/files section, double click the Program Files folder to open it, and double click the Simply Accounting Pro 2007 folder to display the folders.

**WARNING!**
You will be allowed to use the program only for a limited time before entering the registration validation codes. You must have a payroll ID code in order to use the Payroll features of the program.

The Student Version does not require payroll activation.

**NOTES**
The Select Company window shows the version you are using. This window has Pro added to the screen.

In Chapter 4, we show the location of the Select Company option in the View menu.

**Double click** the **Simply Accounting Pro 2007 folder** to list the folders in the large files/folders list in the centre of the window. The Look In field now displays Simply Accounting Pro 2007 as the folder name:

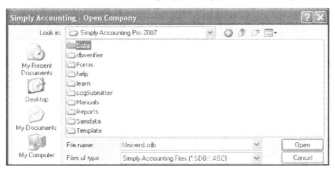

**Click**    the **Data folder** to select it as shown above.

**Click**    **Open** to list the folders containing your workbook data. The folder name Data now appears in the Look In field.

**Click**    the **Start folder** to select it.

**Click**    **Open** to list the Simply Accounting data files contained in this folder and to display the folder name Start in the Look In field. There should be just one file listed, Start (or Start.sdb if you chose to show file name extensions).

You can gain access to the company records through the *.sdb file. Simply Accounting recognizes this file extension as a Simply Accounting format file. Other files that are part of the data set must be located in the same folder.

**Click**    **Start** to select it and add its name to the File Name field as shown:

Substitute the appropriate drive and path or folders for your own setup to access the Simply Accounting Home window. For other applications, substitute the appropriate folder and file name for Start above.

If passwords have been set up for the file, you will see this password entry screen:

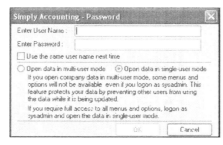

Ask your instructor or site administrator for the name and password you should use (see Appendix G on the Student CD-ROM). Enter your user name and password. Click OK to open the session date screen.

If you see a screen advising that the data has been used in a newer version of the program, your program may be an earlier version of Release B. You will be asked

**NOTES**
The other files will be listed in the Windows Explorer program when you open the Data folder.

**NOTES**
We have not set passwords for any data files in this text, but your site administrator for the network may have done so.
    If you try to open a read-only file, you will see the error message on page 7 instead of the password or session date screen.

if you wish to proceed; click Yes to open the file. If your version of the program is even earlier (Release A), you will be unable to open the data file.

**Click**    **Open** to see the following screen prompting you for the session date:

All date fields in Simply Accounting include a calendar that shows the range of dates you can enter for the data file. The program restricts you from moving to a month beyond the range that is allowed. The list arrow beside the Date field offers a list of dates to choose from. Refer to page 18 for more information on dates in Simply Accounting.

**Click**    **OK** to accept the date shown.

The first time you use the program, you will see a message about automatic program updates. Do not update your program yet. You can download updates periodically (from the Help menu) when you have finished working through the applications in this text. Later updates will download later versions and your answers may not match the screens we show.

**Do not choose automatic updates**. **Click OK** to open the Home window.

Remember to activate the Payroll features. Go to page A-9 in Appendix A in the text for help with this step.

## Simply Accounting Home Window

The Simply Accounting Home window should be open:

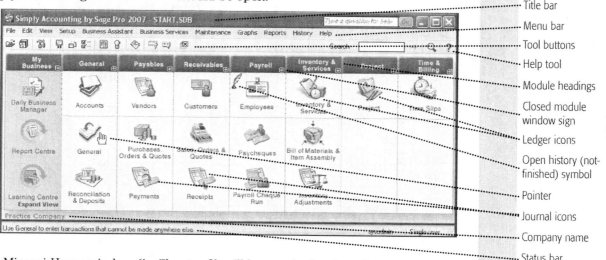

Your Missoni Home window (in Chapter 3) will have only the three icons for the General Ledger — Accounts, General and Reconciliation & Deposits — and the three My Business tab icons. Unused ledgers will be hidden because they are not set up. In this illustration, the Payroll Ledger is not finished. We show it here to illustrate the Open History symbol and the remaining Home window icons.

The Home window is organized as follows: the **title bar** is on top with the program name, Simply Accounting By Sage Pro 2007, the file name, START.SDB, Control Menu icon and size buttons; the **main menu bar** comes next with the **tool bar buttons** below. Tool buttons provide quick access to commonly used menu items. Different Simply Accounting windows have different buttons on the tool bar. The **ledger** or module names come next with their respective icons filling up the major part of the window —

**NOTES**
If your update is later than Release B, you can use the Student Pro Version Release B program that comes with the text.

**NOTES**
The session date is explained in the Missoni Marbleworks application, where you will also learn how to change the session date.

The session date list includes the current session date, the end of the fiscal period and the start of the next fiscal period. The list for any date field includes the dates commonly selected.

*basic* **BASIC VERSION**
You will see an additional message about upgrading to the Pro or Premier version of Simply Accounting.

*basic* **BASIC VERSION**
The program name in the title bar is Simply Accounting by Sage Basic 2007 and you will not see the Time Slips icon.

ledgers in the top row below the ledger or module name and **journal icons** under their respective ledgers in the last two icon rows of the window. Below the journal icons are two more information lines: the company name and the **status bar**. The status bar describes the purpose of the General Journal because the pointer is on the General icon.

The **My Business tab** on the left can be customized to include the icons you use most frequently. You can hide this column if you do not use this feature.

The Pro version also has a **Search field** to look up information in any journal or ledger. In the Basic version, you can access the Search function from the Edit menu.

Hold the mouse pointer on a tool button for a few seconds to see the name or function of the tool button and the keyboard shortcut if there is one. Hold the mouse over an icon to see its description or function in the status bar at the bottom of the window.

**NOTES**
In Windows XP, showing the shortcuts for tool buttons is an optional setting, so you may not see them.

**NOTES**
Many Simply Accounting windows include a Home window tool that brings the Home window to the front without closing the other windows.

## Simply Accounting on the Windows Desktop

**Click**    the **General Journal icon** in the journal part of the window.

**Click**    the **Edit menu**. Your desktop should now look like the one that follows:

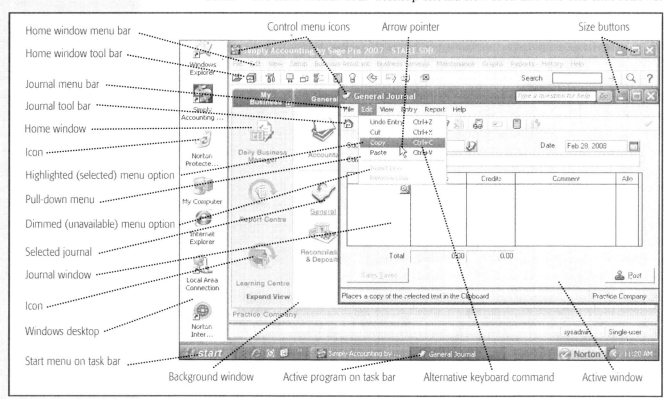

If you need an explanation of terms in this illustration, please refer to Appendix B.

**Click**    ☒ to close the journal window and return to the Home window.

## Simply Accounting Module Window

Each module or ledger can be expanded so that its icons are the only ones displayed. The module heading or module name is used to open the module window or close it if it is open.

**Click**    the **Payables module heading** to open the Payables module window:

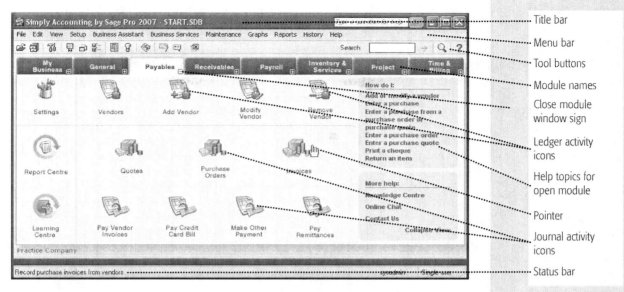

The heading for the open module has the colours reversed, and the boxed plus sign has changed to a minus sign. All activities for the Payables module are represented by separate icons. This view may be easier for new users. To access a function or activity, just click the related icon. However, once you are in a journal such as Invoices, you can switch to Orders or Quotes without returning to this window, or you can close one journal and open the other journal window from the module window. Although the Home window does not appear, it is open in the background, and all its menu and tool bar items are still available.

On the right-hand side, the window includes a list of **How Do I ...** topics to help you get started using the module. Click a topic to see the steps for that activity. The Help window will stay open until you close it. You can keep it open to assist you while you are completing a task or transaction.

To work with another module, click the next module heading you want. To restore the Home window, click the module heading or click **Collapse View** under the More Help list. The module window will close.

> **Click**    **Enter A Purchase** on the How Do I list of topics.
>
> **Read**     the **instructions** and then **close** the **Help window**.
>
> **Click**    the **Payables module heading** ⎡ Payables ⎤ or **click Collapse View** to close the module and restore the Home window.

Open and close some of the other module windows to see their activity icons. Restore the Home window before continuing.

# Simply Accounting Help Features

Simply Accounting provides program assistance in several different ways. You can display or print Help information on many topics. General accounting information, advice topics and Simply Accounting software assistance are included. You can access Help from the Home window at any time.

The most immediate form of help comes from the **status bar** at the bottom of many program windows. It offers a one-line description of the icon or field that the mouse is pointing to. As you move the mouse around the screen, the status bar information changes accordingly. The message in the status bar is connected to the mouse position only. This may not be the same as the position of the cursor or insertion point, which is located wherever the mouse was when you last clicked the mouse button.

We have already seen that each module window includes a **How Do I list** for activities related to that module. In addition, many settings or options windows include a **Help button** that offers context sensitive help for the procedure you are using.

Simply Accounting general help can be accessed several ways:

Click the Learning Centre icon ,

Press (f1),

Choose the Help menu and click Contents, or

Click the Help button [?].

**Click**    the **Learning Centre icon** [Learning Centre]:

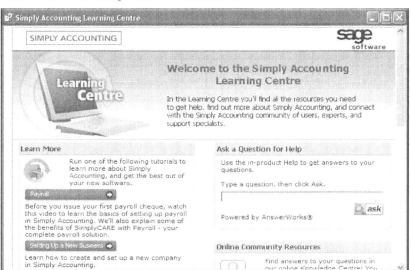

From this centre you can get different types of assistance: you can search for information, run one of the tutorials, or find out about courses and training, contacting a Simply Accounting expert, or providing your feedback to Sage Software. We will demonstrate the Search option.

**Click**    the **Type A Question field**.

**Type**    purchase orders **Click** the **Ask button**:

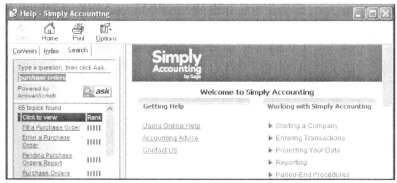

The Help Welcome screen opens and several topics related to purchase orders are listed in the left-hand pane. The topics are shown in order of likely relevance — their **Rank**. Information can be displayed for the underlined topics.

**Click**    **Enter A Purchase Order** to display information for this topic:

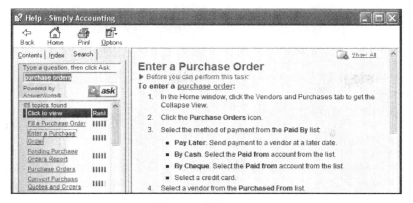

Click any underlined topic in the topics list or in the information display pane to display the information for that newly selected topic.

**Close**    the **Help window** and the **Learning Centre window**.

**Click**    the **Help menu** in the Home window:

The options on this menu include all the ones we saw in the Learning Centre. In addition, you can update the program to a later release, upgrade the program to Premier from Pro or to Pro or Premier from Basic, and see the version number and serial number for your program (About Simply Accounting By Sage).

**Click**    the **Help tool** ?  . The Contents tab "book" menu opens:

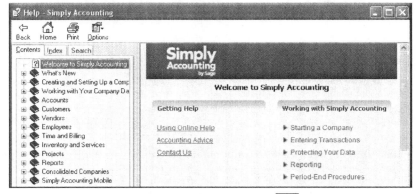

Major topics have a book symbol beside them ▣ .

Click ⊞ beside a topic to see the list of subtopics under that heading (or double click the topic).

When a topic has a question mark beside it ? , there is detailed help on that subject. Click the topic or the question mark symbol to display information on that subject in the right-hand side of the Help window.

Welcome, with a question mark ? beside it, is selected, so this topic is displayed. The Welcome screen has topics to help you get started in Simply

Accounting. Clicking an arrow ▶ beside a topic in the right-hand side display pane expands the list of topics. Clicking underlined text provides further information on that topic.

Click a book title or click ⊟, the boxed minus sign beside it to close the book and hide the list of subtopics.

**Click**    **Vendors**. The list expands with several subtopics.

**Click**    **Purchases** to view the second list of subtopics.

**Click**    **Paying Vendors (Payments)** to view the next list of subtopics.

**Click**    **Paying A Vendor** (with a question mark 🔲 beside it) to see the help information on this topic:

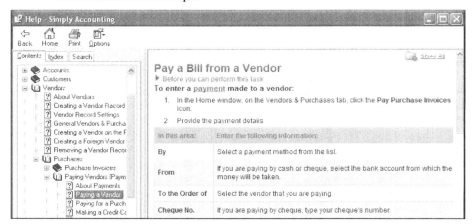

**Click**    the **Index tab** to see an alphabetic list of entries as shown here:

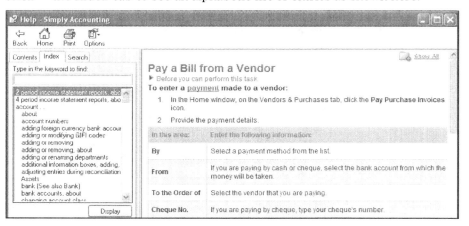

Notice that the previous topic remains on display until you select a new topic.

Click a topic and then click Display to open the help information. Type a letter in the field above the list to advance the alphabetic list quickly.

**Click**    the **Search tab** to open the Search function:

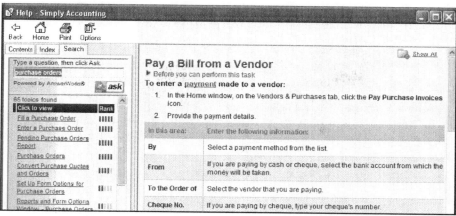

Again, the previous topic remains displayed until you select a new one. The last item you searched for is listed in the Type A Question... field. Purchase orders is still entered.

This screen is the same one we accessed from the Learning Centre.

You can search for a topic by typing it in the **Type A Question** field. Then click the **Ask** button to see the entries that include the topic you typed.

**Click**    the **Type A Question field** and **type**   delete

**Click**    the **Ask button**.

**Click**    **Vendors** to display the information. Vendors is underlined so the information is displayed directly.

**Close**    the **Help windows** when you have finished.

The Simply Accounting program also includes **Advice** on a number of topics.

**Click**    the **Advice tool button** [icon] in Simply Accounting's Home window to access the main Advice menu shown here:

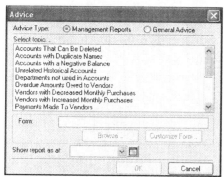

If a Home window ledger or journal icon is selected when you click the Advice tool, you will see the list of Management Reports for only that module or ledger.

General management advice topics are also available from the Business Assistant menu under the Business Advice option.

The default list of topics is the list of Management Reports. Rather than providing general information, these reports relate specifically to the company data set that is in use at the time. Management reports are available only for ledgers that are not hidden, so the list you see is not always complete. The reports combine the company data with forms and reports provided through the Crystal Report Engine. If you have not installed the Crystal Report Engine and the customizable forms, these reports will not be available.

You can click the report or advice topic you want, and then click OK to see the report (or double click the topic).

**Click**    **General Advice** to see the list of topics that provide suggestions about general accounting practices. **Click** the **topic** you want and then **click OK**. **Close** the **advice report windows** when finished.

A final source of general assistance is available as **automatic advice**. This feature can be turned off from the Setup menu (User Preferences, View) in the Home window if it is not needed. We recommend leaving it on. When it is turned on, the Simply Accounting program will provide warning statements as, for example, when you choose a customer who has exceeded their credit limit:

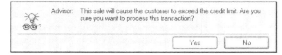

To proceed, you must close the advice screen. In the example shown here, you can click Yes if you want to proceed with the sale, or No if you want to make a change (perhaps by asking for a deposit).

The following warning about an overdrawn chequing account appears when you make a payment from a bank account that exceeds the account balance:

Close this type of message by clicking the advisor icon as indicated [Click Here To Close].

The program also warns when year-end is approaching and it is time to complete year-end adjustments or when inventory items reach the reorder point.

# Date Formats and Settings

Before closing the program we will review date format settings. Simply Accounting has date format control settings within each file that are independent of the display date settings for Windows. When you enter dates using a series of two digits for month, day and year, it is important to know how these will be interpreted. For example, when you type 07-06-05, this date may be June 7, July 6 or June 5 in the year 2005, 1905, 1907 or 2007, depending on whether month, day or year comes first and whether your computer defaults to 1900 dates or is preset for 2000 dates. We always use month, day and year as the order for presenting dates in this text.

Fortunately, Simply Accounting allows you to enter and display dates as text. Thus, you may type June 7, 2007, in a date field. And if you want, you can display this date as Jun 7, 2007, even if you enter numbers in the date field.

All date fields also have a Calendar icon ▦ that you can click to access a month-by-month calendar from which you can select a date. These two options will help you avoid making date errors from incorrect orders. To access the date settings,

**Choose** the **Setup menu**, then **click Settings** as shown:

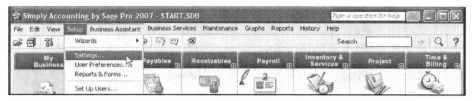

The Settings control window opens:

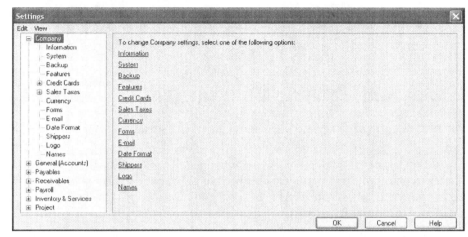

Each entry in the list opens the settings screen for a different part of the program. We want the date format settings.

**Click** **Date Format** (the entry under Company or from the list on the right) to open the Settings window for Dates:

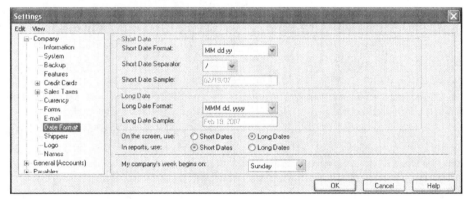

Each field has a drop-down list of format options. The **Short Date Format** uses two digits each for month and day. For the year, you can choose a two-digit or four-digit format. You can choose to begin with month, day or year — the Short Date Format shows which comes first. The **Short Date Separator** character may be a slash, dash or period. This is the character that will appear on the screen regardless of how you entered the date. The sample shows the appearance that you can expect from your selections.

The **Long Date Format** shows the month as a three-letter text abbreviation. Either the month or the day can be the first character in the long date style. The sample shows the result of your selection.

The next section allows you to select the short or long date styles for your screen and reports. You can select different date styles for your reports and screen displays.

We will use the same date format settings for all files to avoid any confusion about dates when the numeric entry might be ambiguous. For reports you can use long or short date formats.

**NOTES**
A final date option allows you to indicate the normal first weekday for the business.

**Click** the **Short Date Format field list arrow**.

**Click** **MM dd yyyy**. Be sure that Month (MM) is the first part of the entry. Showing a four-digit year will ensure that you see whether you are using 1900 or 2000 year dates.

**Click** the **Long Date Format field list arrow**.

**Click** **MMM dd, yyyy**.

**Click** **Long Dates** beside the option On The Screen, Use.

**Click** **OK** to save the settings.

# Saving and Backing Up Your Work

Simply Accounting saves your work automatically at various stages when you are working with the program. For example, when you display or print reports, Simply Accounting writes all the journal transactions to your file to compile the report you want. When you exit from the program properly, Simply Accounting also saves all your work.

On a regular basis, you should also make a backup copy of your files. The Backup command is described in detail in Chapter 3.

**Click** the **Backup tool** 🗗 or **choose** the **File menu** and **click Backup** to start the Backup wizard.

The wizard will create a separate backup folder inside your current working folder so that the backup will remain separate from your working copy.

While **Backup** creates a compressed copy of the files that must be restored with the Restore command before you can use them, the next two options create separate complete working copies of your data files that can be opened directly. Both save the file under a different file name so that you will have two working copies of the files, the original and the copy. You cannot create backups on a CD with the Backup command.

**Save As** makes a copy, closes the original file and lets you continue to work with the new copy. Because the new file becomes your working file, you can use Save As to copy to any medium that you can also work from in Simply Accounting — your hard disk drive or a removable memory stick, but not a CD. **Save A Copy** makes a copy of the file and then allows you to continue working with the original file. You can use Save A Copy to save your files to a CD. You must copy the CD files back to your hard disk drive and remove the read-only property before working with these files.

Because the data files are very large, we recommend using the Backup procedure described in Chapter 3 rather than Save As or Save A Copy for regular backups.

**Choose** the **File menu** and **click Save A Copy** to open the file name window:

You can save the copy in the same folder as the original or use a different folder. We recommend using different folders. To change to a different folder,

**Click** the **Save In field list arrow** and **choose** a different **folder**.

**Double click** the **folder** to open it. To create a new folder inside the one that you have open,

**Click**  the **New Folder icon**   .

**Type**  a **new name** to replace New Folder, the selected text.

**Click**  **Open**.

**Double click**  the file name **NEW** or **NEW.SDB** if you show file extensions.

**Type**  the **new file name**.

**Click**  **Save**.

You will return to your original file and you can continue working.

To save the file under a different name and continue working with the new file, use the Save As command.

**Choose** the **File menu** and **click Save As** to open the file name window.

The remaining steps are the same as Save A Copy, as shown above.

Change folders, create a new folder, rename the folder, open the new folder, type a file name for the copy and click Save. Remember to return to your original working copy before entering any transactions if you use the Save As command.

You can also back up all your data files at the same time by using Windows Explorer Copy and Paste commands as described earlier in this chapter. In this way, you can save the files to a different folder on your hard drive.

## Finishing a Session

**Choose** the **Control Menu icon** and **click Close** or **click** ☒ to close the journal input form or display window you are working in.

You will return to the main Home window.

**Choose** the **Control Menu icon** and **click Close**, or **click** ☒ or **choose** the **File menu** and **click Exit** to close the Home window.

Your work will be saved again automatically when you complete this step. You should now be in the Windows desktop.

## Creating New Folders

You will need to make folders to work with the applications in this workbook. The four setup applications — Toss for Tots, Dorfmann Design, Flabuless Fitness and Stratford Country Inn — will require new folders. In addition, you may want to make folders for backing up individual applications.

In Simply Accounting windows that have a **New Folder tool button**  — the Save As, Save A Copy and Open Company windows — you can make folders. The method for creating new folders in Simply Accounting is the same in all Simply Accounting windows and is described on page 20 for the Save A Copy method and in Chapter 4 using the Save As option.

We will describe the Windows Explorer approach here.

**Double click**  the **My Computer icon** ⬛ on the desktop.

**NOTES**
You may want to use the Save A Copy or Save As command when you are unsure how a journal entry will be posted and you want to experiment with different methods of entering the same transactions.

**WARNING!**
Remember to copy all the files for a company when you use the Copy and Paste commands. Copying the folder will ensure you copy all the necessary files.

**NOTES**
In any Simply Accounting window that has the New Folder tool, you can right-click the mouse and choose New and Folder from the pop-up menu.

**Double click**   the **drive** you want to use and then **double click** the **folder** in the drive where you want to place the new folder (or create the folder at the root of the disk drive, e.g., at C:\).

**Choose**   the **File menu**, then **choose New** and **click Folder** (or **right-click** the mouse and **choose New** and **Folder** from the pop-up menu).

The file menu path should look like the one shown here:

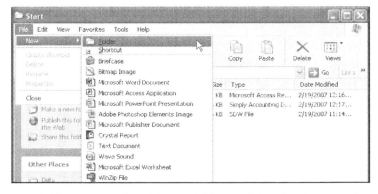

The new folder is placed inside the folder or drive that is open. Its name, New Folder, will be selected so you can type a new folder name immediately.

**Enter**   a **new name** and then **click somewhere else** on the screen to save the name change.

You can create several folders in the same session by repeating these steps.

**Close**   the **My Computer window** when you have finished.

# REVIEW

The Student CD-ROM with Data Files includes Review Questions for this chapter.

# OBJECTIVES

- **plan** and **design** an accounting system for a small business
- **prepare** procedures for converting from a manual system
- **understand** the objectives of a computerized system
- **create** company files
- **set up** company accounts
- **enter** settings for foreign currency transactions
- **prepare** files for foreign currency transactions and importing goods
- **identify** preferred customers for reduced prices
- **enter** preferred customer prices and import duty rates for inventory
- **finish** entering the accounting history for all modules
- **insert** new accounts, vendors, customers and employees as required
- **export** reports
- **use** spreadsheets for analyzing, planning and decision making
- **enter** end-of-accounting-period adjustments
- **perform** end-of-accounting-period closing routines
- **analyze** and **interpret** case studies
- **develop** further group interpersonal skills
- **develop** further oral and written skills

# INTRODUCTION

This application provides a complete accounting cycle for a merchandising business. It is a comprehensive application covering a three-month fiscal period. You will use Simply Accounting to convert a manual accounting system to a computerized accounting system and then enter transactions. The routines in this application are common to many small businesses, so they should be useful. The information in this chapter reflects the business realities in Ontario in 2007.

You may substitute information relevant to other provinces or the latest payroll and tax regulations wherever it is appropriate to do so. Rules for the application of the federal Goods and Services Tax (GST), provincial sales taxes and payroll may vary from one province to another.

Because of the length of the setup, instructions for working with the source documents are presented with those documents on page 689.

# COMPANY INFORMATION

## Company Profile

**F**labuless Fitness, in Hamilton, Ontario, sells a wide range of fitness equipment and accessories for home and light commercial use. Stephen Reeves, the owner, opened his business a few years ago after retiring as a professional athlete, gaining business experience with another store and completing some business courses. Reeves has three employees to assist with the work in the store. They also perform other duties. One employee does the accounting, one teaches yoga classes and one delivers equipment and provides personal training services to clients. Reeves works mostly outside the store, promoting the business.

Several of the equipment suppliers offer discounts to the store for early payment. Two suppliers are located in the United States. Accounts are also set up for other supplies and services that are provided locally. The store uses a credit card for some of these purchases.

Most customers are situated in the Hamilton region but Reeves has recently added two new customers in New York State. All account customers are given discounts for early payment and some preferred customers receive additional discounts. Individual customers usually pay by cash, debit or credit card and do not receive any discounts. Delivery is provided at a small charge and includes equipment setup and a brief demonstration on equipment use.

All items and services sold by the store are set up as inventory so that sales can be monitored. GST is charged on all sales and services, except to foreign customers. PST is charged on sales but not on services. The store pays GST and PST on all taxable purchases, but inventory purchased for resale in the store is exempt from PST.

The owner decided to use Simply Accounting for record keeping after a consultant prepared the report on the following pages. Reeves found an application called Hearth House in an older Simply Accounting textbook. It appeared similar in complexity and structure to Flabuless Fitness and even included complete instructions for creating the data files. Before converting the books for the store, he asked his assistant to work through this application for practice. Next she printed all the relevant business guide information and prepared the following reports to assist with the conversion on April 1, 2009:

- Income Statement
- Business Information
- Chart of Accounts
- Balance Sheet
- Post-Closing Trial Balance

- Vendor Information
- Customer Information
- Employee Information
- Inventory Information
- Accounting Procedures

# MANAGER'S REPORT ON SIMPLY ACCOUNTING

## PREPARED FOR FLABULESS FITNESS

1.  Simply Accounting allows a business to process all source documents in a timely fashion. It can automatically prepare both single-period and comparative accounting reports for planning, decision making and controlling operations within the business.
2.  The software eliminates some of the time-consuming manual clerical functions. For example, it can automatically prepare invoices, cheques and statements, and it can perform all the necessary mathematical calculations. Being freed from these chores, the accountant can extend her role to assume a much higher level of responsibility. For example, the accountant will have more time to spend analyzing reports with the owner and can work directly with the owner in making business decisions.
3.  Simply Accounting can easily export reports to spreadsheets for further analysis, or link with the Internet, with other software programs and with vendors and customers for interactive data exchange. When combined with the graphing, account reconciliation and budgeting features, these reports permit the owner to analyze past trends and to make better predictions about the future behaviour of the business.
4.  As the business grows, the manager can divide work more meaningfully among new accounting personnel. Since Simply Accounting provides subsidiary ledgers that are linked to control accounts in the General Ledger, it automatically coordinates accounting work performed by different individuals. Customizable window backgrounds can even accommodate mood changes of the different users.
5.  Simply Accounting allows the owner to exercise business controls in a number of areas.

## IN GENERAL

- Access to confidential accounting records and editing capability can be restricted to authorized personnel by using passwords.
- Mechanical errors can be virtually eliminated, since journal transactions with unequal debits and credits cannot be posted. Customer, vendor, employee, inventory and jobcost names appear in full on the journal entry input forms, making errors less likely.
- The ability to preview forms, store recurring entries and look up posted invoices makes it possible to avoid errors in repeated information and to double check invoices in response to customer and vendor inquiries.
- Errors in General, Sales, Receipts, Purchases, Payments and Payroll journal entries can be corrected as adjustments or reversed. The software automatically creates and posts the reversing entries.
- Simply Accounting provides an audit trail for all journals.
- Bank account, customer, vendor and inventory records can be set up to calculate many foreign currency transactions automatically, including import duties.
- Daily Business Manager lists and checklists provide reminders of upcoming discounts, recurring entries and routine tasks.
- Business guides, accounting advice and management reports and advice all provide helpful information for running the business.
- Simply Accounting provides a directory of customers, vendors and employees, and can create mailing labels for them.

## GENERAL LEDGER

- The software provides a directory of accounts used by the business, including all linked accounts for the other ledgers in Simply Accounting.
- The information in these accounts can be used to prepare and analyze financial reports such as the Balance Sheet and Income Statement.

## RECEIVABLES LEDGER

- Credit limit entries for each customer should reduce the losses from non-payment of accounts. Customers with poor payment histories can have their credit limits reduced or their credit purchase privileges removed.
- Preferred customers can be identified so that they automatically receive lower prices.
- Sales quote and order entries result in automatic Sales Journal entries when the quotes or orders are filled.
- Tax codes and accounts can be entered in the customer record so that they are automatically entered for sales when the customer is selected.
- Accounts receivable can be aged, and each customer's payment behaviour can be analyzed. This feature allows for the accurate calculation of provisions for bad debts.

## PAYABLES LEDGER

- The information from the review of transactions with vendors and from the accounts payable aged analysis can be combined with detailed cash flow reports to make payment decisions. Simply Accounting helps to predict short-term cash needs in order to establish priorities for making payments and to schedule payments to vendors.
- The GST remittance or refund is calculated automatically because of the linked GST accounts in the Payables and Receivables ledgers.
- Simply Accounting purchase quote and order entries result in automatic Purchases Journal entries when quotes or orders are filled.
- The usual tax code and expense account for a vendor can be entered in the vendor record so that they are entered automatically for purchases when the vendor is selected.

## PAYROLL LEDGER

- Simply Accounting maintains employee records with both personal and payment information for personnel files.
- Paycheques for several employees can be processed in a single entry with direct payroll deposit.
- Once records are set up, the program automatically withholds employee deductions including income tax, CPP (Canada Pension Plan) and EI (Employment Insurance) and is therefore less prone to error. Updated tax tables can be obtained from Sage Software, Inc.

▶

## PAYROLL LEDGER CONTINUED

- Payroll summaries permit easy analysis of compulsory and optional payroll expenses and benefits, employee contributions and entitlements.
- Different kinds of income can be linked to different expense accounts. In addition, the wages for different employees can be linked to different expense accounts, again permitting better tracking of payroll expenses.
- Simply Accounting automatically links payroll with control accounts in the General Ledger. Remittance amounts are tracked and linked with the corresponding payroll authorities for monthly or quarterly remittance.

## INVENTORY LEDGER

- The software provides an inventory summary or database of all inventory items.
- Services can be set up as inventory and tracked the same way as inventory items.
- Inventory reports flag items that need to be re-ordered, and the reports can be used to make purchase decisions.
- Import duty rates and different price list prices in home and foreign currencies can be set up in the ledger so they appear automatically in the journals.
- Inventory codes can be matched to the vendor and customer item codes so that common order forms are created automatically.
- The software calculates inventory variance costs when the items sold are out of stock and later purchased at different prices.
- Simply Accounting automatically updates inventory records when inventory is purchased, sold, transferred, lost, recovered or returned. It warns when you try to oversell inventory.
- Different units for stocking, selling and buying items can be saved for inventory items so that prices are automatically entered correctly for both sales and purchases. Reports can be prepared for any of the units on record.
- Inventory tracking reports can monitor sales and purchase activity on individual inventory items to see which ones are selling well and which are not. These reports can be used to determine optimum inventory buying patterns to reduce storage costs.

6. In summation, Simply Accounting provides an integrated management accounting information system.

## INCOME STATEMENT

### FLABULESS FITNESS

January 1 to March 31, 2009

| | | | |
|---|---|---|---|
| **Revenue** | | | |
| 4000 | GENERAL REVENUE | | |
| 4020 | Revenue from Sales | $78 450.00 | |
| 4040 | Revenue from Services | 8 335.00 | |
| 4060 | Sales Discounts | −965.00 | |
| 4100 | Net Sales | | $85 820.00 |
| 4120 | Exchange Rate Differences | | −12.00 |
| 4150 | Interest Revenue | | 1 980.00 |
| 4180 | Sales Tax Compensation | | 248.00 |
| 4200 | Freight Revenue | | 379.00 |
| 4390 | TOTAL GENERAL REVENUE | | $88 415.00 |
| TOTAL REVENUE | | | $88 415.00 |
| **Expense** | | | |
| 5000 | OPERATING EXPENSES | | |
| 5010 | Advertising and Promotion | | $ 530.00 |
| 5020 | Bank Charges | | 128.00 |
| 5030 | Credit Card Fees | | 1 480.00 |
| 5040 | Damaged Inventory | $ 80.00 | |
| 5050 | Cost of Goods Sold: Accessories | 5 395.00 | |
| 5060 | Cost of Goods Sold: Equipment | 3 149.00 | |
| 5070 | Cost Variance | 64.00 | |
| 5080 | Freight Expense | 432.00 | |
| 5090 | Purchase Discounts | −524.00 | |
| 5100 | Purchases Returns & Allowances | −367.00 | |
| 5110 | Net Cost of Goods Sold | | 8 229.00 |
| 5120 | Depreciation: Cash Registers | 300.00 | |
| 5130 | Depreciation: Computer Equipment | 150.00 ▶ | |

| | | | |
|---|---|---|---|
| ▶ 5140 | Depreciation: Furniture & Fixtures | 80.00 | |
| 5150 | Depreciation: Retail Premises | 2 440.00 | |
| 5160 | Depreciation: Van | 190.00 | |
| 5180 | Net Depreciation | | 3 160.00 |
| 5190 | Delivery Expense | | 63.00 |
| 5200 | Hydro Expense | | 528.00 |
| 5210 | Insurance Expense | | 1 200.00 |
| 5220 | Interest on Loan | | 1 240.00 |
| 5230 | Interest on Mortgage | | 5 600.00 |
| 5240 | Maintenance of Premises | | 1 055.00 |
| 5250 | Supplies Used | | 165.00 |
| 5260 | Property Taxes | | 2 700.00 |
| 5270 | Uncollectable Accounts Expense | | 500.00 |
| 5280 | Telephone Expense | | 295.00 |
| 5285 | Van Maintenance & Operating Expense | | 638.00 |
| 5290 | TOTAL OPERATING EXPENSES | | $27 511.00 |
| 5295 | PAYROLL EXPENSES | | |
| 5300 | Wages | | 8 295.20 |
| 5305 | Salaries | | 22 800.00 |
| 5310 | Commissions & Bonuses | | 284.80 |
| 5320 | EI Expense | | 998.00 |
| 5330 | CPP Expense | | 1 201.00 |
| 5340 | WSIB Expense | | 379.00 |
| 5360 | EHT Expense | | 309.00 |
| 5370 | Gp Insurance Expense | | 105.00 |
| 5490 | TOTAL PAYROLL EXPENSES | | $34 372.00 |
| TOTAL EXPENSE | | | $61 883.00 |
| NET INCOME | | | $26 532.00 |

## BUSINESS INFORMATION

### FLABULESS FITNESS

**USER PREFERENCES: Options**
Use Accounting Terms
Automatically save changes to records

**View**
Daily Business Manager   Turned off
Checklists   Turned off

**COMPANY SETTINGS: Information**

Address      199 Warmup Rd., Unit 500
             Hamilton, Ontario L8T 3B7
Tel 1        (905) 642-2348 (B-FIT)
Tel 2        (800) 448-2348 (B-FIT)
Fax          (905) 642-9100
Industry     Retail
Business No. 245 138 121 RT0001
Business Province: Ontario
Fiscal Start   04-01-2009
Earliest Transaction   04-01-2009
Fiscal End   06-30-2009

**System**
Warn if accounts not balanced

**Backup**
Backup Semi-monthly
Display a backup reminder

**Features**
All used

**Forms Settings (Next Number)**
Sales Invoices   No. 3000
Sales Quotes   No. 41
Receipts   No. 39
Customer Deposits   No. 15
Purchase Orders   No. 25
Direct Deposits   No. 19

**Date Format**
Use Long Dates on the screen

**Logo**
Data\Setup\logos\flab.bmp

**Names**
Additional Field: Ref. Number

**Credit Card Information**
Used: Visa
Payable  2250   Expense  5030

| Accept: | Visa | Interac |
|---|---|---|
| Fee | 2.5% | 0% |
| Expense | 5030 | 5030 |
| Asset | 1120 | 1120 |

**Sales Taxes**

| Tax | ID on forms | Track: | Purch | Sales |
|---|---|---|---|---|
| GST | 245 138 121 | | 2670 | 2650 |
| PST | | | | 2640 |

| | Taxable? | Exempt? | Report? |
|---|---|---|---|
| GST | No | No | Yes |
| PST | No | No | Yes |

**Tax Codes:**
G: GST, taxable, 6%, not included, refundable
GP: GST, taxable, 6%, not included, refundable
  PST, taxable, 8% not included,
    not refundable
IN: GST, taxable, 6%, included, refundable
  PST, taxable, 8%, included, not refundable

**Foreign Currency**
USD   United States Dollars
Tracking Account   4120
Exchange Rate on 04/01/09   1.185

**GENERAL SETTINGS**   No changes

**PAYABLES SETTINGS: Options**
Aging periods: 15, 30, 60 days
Discounts before tax: Yes

**Import Duty**
Track import duty
Linked account:  2220

**RECEIVABLES SETTINGS: Options**
Aging periods: 10, 30, 60 days
Interest charges: 1.5% after 30 days
Statements include invoices for 31 days
Use code GP for new customers

**Discount**
Payment terms: 2/10, n/30
Discounts before tax: No
Line Discounts: Not used

**Comments**
On Sales Invoice   Interest @ 1.5% per month
  charged on accounts over 30 days.

**PAYROLL SETTINGS**
**Names: Income and Deduction**
Income 1   Salary
Income 2   Commission
Income 3   No. Clients
Income 4   Bonus
Income 5   Tuition
Income 6   Travel Exp
Deduction 1   RRSP
Deduction 2   CSB Plan
Deduction 3   Garnishee

**Names: Additional Payroll**
Field 1   Emergency Contact
Field 2   Contact Number
User Expense 1   Gp Insurance
Entitlement 1   Vacation
Entitlement 2   Sick Leave
Entitlement 3   PersonalDays

**Incomes**

| Income | Type | Taxable | Vac. Pay |
|---|---|---|---|
| Regular | Income | Yes | Yes |
| Overtime 1 | Income | Yes | Yes |
| Salary | Income | Yes | No |
| Commission | Income | Yes | No |
| Bonus | Income | Yes | No |
| No. Clients | Piece Rate | Yes | Yes |
| Tuition | Income | Yes | No |
| Travel Exp | Reimburse | No | No |

**Deductions**
RRSP   Before tax, after other deductions
CSB Plan   After tax and other deductions
Garnishee   After tax and other deductions

**Taxes**
EI factor  1.4
EHT factor  0.98
WSIB rate  1.29
Prov. Tax   Not applicable

**Entitlements**

| Name | Track % | Max Days | Clear |
|---|---|---|---|
| Vacation | 8.0% | 25 | No |
| Sick Leave | 5.0% | 15 | No |
| PersonalDays | 2.5% | 5 | No |

**Remittance**

| Payroll Liability | Payroll Authority |
|---|---|
| EI, CPP, Income Tax | Receiver General |
| EHT, PST | Minister of Finance |
| WSIB | Workplace Safety & Insurance Board |
| Gp Insurance, RRSP | Ancaster Insurance |
| CSB | Mt. Hope Investment |
| Garnishee | Receiver General |

**Job Categories**
Sales: employees are salespersons
All employees are in Sales category

**INVENTORY SETTINGS**
Profit evaluation by markup
Sort inventory by number
Allow inventory levels to go below zero
Foreign prices from inventory records

**ACCOUNT CLASS SETTINGS**
Bank
  1060 Bank: Hamilton Trust Chequing  (CAD)
           Next cheque no.   101
           Next deposit no.   14
  1080 Bank: Hamilton Trust Savings  (CAD)
  1140 Bank: USD Chequing  (USD)
           Next cheque no.   346
Cash
  1030 Undeposited Cash and Cheques
Credit Card Receivable
  1120 Bank: Visa and Interac
Credit Card Payable
  2250 Credit Card Payable
All Postable Expense Accounts
  Expense or Operating Expense class

**LINKED ACCOUNTS FOR LEDGERS**
See pages 651–655, 661–662

# CHART OF ACCOUNTS

## FLABULESS FITNESS

### ASSETS
- 1000 CURRENT ASSETS [H]
- 1010 Test Balance Account
- 1030 Undeposited Cash and Cheques [A]
- 1060 Bank: Hamilton Trust Chequing [A]
- 1080 Bank: Hamilton Trust Savings [A]
- 1120 Bank: Visa and Interac [A]
- 1140 Bank: USD Chequing [A]
- 1150 Net Bank [S]
- 1200 Accounts Receivable [A]
- 1210 Allowance for Doubtful Accounts [A]
- 1220 Advances Receivable [A]
- 1230 Interest Receivable [A]
- 1240 Net Receivables [S]
- 1250 Purchase Prepayments
- 1260 Office Supplies
- 1265 Linen Supplies
- 1270 Prepaid Advertising
- 1280 Prepaid Insurance
- 1300 TOTAL CURRENT ASSETS [T]

- 1500 INVENTORY ASSETS [H]
- 1520 Accessories
- 1540 Fitness Equipment
- 1580 TOTAL INVENTORY ASSETS [T]

- 1600 CENTRE & EQUIPMENT [H]
- 1610 Cash Registers [A]
- 1620 Accum Deprec: Cash Registers [A]
- 1630 Net Cash Registers [S]
- 1640 Computer Equipment [A]
- 1650 Accum Deprec: Computer Equipment [A]
- 1660 Net Computer Equipment [S]
- 1670 Furniture & Fixtures [A]
- 1680 Accum Deprec: Furniture & Fixtures [A]
- 1690 Net Furniture & Fixtures [S]
- 1700 Retail Premises [A]
- 1710 Accum Deprec: Retail Premises [A]
- 1720 Net Retail Premises [S]
- 1730 Van [A]
- 1740 Accum Deprec: Van [A]
- 1750 Net Van [S]
- 1890 TOTAL CENTRE & EQUIPMENT [T] ▶

### ▶LIABILITIES
- 2000 CURRENT LIABILITIES [H]
- 2100 Bank Loan
- 2200 Accounts Payable
- 2210 Prepaid Sales and Deposits
- 2220 Import Duty Payable
- 2250 Credit Card Payable
- 2300 Vacation Payable
- 2310 EI Payable [A]
- 2320 CPP Payable [A]
- 2330 Income Tax Payable [A]
- 2350 Receiver General Payable [S]
- 2380 EHT Payable
- 2400 RRSP Payable
- 2410 CSB Plan Payable
- 2420 Group Insurance Payable
- 2430 Garnisheed Wages Payable
- 2460 WSIB Payable
- 2500 Business Income Tax Payable
- 2640 PST Payable
- 2650 GST Charged on Sales [A]
- 2670 GST Paid on Purchases [A]
- 2750 GST Owing (Refund) [S]
- 2790 TOTAL CURRENT LIABILITIES [T]

- 2800 LONG TERM LIABILITIES [H]
- 2820 Mortgage Payable
- 2890 TOTAL LONG TERM LIABILITIES [T]

### EQUITY
- 3000 OWNER'S EQUITY [H]
- 3560 S. Reeves, Capital
- 3600 Current Earnings [X]
- 3690 TOTAL OWNER'S EQUITY [T]

### REVENUE
- 4000 GENERAL REVENUE [H]
- 4020 Revenue from Sales [A]
- 4040 Revenue from Services [A]
- 4060 Sales Discounts [A]
- 4100 Net Sales [S]
- 4120 Exchange Rate Differences
- 4150 Interest Revenue
- 4180 Sales Tax Compensation
- 4200 Freight Revenue
- 4390 TOTAL GENERAL REVENUE [T] ▶

### ▶EXPENSE
- 5000 OPERATING EXPENSES [H]
- 5010 Advertising and Promotion
- 5020 Bank Charges
- 5030 Credit Card Fees
- 5040 Damaged Inventory [A]
- 5050 Cost of Goods Sold: Accessories [A]
- 5060 Cost of Goods Sold: Equipment [A]
- 5065 Cost of Services [A]
- 5070 Cost Variance [A]
- 5080 Freight Expense [A]
- 5090 Purchase Discounts [A]
- 5100 Purchases Returns & Allowances [A]
- 5110 Net Cost of Goods Sold [S]
- 5120 Depreciation: Cash Registers [A]
- 5130 Depreciation: Computer Equipment [A]
- 5140 Depreciation: Furniture & Fixtures [A]
- 5150 Depreciation: Retail Premises [A]
- 5160 Depreciation: Van [A]
- 5180 Net Depreciation [S]
- 5190 Delivery Expense
- 5200 Hydro Expense
- 5210 Insurance Expense
- 5220 Interest on Loan
- 5230 Interest on Mortgage
- 5240 Maintenance of Premises
- 5250 Supplies Used
- 5260 Property Taxes
- 5270 Uncollectable Accounts Expense
- 5280 Telephone Expense
- 5285 Van Maintenance & Operating Expense
- 5290 TOTAL OPERATING EXPENSES [T]

- 5295 PAYROLL EXPENSES [H]
- 5300 Wages
- 5305 Salaries
- 5310 Commissions & Bonuses
- 5320 Travel Expenses
- 5330 EI Expense
- 5340 CPP Expense
- 5350 WSIB Expense
- 5360 EHT Expense
- 5370 Gp Insurance Expense
- 5380 Employee Benefits

**NOTES:** The Chart of Accounts includes all accounts and Net Income. Group account types are not marked. Other account types are marked as follows: [H] Heading, [A] subgroup Account, [S] Subgroup total, [T] Total, [X] Current Earnings.

## BALANCE SHEET

### FLABULESS FITNESS

March 31, 2009

Assets

| | | | | |
|---|---|---|---|---|
| 1000 | CURRENT ASSETS | | | |
| 1060 | Bank: Hamilton Trust Chequing | $ 77 988.00 | | |
| 1080 | Bank: Hamilton Trust Savings | 108 250.00 | | |
| 1120 | Bank: Visa and Interac | 8 635.00 | | |
| 1140 | Bank: USD (8 020 USD) | 9 500.00 | | |
| 1150 | Net Bank | | $204 373.00 | |
| 1200 | Accounts Receivable | 17 280.00 | | |
| 1210 | Allowance for Doubtful Accounts | −800.00 | | |
| 1220 | Advances Receivable | 100.00 | | |
| 1230 | Interest Receivable | 420.00 | | |
| 1240 | Net Receivables | | 17 000.00 | |
| 1260 | Office Supplies | | 300.00 | |
| 1265 | Linen Supplies | | 450.00 | |
| 1270 | Prepaid Advertising | | 180.00 | |
| 1280 | Prepaid Insurance | | 4 800.00 | |
| 1300 | TOTAL CURRENT ASSETS | | $227 103.00 | |
| | | | | |
| 1500 | INVENTORY ASSETS | | | |
| 1520 | Accessories | | 15 270.00 | |
| 1540 | Fitness Equipment | | 78 616.00 | |
| 1580 | TOTAL INVENTORY ASSETS | | $93 886.00 | |
| | | | | |
| 1600 | CENTRE & EQUIPMENT | | | |
| 1610 | Cash Registers | 5 000.00 | | |
| 1620 | Accum Deprec: Cash Registers | −1 000.00 | | |
| 1630 | Net Cash Registers | | 4 000.00 | |
| 1640 | Computer Equipment | 3 000.00 | | |
| 1650 | Accum Deprec: Computer Equip | −1 000.00 | | |
| 1660 | Net Computer Equipment | | 2 000.00 | |
| 1670 | Furniture & Fixtures | 2 000.00 | | |
| 1680 | Accum Deprec: Furn & Fixtures | −400.00 | | |
| 1690 | Net Furniture & Fixtures | | 1 600.00 | |
| 1700 | Retail Premises | 200 000.00 | | |
| 1710 | Accum Deprec: Retail Premises | −5 000.00 | | |
| 1720 | Net Retail Premises | | 195 000.00 | |
| 1730 | Van | 30 000.00 | | |
| 1740 | Accum Deprec: Van | −5 000.00 | | |
| 1750 | Net Van | | 25 000.00 | |
| 1890 | TOTAL CENTRE & EQUIPMENT | | $227 600.00 | |

TOTAL ASSETS    $548 589.00 ▶

Liabilities

| | | | | |
|---|---|---|---|---|
| ▶ 2000 | CURRENT LIABILITIES | | | |
| 2100 | Bank Loan | | $ 50 000.00 | |
| 2200 | Accounts Payable | | 16 960.00 | |
| 2250 | Credit Card Payable | | 220.00 | |
| 2300 | Vacation Payable | | 371.84 | |
| 2310 | EI Payable | $ 563.28 | | |
| 2320 | CPP Payable | 824.77 | | |
| 2330 | Income Tax Payable | 1 755.60 | | |
| 2350 | Receiver General Payable | | 3 143.65 | |
| 2380 | EHT Payable | | 320.50 | |
| 2400 | RRSP Payable | | 350.00 | |
| 2410 | CSB Plan Payable | | 350.00 | |
| 2420 | Group Insurance Payable | | 39.00 | |
| 2430 | Garnisheed Wages Payable | | 200.00 | |
| 2460 | WSIB Payable | | 392.51 | |
| 2500 | Business Income Tax Payable | | 3 600.00 | |
| 2640 | PST Payable | | 2 470.00 | |
| 2650 | GST Charged on Sales | 2 940.00 | | |
| 2670 | GST Paid on Purchases | −1 260.00 | | |
| 2750 | GST Owing (Refund) | | 1 680.00 | |
| 2790 | TOTAL CURRENT LIABILITIES | | $80 097.50 | |
| | | | | |
| 2800 | LONG TERM LIABILITIES | | | |
| 2820 | Mortgage Payable | | 180 000.00 | |
| 2890 | TOTAL LONG TERM LIABILITIES | | $180 000.00 | |

TOTAL LIABILITIES    $260 097.50

Equity

| | | | |
|---|---|---|---|
| 3000 | OWNER'S EQUITY | | |
| 3560 | S. Reeves, Capital | $261 129.50 | |
| 3600 | Current Earnings | 26 532.00 | |
| 3690 | TOTAL OWNER'S EQUITY | $288 491.50 | |

TOTAL EQUITY    $288 491.50

LIABILITIES AND EQUITY    $548 589.00

## POST-CLOSING TRIAL BALANCE

### FLABULESS FITNESS

| March 31, 2009 | | Debits | Credits | | | | Debits | Credits |
|---|---|---|---|---|---|---|---|---|
| 1060 | Bank: Hamilton Trust Chequing | $ 77 988.00 | | ▶ 1730 | Van | | 30 000.00 | |
| 1080 | Bank: Hamilton Trust Savings | 108 250.00 | | 1740 | Accum Deprec: Van | | | 5 000.00 |
| 1120 | Bank: Visa and Interac | 8 635.00 | | 2100 | Bank Loan | | | 50 000.00 |
| 1140 | Bank: USD Chequing (8 020 USD) | 9 500.00 | | 2200 | Accounts Payable | | | 16 960.00 |
| 1200 | Accounts Receivable | 17 280.00 | | 2250 | Credit Card Payable | | | 220.00 |
| 1210 | Allowance for Doubtful Accounts | | $ 800.00 | 2300 | Vacation Payable | | | 371.84 |
| 1220 | Advances Receivable | 100.00 | | 2310 | EI Payable | | | 563.28 |
| 1230 | Interest Receivable | 420.00 | | 2320 | CPP Payable | | | 824.77 |
| 1260 | Office Supplies | 300.00 | | 2330 | Income Tax Payable | | | 1 755.60 |
| 1265 | Linen Supplies | 450.00 | | 2380 | EHT Payable | | | 320.50 |
| 1270 | Prepaid Advertising | 180.00 | | 2400 | RRSP Payable | | | 350.00 |
| 1280 | Prepaid Insurance | 4 800.00 | | 2410 | CSB Plan Payable | | | 350.00 |
| 1520 | Accessories | 15 270.00 | | 2420 | Group Insurance Payable | | | 39.00 |
| 1540 | Fitness Equipment | 78 616.00 | | 2430 | Garnisheed Wages Payable | | | 200.00 |
| 1610 | Cash Registers | 5 000.00 | | 2460 | WSIB Payable | | | 392.51 |
| 1620 | Accum Deprec: Cash Registers | | 1 000.00 | 2500 | Business Income Tax Payable | | | 3 600.00 |
| 1640 | Computer Equipment | 3 000.00 | | 2640 | PST Payable | | | 2 470.00 |
| 1650 | Accum Deprec: Computer Equipment | | 1 000.00 | 2650 | GST Charged on Sales | | | 2 940.00 |
| 1670 | Furniture & Fixtures | 2 000.00 | | 2670 | GST Paid on Purchases | | 1 260.00 | |
| 1680 | Accum Deprec: Furniture & Fixtures | | 400.00 | 2820 | Mortgage Payable | | | 180 000.00 |
| 1700 | Retail Premises | 200 000.00 | | 3560 | S. Reeves, Capital | | | 288 491.50 |
| 1710 | Accum Deprec: Retail Premises | | 5 000.00 ▶ | | | | $563 049.00 | $563 049.00 |

## VENDOR INFORMATION

### FLABULESS FITNESS

| Vendor Name (Contact) | Address | Phone No. Fax No. | E-mail Web Site | Terms Tax ID | Expense Acct Tax Code |
|---|---|---|---|---|---|
| Ancaster Insurance (Feulle Cuvver) | 718 Montgomery Dr. Ancaster, ON L9G 3H5 | Tel: (905) 588-1773 Fax: (905) 588-1624 | fc@ancaster.insur.ca www.ancaster.insur.ca | net 1 | no tax (not exempt) |
| Bell Canada (Noel Coller) | 100 James St. N. Hamilton, ON L8R 2K5 | Tel: (905) 525-2355 | www.bell.ca | net 1 | 5280 GP |
| City of Hamilton Treasurer (Budd Jett) | 53 Main St. W. Hamilton, ON L8P 2Z3 | Tel: (905) 461-0063 Fax: (905) 461-9204 | www.hamilton.city.ca | net 1 | 5260 no tax (exempt) |
| Energy Source (Manny Watts) | 91 NacNab St. Hamilton, ON L8R 2L9 | Tel: (905) 463-2664 | watts@energysource.ca www.energysource.ca | net 1 | 5200 G |
| Feelyte Gym Accessories (Stretch Theraband) | 7 Onondaga Dr. Ancaster, ON L9G 4S5 | Tel: (905) 588-3846 Fax: (905) 588-7126 | stretch@feelyte.com www.feelyte.com | 2/10, n/30 (before tax) 466 254 108 | G |
| Footlink Corporation (Onna Treadmill) | 39 Treadwell St. Oakville, ON L6M 3K9 | Tel: (905) 777-8133 Fax: (905) 777-8109 | onna@footlink.com www.footlink.com | 1/15, n/30 (before tax) 274 309 481 | G |
| Hamilton Spectator (Dawn Newsman) | 15 Wentworth St. N. Hamilton, ON L8L 5T8 | Tel: (905) 525-1800 Fax: (905) 525-1816 | newsman@spectator.ca www.spectator.ca | net 10 | 1270 GP |
| Minister of Finance (N.O. Money) | 631 Queenston Rd. Hamilton, ON L8K 6R5 | Tel: (905) 462-5555 | www.gov.on.ca/fin | net 1 | no tax (exempt) |
| Mt. Hope Investment Corp. (P. Cuniary) | 122 King St. W. Hamilton, ON L8P 4V2 | Tel: (905) 462-3338 Fax: (905) 461-2116 | pc@mt.hope.invest.ca www.mt.hope.invest.ca | net 15 | 2410 no tax (exempt) |

▶

| Vendor Name (Contact) | Address | Phone No. Fax No. | E-mail Web Site | Terms Tax ID | Expense Acct Tax Code |
|---|---|---|---|---|---|
| Prolife Exercisers Inc. (C. Glider) (USD vendor) | 1500 Redmond Road Suite 100, Woodinville Washington  98072  USA | Tel: (509) 628-9163 Fax: (509) 629-7164 | glider@prolife.ex.com www.prolife.ex.com | 2/10, n/30 (before tax) | G |
| Receiver General for Canada | Sudbury Tax Services Office PO Box 20004 Sudbury, ON  P3A 6B4 | Tel 1: (800) 561-7761 Tel 2: (800) 959-2221 | www.cra-arc.gc.ca | net 1 | no tax (exempt) |
| Redux Home Gym Wholesalers (Bi Sepps) (USD vendor) | 4900 Columbia St., #650 El Cerrito, California 94533  USA | Tel 1: (510) 525-4327 Tel 2: (800) 567-9152 Fax: (510) 526-1135 | bisepps@redux.com www.redux.com | 2/10, n/30 (before tax) | G |
| Scandia Weights Co. (B. Fitt) | 82 Nordica Lane Hamilton, ON  L8P 2G6 | Tel: (905) 465-6247 Fax: (905) 466-3554 | fitt@scandiawts.com www.scandiawts.com | net 30 372 640 813 | G |
| Trufit Depot (Varry Shapely) | 43 Paling Ave. Hamilton, ON  L8H 5J5 | Tel: (905) 529-7235 Fax: (905) 529-2995 | shapely@trufitdepot.ca www.trufitdepot.ca | 2/5, n/30 (before tax) 244 573 650 | G |
| Waterdown Sunoco (Mick Annick) | 101 Niska Dr. Waterdown, ON  L0R 2H3 | Tel: (905) 622-6181 Fax: (905) 622-4777 | mick@goodforcars.com www.goodforcars.com | net 1 | 5285 IN |
| Westdale Office Supplies (Clip Papers) | 26 Dalewood Ave. Hamilton, ON  L8S 1Y7 | Tel: (905) 528-8199 Fax: (905) 528-8221 | papers@wos.com www.wos.com | net 30 259 491 820 | 1260 GP |
| Workplace Safety & Insurance Board (I.M. Hurt) | PO Box 2099 Hamilton, ON  L8N 4C5 | Tel: (800) 525-9100 Fax: (905) 523-1824 | www.wsib.on.ca | net 1 | 2460 no tax (exempt) |

**NOTES:** Year-to-date purchases and payments are not recorded because this is a new fiscal period.

## OUTSTANDING VENDOR INVOICES

### FLABULESS FITNESS

| Vendor Name | Terms | Date | Inv/Chq No. | Amount | Tax | Total |
|---|---|---|---|---|---|---|
| Feelyte Gym Accessories | 2/10, n/30 (before tax) | Mar. 30/09 | FG-1611 | $1 000 | $60 | $1 060 |
| Footlink Corporation | 1/15, n/30 (before tax) | Mar. 20/09 Mar. 21/09 | FC-618 Chq 96 Balance Owing | $10 000 2 120 | $600 | $10 600 2 120 $8 480 |
| Redux Home Gym Wholesalers | 2/10, n/30 (before tax) | Mar. 28/09 | R-914 | $5 910 USD | 354.60 USD | $7 420 CAD |
| | | | | Grand Total | | $16 960 |

## CUSTOMER INFORMATION

### FLABULESS FITNESS

| Customer Name (Contact) | Address | Phone No. Fax No. | E-mail Web Site | Terms Tax Code | Credit Limit |
|---|---|---|---|---|---|
| *Buffalo Health Clinic (Minnie Mussle) | 75 Brawn Ave. Buffalo, New York 14202 USA | Tel: (716) 367-7346 Fax: (716) 367-8258 | mmussle@buffalohealth.com www.buffalohealth.com Currency: USD | 2/10, n/30 no tax | $12 000 ($10 500 USD) |
| *Chedoke Health Care (Wade Less) | 13 Wellspring Dr. Hamilton, ON  L8T 3B8 | Tel: (905) 526-3344 Fax: (905) 525-1166 | less@chedoke.healthcare.ca www.chedoke.healthcare.ca | 2/10, n/30 GP | $12 000 |
| Dundas Recreational Centre (X.S. Wayte) | 190 Playtime Circle Dundas, ON  L8C 2V8 | Tel: (905) 466-5576 Fax: (905) 466-7284 | xswayte@dundas.reccentre.ca www.dundas.reccentre.ca | 2/10, n/30 GP | $12 000 |
| Hamilton District Bd of Education (Nott Skinny) | 10 James St. S. Hamilton, ON  L8K 4G2 | Tel: (905) 461-5997 Fax: (905) 461-6936 | nskinny@hdsb.ca www.hdsb.ca | 2/10, n/30 GP | $12 000 |

| Customer Name (Contact) | Address | Phone No. Fax No. | E-mail Web Site | Terms Tax Code | Credit Limit |
|---|---|---|---|---|---|
| Lockport Gymnasium (B. Phatt) | 62 Sweats St. Niagara Falls, New York 14301 USA | Tel: (716) 399-1489 Fax: (716) 399-2735 | phatt@lockportgym.com www.lockportgym.com Currency: USD | 2/10, n/30 no tax | $12 000 ($10 500 USD) |
| *McMaster University (Outov Shape) | Kinesiology Dept. McMaster University Hamilton, ON  L8V 3M9 | Tel 1: (905) 529-3000 Tel 2: (905) 529-3198 Fax: (905) 529- 3477 | oshape@mcmasteru.ca www.mcmasteru.ca | 2/10, n/30 GP | $12 000 |
| *Mohawk College (Phat Nomore) | Physical Education Dept. Mohawk College Hamilton, ON  L8F 7F2 | Tel 1: (905) 622-9250 Tel 2: (905) 622-9238 Fax: (905) 622-9729 | nomore@mohawkcoll.ca www.mohawkcoll.ca | 2/10, n/30 GP | $12 000 |
| *Stelco Health Club (Les Pound) | 1 Stelco Rd. Hamilton, ON  L8P 6N6 | Tel: (905) 524-1000 Fax: (905) 524-1924 | pound@stelco.health.com www.stelco.health.com | 2/10, n/30 GP | $12 000 |
| Stoney Creek Sports Arena (B. Thin) | 93 Workout Rd. Stoney Creek, ON  L7M 5C7 | Tel: (905) 838-1800 Fax: (905) 838-1278 | bthin@scsa.com www.scsa.com | 2/10, n/30 GP | $12 000 |
| Cash and Interac Customers Visa Sales (for Visa customers) | | | | net 1 net 1 | GP GP |

**NOTES:** Preferred price list customers are marked with an asterisk (*). The ship-to address is the same as the mailing address for all customers.

## OUTSTANDING CUSTOMER INVOICES

### FLABULESS FITNESS

| Customer Name | Terms | Date | Inv/Chq No. | Amount | Total |
|---|---|---|---|---|---|
| Chedoke Health Care | 2/10, n/30 (after tax) | Mar. 30/09 Mar. 30/09 | 2199 Chq 488 Balance Owing | $9 120 2 100 | $7 020 |
| Mohawk College | 2/10, n/30 (after tax) | Mar. 26/09 | 2194 | $5 700 | $5 700 |
| Stoney Creek Sports Arena | 2/10, n/30 (after tax) | Mar. 23/09 | 2191 | $4 560 | $4 560 |
| | | | | Grand Total | $17 280 |

## EMPLOYEE INFORMATION SHEET

### FLABULESS FITNESS

| Employee | George Schwinn | Nieve Prekor | Assumpta Kisangel |
|---|---|---|---|
| Position | Shipping/Trainer | Sales/Yoga Instructor | Sales/Accounting |
| Address | 55 Carter St. Hamilton, ON  L8B 2V7 | 2 Meditation Circle Hamilton, ON  L8B 7C1 | 300 Track Rd. Hamilton, ON  L9G 4K8 |
| Telephone | (905) 426-1817 | (905) 527-4412 | (905) 688-5778 |
| Social Insurance No. | 532 548 625 | 783 455 611 | 488 655 333 |
| Date of Birth (mm-dd-yy) Date of Hire (mm-dd-yy) | 09/18/69 01/06/03 | 03/15/72 02/15/00 | 05/24/75 08/25/03 |
| Federal (Ontario) Tax Exemption - TD1    Basic Personal    Spousal    Other    Total Exemptions | $8 929 (8 533) – – $8 929 (8 533) | $8 929 (8 533) – – $8 929 (8 533) | $8 929 (8 533) $7 581 (7 262) $4 019 (4 031) $20 529 (19 826) |
| Additional Federal Tax | – | $50.00 | – |

| Employee | George Schwinn | Nieve Prekor | Assumpta Kisangel |
|---|---|---|---|
| **Employee Taxes** | | | |
| Historical Income tax | $1 562.21 | $2 392.08 | $1 537.85 |
| Historical EI | $217.54 | $270.00 | $248.96 |
| Historical CPP | $375.20 | $478.38 | $438.16 |
| Deduct EI; EI Factor | Yes; 1.4 | Yes; 1.4 | Yes; 1.4 |
| Deduct CPP | Yes | Yes | Yes |
| **Employee Income** | | | |
| Advances: Historical Amount | $100.00 | (use) ✓ | (use) ✓ |
| Benefits Per Period | $5.00 | $12.00 | $12.00 |
| Benefits: Historical Amount | $35.00 | $36.00 | $36.00 |
| Vacation Pay Owed | $371.84 | (do not use) | (do not use) |
| Vacation Paid | $385.92 | (do not use) | (do not use) |
| Regular Wage Rate (Hours per Period) | $16.00/hr  (80 hours) | (do not use) | (do not use) |
| Regular Wages: Historical Amount | $8 960.00 | (do not use) | (do not use) |
| Overtime 1 Wage Rate | $24.00/hr | (do not use) | (do not use) |
| Overtime 1 Wages: Historical Amount | $336.00 | (do not use) | (do not use) |
| Salary (Hours Per Period) | (do not use) | $4 000.00 (150 Hours) | $3 600.00 (150 hours) |
| Salary: Historical Amount | (do not use) | $12 000.00 | $10 800.00 |
| Commission | (do not use) | (do not use) | (use) ✓ 2% (service revenue) |
| Commissions: Historical Amount | (do not use) | (do not use) | $285.00 |
| No. Clients (piece rate) | $10 | $10 | $10 |
| Bonus: | (use) ✓ | (use) ✓ | (use) ✓ |
| Tuition: Historical Amount | (use) ✓ | (use) ✓ | $440 |
| Travel Exp.: Historical Amount | (use) ✓ | $120.00 | (use) ✓ |
| Pay Periods | 26 | 12 | 12 |
| Vacation Rate | 6% retained | 0% not retained | 0% not retained |
| Record Wage Expenses in | Linked Accounts | Linked Accounts | Linked Accounts |
| **Deductions** | | | |
| RRSP (Historical Amount) | $50.00 ($350.00) | $100.00 ($300.00) | $100.00 ($300.00) |
| CSB Plan (Historical Amount) | $50.00 ($350.00) | $100.00 ($300.00) | $100.00 ($300.00) |
| Garnishee (Historical Amount) | (do not use) | $200.00 ($400.00) | (do not use) |
| **WSIB and Other Expenses** | | | |
| WSIB Rate | 1.29 | 1.29 | 1.02 |
| Group Insurance (Historical Amount) | $5.00 ($35.00) | $12.00 ($36.00) | $12.00 ($36.00) |
| **Entitlements: Rate, Maximum Days, Clear? (Historical Amount)** | | | |
| Vacation | – | 8%, 25 days, No (15) | 8%, 25 days, No (15) |
| Sick Leave | 5%, 15 days, No (12) | 5%, 15 days, No (10) | 5%, 15 days, No (8) |
| Personal Days | 2.5%, 5 days, No (4) | 2.5%, 5 days, No (2) | 2.5%, 5 days, No (3) |
| **Direct Deposit** | | | |
| Yes/No | Yes | Yes | Yes |
| Bank, Transit, Account No. | 102, 89008, 2998187 | 102, 89008, 3829110 | 102, 89008, 2309982 |
| Percent | 100% | 100% | 100% |
| **Additional Information** | | | |
| Emergency Contact & Number | Adrian Ingles (905) 722-0301 | Alex Prekor (905) 548-2973 | Martha Kisangel (905) 688-5778 |
| **T4 and RL-1 Reporting** | | | |
| EI Insurable Earnings | $9 681.92 | $12 000.00 | $11 085.00 |
| Pensionable Earnings | $9 716.92 | $12 156.00 | $11 561.00 |
| Withheld | $2 854.95 | $4 140.46 | $2 824.97 |
| Net Pay | $6 926.97 | $7 979.54 | $8 700.03 |

# Employee Profiles and TD1 Information

**All Employees**    Flabuless Fitness pays group insurance premiums for all employees. They also are reimbursed for tuition fees when they successfully complete a university or college course. These benefits are both taxable. In addition, when they use their personal vehicles for company business, they are reimbursed for car expenses.

All employees are entitled to three weeks' vacation, ten days' sick leave and five personal days of leave per year. All three employees have sick leave and personal days that they can carry forward from the previous year. The two salaried employees take three weeks' vacation as paid time and the hourly employee receives 6 percent of his wages as vacation pay when he takes his vacation.

Starting in April, as an incentive to provide excellent customer service, all employees will receive a quarterly bonus of $10 for every completed satisfactory customer survey.

**George Schwinn**    is responsible for shipping, receiving, delivery and equipment setup for customers. He also works as the personal trainer in the store. He is single, so he uses only the basic tax claim amount. Every two weeks his pay, at the rate of $16 per hour, is deposited to his account. For the hours beyond 40 hours in a week, he receives an overtime rate of $24 per hour. He is owed three months of vacation pay. He contributes to his RRSP and Canada Savings Bond plan through payroll deductions. He still owes $100 from an advance of $200 and will pay back $50 of the advance in each of the next two pay periods.

**NOTES**
Wages may be garnisheed by any creditor, but the most common one is the Receiver General to pay back-taxes owing.

**Nieve Prekor**    is the store manager and yoga instructor for Flabuless Fitness, and she assists with store sales. Her monthly salary of $4 000 is deposited directly into her bank account. Prekor is married with one child but uses the basic single claim amount because her husband is also employed. Her payroll deductions include additional federal income tax for other income, wages garnisheed to pay for prior taxes owing and regular contributions to her Registered Retirement Savings Plan and Canada Savings Bonds.

**Assumpta Kisangel**    does the accounting and manages the Payables, Receivables and Payroll in addition to sales in the store. Although she is single, she supports her infirm mother so she has the spousal equivalent claim and a caregiver amount in addition to the basic single claim amount. A commission of 2 percent of revenue from services supplements her monthly salary of $3 600 that is deposited directly into her bank account. She has RRSP and CSB contributions withheld from her paycheques.

## INVENTORY INFORMATION

### FLABULESS FITNESS

| Code | Description | Min Stock | CAD Prices Reg | (Pref) | USD Prices Reg. | (Pref) | Stock/Sell Unit | Buying Unit | Relationship | Qty on Hand | Total (Cost) |
|------|-------------|-----------|------|--------|------|--------|------|------|------|------|------|
| **Accessories**: Total asset value $15 270  (Linked Accounts: Asset 1520; Revenue 4020, COGS 5050, Variance 5070) | | | | | | | | | | | |
| A010 | Body Fat Scale | 2 | $ 100 | ($ 90) | $ 85 | ($ 77) | unit | carton | 12/carton | 10 | $ 400 |
| A020 | Yoga Mats | 3 | 30 | (27) | 26 | (24) | unit | box | 10/box | 40 | 480 |
| A030 | Dumbbells: pair | 25 | 1.50 | (1.40) | 1.30 | (1.20) | kg | 100kg | 100/100kg | 400 | 300 |
| A040 | Dumbbells: 5kg set | 5 | 15 | (13) | 13 | (12) | set | | same | 25 | 150 |
| A050 | Dumbbells: 10kg set | 5 | 25 | (22) | 21 | (19) | set | | same | 25 | 250 |
| A060 | Dumbbells: 15kg set | 5 | 40 | (36) | 34 | (31) | set | | same | 25 | 400 |
| A070 | Glide Slidetrak | 3 | 50 | (45) | 42 | (38) | each | | same | 20 | 500 |
| A080 | Heart Rate Monitor | 2 | 75 | (68) | 63 | (57) | unit | carton | 12/carton | 10 | 300 |
| A090 | Power Blocks up to 100 kg | 3 | 160 | (144) | 134 | (121) | set | | same | 10 | 800 |
| A100 | Power Blocks up to 200 kg | 3 | 300 | (270) | 260 | (236) | set | | same | 10 | 1500 |

▶

| Code | Description | Min Stock | CAD Prices Reg. | (Pref) | USD Prices Reg. | (Pref) | Stock/Sell Unit | Buying Unit | Relationship | Qty on Hand | Total (Cost) |
|------|-------------|-----------|-----------------|--------|-----------------|--------|-----------------|-------------|--------------|-------------|--------------|
| **Accessories**: Continued | | | | | | | | | | | |
| A110 | Stability Balls | 5 | $ 10 | ($ 9) | $ 9 | ($ 8) | each | | same | 25 | 100 |
| A120 | Wavemaster | 2 | 150 | (135) | 130 | (119) | unit | | same | 10 | 750 |
| A130 | Weight Plates | 25 | 1.20 | (1.10) | 1.00 | (0.90) | kg | 100kg | 100/100kg | 400 | 240 |
| A140 | Weights: Olympic 75 kg | 5 | 150 | (135) | 132 | (119) | set | | same | 20 | 1 500 |
| A150 | Weights: Olympic 100 kg | 5 | 200 | (180) | 170 | (151) | set | | same | 20 | 2 000 |
| A160 | Weights: Olympic 125 kg | 5 | 250 | (225) | 210 | (190) | set | | same | 20 | $2 500 |
| A170 | Weights: Olympic 150 kg | 5 | 300 | (270) | 260 | (232) | set | | same | 20 | 3 000 |
| A180 | Workout Gloves: all sizes | 5 | 10 | (9) | 9 | (8) | pair | box | 10/box | 25 | 100 |
| **Fitness Equipment**: Total asset value $78 616  (Linked Accounts: Asset 1540; Revenue 4020, COGS 5060, Variance 5070) | | | | | | | | | | | |
| Elliptical Exercisers | | | | | | | | | | | |
| E010 | Elliptical Exerciser: ME-100 | 2 | 1 100 | (1 000) | 925 | (830) | unit | | same | 5 | 2 200 |
| E020 | Elliptical Exerciser: AE-200 | 2 | 1 700 | (1 550) | 1 430 | (1 285) | unit | | same | 5 | 3 400 |
| E030 | Elliptical Exerciser: DE-300 | 2 | 2 000 | (1 875) | 1 680 | (1 512) | unit | | same | 5 | 4 000 |
| E040 | Elliptical Exerciser: LE-400 | 2 | 2 200 | (2 000) | 1 850 | (1 663) | unit | | same | 5 | 4 400 |
| Exercise Bicycles | | | | | | | | | | | |
| E050 | Bicycle: Calorie Counter CC-60 | 2 | 400 | (360) | 336 | (302) | unit | | same | 10 | 1 600 |
| E060 | Bicycle: Dual Action DA-70 | 2 | 600 | (540) | 505 | (455) | unit | | same | 10 | 2 400 |
| E070 | Bicycle: Recumbent R-80 | 2 | 750 | (680) | 630 | (567) | unit | | same | 10 | 3 000 |
| Exercise Equipment: Home Gyms | | | | | | | | | | | |
| E080 | Home Gym: Basic HG-1400 | 2 | 1 000 | (900) | 840 | (755) | set | | same | 5 | $2 000 |
| E090 | Home Gym: Deluxe HG-1401 | 2 | 1 500 | (1 400) | 1 310 | (1 180) | set | | same | 5 | 3 000 |
| E100 | Home Gym: Multi HG-1402 | 2 | 2 000 | (1 875) | 1 680 | (1 512) | set | | same | 5 | 4 000 |
| Riders, Walkers and Rowing Machines | | | | | | | | | | | |
| E110 | Rider: Airwalker RA-900 | 3 | 300 | (270) | 265 | (237) | unit | | same | 8 | 960 |
| E120 | Rider: Powerglider RP-1500 | 3 | 350 | (315) | 305 | (275) | unit | | same | 8 | 1 120 |
| E130 | Rowing Machine: RM-1000 | 3 | 480 | (435) | 400 | (360) | unit | | same | 8 | 1 536 |
| Ski Exercisers | | | | | | | | | | | |
| E140 | Ski Exerciser: Skitrek SE-680 | 3 | 400 | (360) | 335 | (302) | unit | | same | 10 | 1 600 |
| E150 | Ski Exerciser: Linked SE-780 | 3 | 450 | (410) | 380 | (340) | unit | | same | 10 | 1 800 |
| E160 | Ski Exerciser: Independent SE-880 | 3 | 600 | (550) | 505 | (455) | unit | | same | 10 | 2 400 |
| Stair Climbers | | | | | | | | | | | |
| E170 | Stair Climber: Adjustable SC-A60 | 2 | 1 500 | (1 375) | 1 310 | (1 180) | unit | | same | 5 | 3 000 |
| E180 | Stair Climber: Unlinked SC-U75 | 2 | 2 100 | (1 925) | 1 735 | (1 560) | unit | | same | 5 | 4 200 |
| Treadmills | | | | | | | | | | | |
| E190 | Treadmill: Basic T-800B | 3 | 1 200 | (1 100) | 1 000 | (900) | unit | | same | 10 | 4 800 |
| E200 | Treadmill: Basic Plus T-910P | 3 | 1 600 | (1 450) | 1 315 | (1 180) | unit | | same | 10 | 6 400 |
| E210 | Treadmill: Deluxe T-1100D | 3 | 2 400 | (2 200) | 2 015 | (1 810) | unit | | same | 10 | 9 600 |
| E220 | Treadmill: Deluxe Plus T-1200P | 3 | 2 800 | (2 600) | 2 360 | (2 125) | unit | | same | 10 | 11 200 |
| **Services** (Linked Accounts: Revenue 4040, COGS 5065) | | | | | | | | | | | |
| S010 | Personal Trainer: 1 hour | | 75 | (70) | | | hour | | PST Tax Exempt | | |
| S020 | Personal Trainer: 1/2 day | | 200 | (190) | | | 1/2 day | | PST Tax Exempt | | |
| S030 | Personal Trainer: full day | | 400 | (380) | | | day | | PST Tax Exempt | | |
| S040 | Yoga Instructor: 1 hour | | 100 | (95) | | | hour | | PST Tax Exempt | | |
| S050 | Yoga Instructor: 1/2 day | | 200 | (190) | | | 1/2 day | | PST Tax Exempt | | |

**NOTES:**  No duty is charged on items imported from the United States. The duty rate is 0%.
Stocking and selling units are the same for all items.
Buying units and the relationship to stocking units are entered only when these are different from the stocking/selling units.
"Same" is entered in the relationship column when the same unit is used for all measures.

# Accounting Procedures

### The Goods and Services Tax (GST)

GST at the rate of 6 percent is applied to all goods and services offered by Flabuless Fitness. Flabuless Fitness uses the regular method for remittance of the Goods and Services Tax. GST collected from customers is recorded as a liability in *GST Charged on Sales*. GST paid to vendors is recorded in *GST Paid on Purchases* as a decrease in liability to Canada Revenue Agency (CRA). These two postable accounts are added together in the subgroup total account *GST Owing (Refund)*. The balance of GST to be remitted or the request for a refund is sent to the Receiver General for Canada by the last day of the current month for the previous month.

Tax calculations will be correct only for customers and vendors for whom the tax exempt option was set as No. The GST Report available from the Reports menu will include transactions completed in the Sales, Purchases and General journals, but the opening historical balances will not be included. Therefore, the amounts shown in the GST Report may differ from the balances in the General Ledger GST accounts. You should use the General Ledger accounts to verify the balance owing (or refund due) and make adjustments to the report manually as necessary.

After the report is filed, clear the GST Report (choose the Maintenance menu, then Clear Data and click Clear Tax Report and select GST). Enter the last day of the previous month as the date for clearing. Always back up your files before clearing the GST Report.

### Provincial Sales Tax (PST)

Provincial Sales Tax of 8 percent is applied to the sales of all goods but not services provided by Flabuless Fitness. It is applied to the amount of the sale without GST included and is not applied to freight. The PST collected must be remitted monthly to the Minister of Finance. Provincial Sales Taxes to be remitted must be set up as a liability owing to the vendor, Minister of Finance, in the Purchases Journal. The General Ledger balance for *PST Payable* for the last day of the previous month will provide the total owing. You may display or print this account for reference. A 5 percent sales tax compensation is earned if the remittance is made before the due date assigned to the business.

### Business Income Tax

Flabuless Fitness pays income tax in quarterly instalments to the Receiver General based on its previous year's net income.

### The Employer Health Tax (EHT)

The Employer Health Tax (EHT) is paid by all employers permanently established in Ontario to provide Ontario Health Insurance Plan (OHIP) coverage for all eligible Ontario residents. The EHT is based on the total annual remuneration paid to employees. Employers whose total payroll exceeds $400 000 must pay EHT. Although the payroll for Flabuless Fitness is less than this amount, we show the application of EHT so that you can learn how to set up the expense and make the remittances. In this application, EHT will be remitted quarterly. *EHT Payable* is set up as a liability owing to the vendor, Minister of Finance. The Remittance Payments Journal will provide you with the balance owing to the Minister of Finance when the liability is linked to this vendor.

### Aging of Accounts

Flabuless Fitness uses aging periods that reflect the payment terms it provides to customers and receives from vendors. For customers, this will be 10, 30 and 60 days, and for vendors, 15, 30 and 60 days. Interest at 1.5 percent is charged on customer accounts that are not paid within 30 days. Regular customer statements show interest amounts, and invoices are then prepared to add the interest to the amount owing in the ledger record.

### Discounts

Flabuless Fitness offers a 2 percent discount to regular account customers if they settle their accounts within 10 days. Full payment is requested within 30 days. These payment terms are set up as defaults. When the receipt is entered and the discount is still available, the program shows the amount of the discount and the net amount owing. No discounts are given on cash or credit card sales. Customer discounts are calculated on after-tax amounts.

Some customers receive preferred customer prices, approximately 10 percent below the regular prices. These customers are identified in the ledger records and the preferred prices are set up in the inventory ledger records.

Some vendors also offer discounts for early settlement of accounts. Again, when the terms are entered for the vendor and payment is made before the discount period expires, the program displays the discount as available and automatically calculates a net balance owing. Payment terms vary from vendor to vendor. Most vendor discounts are calculated on before-tax amounts but some are based on after-tax amounts.

### Freight

When a business purchases inventory items, the cost of any freight that cannot be directly allocated to a specific item must be charged to *Freight Expense*. This amount will be regarded as a general expense rather than being charged to the costs of any inventory asset account. Customers also pay for delivery and setup. GST is charged on freight for both sales and purchases but there is no PST on freight. The tax code for all freight charges is code G.

### Bank Deposits

Deposit slips are prepared weekly when cash and cheques are received. Receipts are debited to *Undeposited Cash and Cheques* and transferred weekly to *Bank: Hamilton Trust Chequing*.

### Imported Inventory

Some inventory items are imported from the United States. The bank accounts, vendor records and inventory records are modified to accommodate the foreign currency transactions and import duties automatically.

### Purchase Returns and Allowances

A business will sometimes return inventory items to vendors because of damage, poor quality or shipment of the wrong items. Usually a business records these returns after it receives a credit note from a vendor. The return of inventory is entered in the Purchases Journal as an inventory purchase:

- Select the item in the Item field and enter the quantity returned as a **negative** amount in the Quantity field. The program will automatically calculate a negative amount as a default in the Amount field. You cannot change the account number.
- Accept the default amount and enter other items returned to the vendor.

**NOTES**
Daily Business Manager lists are helpful for making sure that you take advantage of available discounts.

**NOTES**
Although import duties are not charged on the items imported by Flabuless Fitness from the United States, we show the setup of import duties and set the rates at zero so that no tax will be charged.

• Enter the appropriate tax code for each item returned.

The program will create a negative invoice to reduce the balance owing to the vendor and will reduce the applicable inventory asset accounts, the freight accounts, *GST Paid on Purchases* and the quantity of items in the Inventory Ledger database.

Purchase allowances for damaged merchandise that is not returned are entered as non-inventory negative purchase invoices. Enter the amount of the allowance as a **negative** amount in the Amount field and leave the tax fields blank (i.e., treat it as non-taxable). Enter *Purchases Returns and Allowances* in the Account field.

### Sales Returns and Allowances

Sometimes customers will return inventory items. Usually, a business records the return after it has issued a credit note. The return is entered in the Sales Journal as a negative inventory sale for the customer:

• Select the appropriate item in the Item field.
• Enter the quantity returned with a **negative** number in the Quantity field.
• The price of the item appears as a positive number in the Price field, and the Amount field is calculated automatically as a negative amount that should be correct. If it is not, you can change it.
• Enter the tax code for the sale and the account number for *Sales Returns & Allowances.*

The program will create a negative invoice to reduce the balance owing by the customer, and *Cost of Goods Sold*, *GST Charged on Sales* and *PST Payable*. The applicable inventory asset accounts and the quantity of items in the Inventory Ledger database will be increased.

Sales allowances are entered as non-taxable, non-inventory negative sales invoices, creating a debit entry for *Sales Returns & Allowances* and a credit for *Accounts Receivable*. If the allowance is paid by cheque, enter the allowance in the Payments Journal as an Other Payment paid by cheque.

### NSF Cheques

If a cheque is deposited from an account that does not have enough money to cover it, the bank returns it to the depositor as NSF (non-sufficient funds). If the cheque was in payment for a cash sale, you must process the NSF cheque through the Sales Journal because there was no Receipts Journal entry. Create a customer record if necessary and enter a positive amount for the amount of the cheque. Choose *Bank: Hamilton Trust Chequing* as the account. Choose Pay Later as the method of payment. If the customer is expected to pay the bank charges, enter these on the second invoice line as a positive amount and select the appropriate revenue account.

If the NSF cheque was deposited to a different account than the one used in the Receipts Journal, create a negative receipt to reverse the cheque. Choose Include Fully Paid Invoices. Click the invoice line that this cheque was applied to. Enter the discount taken as a negative amount. Enter the Payment Amount as a negative amount. Choose the correct Bank Account from the Deposit To field.

### Adjustments for Bad Debt

Most businesses set up an allowance for doubtful accounts or bad debts, knowing that some customers will fail to pay. When the allowance is set up, a bad debts or uncollectable accounts expense account is debited. When a business is certain that a customer will not pay its account, the debt should be written off by crediting *Accounts Receivable* and debiting *Allowance for Doubtful Accounts*. When taxes apply, an extra step is required. Part of the original sales invoice was entered as a credit (increase) to *GST Charged on Sales* and to *PST Payable*. By entering the full amount and the tax

**NOTES**

The sales tax rules for credits, allowances and discounts are complex. They may be different for provincial and federal taxes and they may differ from one province to another. Adjusting General Journal entries may be required to adjust the amount of tax owing and calculate the tax remittance. We have chosen to leave out the tax component for transactions of this type. Refer to Chapter 2 for more information about sales taxes.

**NOTES**

Allowance for Doubtful Accounts is a contra-asset account that normally has a credit balance. Therefore, a debit entry will reduce this credit balance.

code for taxes included, the GST and PST payable amounts will automatically be reduced. In Simply Accounting, record the write-off of the debt in the Sales Journal using the following steps:

- Select the customer whose debt will not be paid.
- Enter a source document number to identify the transaction (e.g., memo).
- Enter a **negative** amount for the total unpaid invoice in the Amount field.
- Enter *Allowance for Doubtful Accounts* in the Account field.
- Enter the tax code **IN** (taxes included).

If the customer was also charged for the NSF fees, enter this information on the next invoice line:

- Enter a **negative** amount for the total NSF charge in the Amount field.
- Enter *Allowance for Doubtful Accounts* in the Account field.
- Enter the tax code **No tax**.

Review the transaction. *Accounts Receivable* is credited (reduced) by the full amount of the invoice to remove the balance owing by this customer. *Allowance for Doubtful Accounts* has been debited (reduced) by the amount of the invoice minus taxes. *GST Charged on Sales* and *PST Payable* have been debited for the tax portion of the invoice to reduce the tax liabilities.

After recording the write-off, "pay" both the original invoice and the write-off in the Receipts Journal. The balance will be zero and there will be no journal entry. This step removes the items from the journal for the customer so that you can clear the paid transactions and later remove the customer's record.

Manually you would complete the entry as follows:

---

**1.** Set up the Allowance for Bad Debts.

| Date | Particulars | Debit | Credit |
|------|-------------|-------|--------|
| xx/xx | Uncollectable Accounts Expense | 1 000.00 | |
| | Allowance for Doubtful Accounts | | 1 000.00 |

**2.** Customer G. Bell declares bankruptcy. Write off outstanding balance, $228, including GST and PST.

| Date | Particulars | Debit | Credit |
|------|-------------|-------|--------|
| xx/xx | Allowance for Doubtful Accounts | 200.00 | |
| | GST Charged on Sales | 12.00 | |
| | PST Payable | 16.00 | |
| | Accounts Receivable, G. Bell | | 228.00 |

---

Occasionally, a bad debt is recovered after it has been written off. When this occurs, the above procedure is reversed and the GST and PST liabilities must also be restored. The recovery is entered as a non-inventory sale in the Sales Journal using the following steps:

- Select the customer and enter the date and source document number.
- Type an appropriate comment such as "Debt recovered" as the Description.
- Enter a **positive** amount for the total invoice amount in the Amount field.
- Enter the tax code **IN** (taxes included).
- Enter *Allowance for Doubtful Accounts* in the Account field.

Review the transaction. You will see that *Accounts Receivable* has been debited for the full amount of the invoice. *Allowance for Doubtful Accounts* has been credited for the amount of the invoice minus taxes. *GST Charged on Sales* and *PST Payable* have been credited for the tax portion of the invoice to restore the tax liabilities.

As the final step, record the customer's payment in the Receipts Journal as you would record any other customer payment.

## Remittances

The Receiver General for Canada:
- Monthly EI, CPP and income tax deductions withheld from employees must be paid by the 15th of each month for the previous month.
- Monthly GST owing or requests for refunds must be filed by the end of each month for the previous month.
- Business income tax is paid in quarterly instalments.
- Garnisheed wages are submitted by the 15th of each month for the previous month. A separate cheque is issued for this remittance.

The Minister of Finance:
- Quarterly Employer Health Tax (EHT) deductions must be paid by the 15th of April, July, October and January for the previous quarter.
- Monthly Provincial Sales Taxes (PST) on revenue from sales must be paid by the 23rd of the month for the previous month. A 5 percent sales tax compensation is earned for prompt payment of PST.

Ancaster Insurance:
- Monthly Registered Retirement Savings Plan (RRSP) deductions withheld from employees must be paid by the 15th of the month for the previous month.
- Group insurance contributions paid by the employer must be paid by the 15th of the month for the previous month.

The Mt. Hope Investment Corporation:
- Monthly Canada Savings Bond Plan (CSB Plan) deductions withheld from employees must be paid by the 15th of the month for the previous month.

The Workplace Safety and Insurance Board:
- Quarterly Workplace Safety and Insurance Board (WSIB) assessment for employees must be paid by the 15th of the month for the previous quarter.

---

### SPECIAL DATA FILES FOR FLABULESS FITNESS

Detailed keystroke instructions are included for you to set up the Flabuless Fitness application files. However, the Data CD also includes files for this application so that you can complete segments of the application rather than having to work through it entirely. Each file stands alone so you can work through any month at your discretion.

| To Enter | For (Period Covered) | Use (File Name on Data CD) |
|---|---|---|
| Transactions: | April 1–April 30 | setup\flab\flab-apr.sdb |
| Transactions: | May 1–May 31 | setup\flab\flab-may.sdb |
| Transactions: | June 1–June 30 | setup\flab\flab-jun.sdb |

---

# INSTRUCTIONS FOR SETUP

**Set up** the **company accounts** in Simply Accounting using the Business Information, Chart of Accounts, Balance Sheet, Income Statement, Post-Closing Trial Balance and Vendor, Customer, Employee and Inventory Information provided above for March 31, 2009. Instructions to assist you in setting up the company accounts follow. The setup of the Inventory Ledger is given in detail. Abbreviated instructions are included for the remaining steps. Refer to the Toss for Tots (Chapter 4), Dorfmann Design (Chapter 7) and Lime Light Laundry (Chapter 9) applications if you need more detailed explanations.

# KEYSTROKES FOR SETUP

## Creating Company Files

We will create the company files from scratch. Once we create the files and define the defaults, we will add the accounts, define linked accounts for all ledgers, set up additional features, create vendor, customer, employee and inventory records and add historical data.

**NOTES** Refer to page 216 for detailed instructions on creating company files.

Save your work and update your backup copy frequently as you work through the setup.

**Start**  the **Simply Accounting program**. You should see the Select Company window.

**Click**  **Create A New Company**.

**Click**  **OK**. You will see the Setup wizard welcome screen.

**Click**  **Next** to open the Company Name and Address screen. The default name (the template name) is selected for editing.

**Type**  Flabuless Fitness (and your own name)  **Press** (tab) to advance to the Street 1 address field.

**Type**  199 Warmup Rd. **Press** (tab).

**Type**  Unit 500 **Press** (tab).

**Type**  Hamilton **Press** (tab).

**Type**  o  to enter the province code (ON) and province (Ontario).

**Click**  the Postal Code field.

**Type**  l8t3b7 **Press** (tab).

**Type**  Canada **Press** (tab).

**Type**  9056422348 **Press** (tab) to enter the first phone number.

**Type**  8004482348 **Press** (tab) to enter the second phone number.

**Type**  9056429100  to enter the fax number.

**Click**  **Next** to open the company Dates window.

**NOTES** You cannot complete the company setup in multi-user mode. Many of the settings options are dimmed and unavailable when you are working in multi-user mode.

**NOTES** Add your own name to the company name to personalize your data files.

**NOTES** Because we select Ontario as the province, some defaults will be added to the data file. Province fields are completed automatically in all the ledgers. WCB will be renamed WSIB.

Ttthe city and country will be added as defaults once we save the company information.

The cursor is in the Fiscal Year Start field, the date on which the business begins its fiscal year. Flabuless Fitness closes its books quarterly and is beginning a new quarter in April. To be certain that you have the correct year, you should type four digits for the year. Until we change the date format, they are displayed in the short form, but the order is still month/day/year.

**Enter**  the **fiscal dates** as follows:

• Fiscal Start: April 1, 2009
• Earliest Transaction date: April 1, 2009
• Fiscal End: June 30, 2009

Remember that you can edit the company information and fiscal dates later from the Setup menu, Settings option (choose Company and Information). If you later change the province, you may have to change some settings linked to the province selection.

| Click | Next. |
|---|---|
| **Click** | **Let Me Build The List Of Accounts Myself.... Click Next**. |
| **Click** | **Yes** to confirm your selection and continue to the industry type list. |
| **Choose** | **Retail** as the Industry for the business. **Click Next**. |
| **Type** | flabless  to replace the default entry for the file name. |
| **Drag through** | **Tess** in the folder name field (or the folder you last worked with). |
| **Type** | FLABLESS\ |

If you are using an alternative location for your company files, substitute the appropriate path, folder or drive in the example.

You can also type the complete path in the File Location field (e.g., Type c:\program files\simply accounting pro 2007\data\flabless\).

| Click | Next. |
|---|---|
| **Click** | **Yes** to confirm that you are creating a new folder. |
| **Click** | **Finish** to save the information. **Be patient**, wait for Simply Accounting to finish creating the data files. |
| **Click** | **Close** to advance to the Home window. |
| **Click** | **Collapse View** below the More Help list to close the My Business tab window. |

> **NOTES**
> You can also select another folder by clicking Browse to open the folder path screen and then clicking the folder you want to use. Click OK to return to the File Name screen.
> If the folder you want does not yet exist, click the folder you want to place the new folder in and click OK. Type FLABLESS\ at the end of the path in the Location field.

The program will automatically set up defaults for the session date and for the city, province and country fields for customers, vendors and employees based on the information you have just entered.

You will now see the Home window with the name Flabless at the top of the window and non-accounting term labels for the icons.

## Preparing the System

The next step involves changing the defaults. Change the defaults to suit your own work environment if you have more than one printer or if you are using forms for cheques, invoices or statements. The keystroke instructions are given for computer-generated cheques, invoices and statements. Refer to the Business Information Chart on page 623 for the company default settings.

## Changing the User Preference Settings

> **NOTES**
> Use the Backup feature frequently while setting up your files to update your backup copy.
> Save your work frequently by choosing the Save command. You will also save your work by finishing your session properly. You may finish your session at any time while completing the setup.
> Simply open the data file, accept the session date and continue from where you left off.

You should make the following changes to the User Preferences from the Setup menu. Refer to Chapter 4, page 85, for assistance if necessary.

| Choose | the **Setup menu** and **click User Preferences** to open the Options screen. |
|---|---|
| **Click** | **Use Accounting Terms**. |
| **Click** | **Automatically Save Changes To Vendor....** |
| **Click** | **View**. |
| **Click** | **After Changing Session Date** for **Daily Business Manager** and for **Checklists** to turn off these features and remove the ✓'s. |

If you would like to hide the unused modules,

**Click**    **Project** in the **Module column** to hide the module.

**Click**    **Time & Billing** in the **Module column** to hide the module.

You may show the My Business Tab or hide it. If you want to hide it, click My Business Tab and click Show My Business Tab to remove the ✓.

**Click**    **OK** to save the settings and return to the Home window.

Notice that ledger and journal icons in the Home window have accounting term labels after you change these settings. The user preference settings can be modified at any time by repeating these steps.

## Changing Company Defaults

### *Correcting Company Information*

Click OK at any time to save the settings and close the Settings window. To continue later, you can use the Setup tool to access Settings. If a ledger icon is selected in the Home window, click the Setup tool to display the Settings for that ledger. If no ledger icon is highlighted, click the Setup tool, select the ledger from the list and click Select to display the Settings for the ledger.

**Choose** the **Setup menu**, then **click Settings**. **Click Information**.

**Click**    the **Business No. field**. **Type**  245 138 121 RT0001

### *Changing System Settings*

**Click**    **System**. Use the following System settings:

• Use Cheque No. As The Source Code For Cash Purchases And Sales
• Do Not Allow Transactions Dated Before April 1, 2009
• Allow Transactions In The Future (Beyond The Session Date)
• Warn If Transactions Are More Than 7 Days In The Future
• Warn If Accounts Are Not Balanced When Entering A New Month

### *Changing Backup Settings*

**Click**    **Backup**. Use the following Backup settings:

• Semi-monthly Backup Frequency
• Display a Backup Reminder When Closing This Company

**Click**    **Automatically Back Up This File** to remove the ✓. We do not want to schedule automatic backups for instructional files.

### *Changing Features Settings*

Flabuless uses all features of the program except Projects — orders, quotes and language options should be selected. Project and Packing slips may be left unselected.

**Click**    **Features**.

**Click**    **each feature** to change its setting.

### *Changing Default Settings for Forms*

**Click**    **Forms** to display the defaults.

**NOTES**
Even if you are not using the Project and Time Slips ledgers, you do not need to hide them to finish the history because they have no linked accounts.

**WARNING!**
Do not skip any ledger icon windows before completing the setup.

**NOTES**
Remember that if you select a journal from the Select Setup list you will open the Linked Accounts window for that journal instead of the Settings window for the ledger.

**NOTES**
If you chose to hide the Project module, Projects will not appear in the Features Settings window.

**NOTES**
Credit Cards, Sales Taxes and Currency settings require linked accounts, so we will set them after creating accounts.

Use the Forms options to set up the automatic numbering and printing of all cheques and invoices. They apply only to numerical invoices.

If you want to use automatic invoice numbering, type the next number from the source documents so the automatic numbering system can take over from the manual system. Using automatic numbering reduces the risk of typing and recording an incorrect invoice or cheque number even when you are not printing cheques and invoices through the program. For Flabuless Fitness, the next invoice is #3000.

> **Click**   1 in the **Invoices Number field**.
>
> **Type**   3000
>
> **Click**   the **Sales Quotes Number field**. **Type**   41
>
> **Click**   the **Receipts Number field**. **Type**   39
>
> **Click**   the **Customer Deposits Number field**. **Type**   15
>
> **Click**   the **Purchase Orders Number field**. **Type**   25
>
> **Click**   the **Direct Deposit Stubs Number field**. **Type**   19

Leave selected the option to verify number sequences for all forms so that the program will warn you if you skip or duplicate a number.

> **Click**   **Verify Number Sequence for Deposit Slips**.

Click a check box to add other features or to turn off an option once it is selected. The ✓ in the appropriate boxes indicates a feature is being used.

The option to Confirm Printing/E-mail will warn you to print before posting a transaction. When printing invoices, statements or cheques, you should include the company address, unless it is already printed on your forms.

> If you print or e-mail invoices and cheques through the computer, you should turn on the option to Confirm Printing/E-mail.

We want to allow batch printing, printing several forms at once, after posting instead of one at a time while entering a transaction.

> **Click**   the **Print In Batches check box** for each form to add a ✓ to each box.

We should also check for duplicate numbers. This control is not selected by default.

> **Click**   the **Check For Duplicates check box for Invoices and Receipts**.

### Changing Date Format Settings

> **Click**   **Date Format**.

We want to use the long date form for all dates on the screen to verify that we are entering dates correctly. For the reports, you may use either the long or short form.

> **Click**   **Long Dates** as the setting for On The Screen, Use.

### Adding the Company Logo

> **Click**   **Logo**.
>
> **Click**   **Browse**. **Click** the **Up One Level tool** 🔼 .
>
> **Double click**   the **Data folder**.
>
> **Double click**   the **Setup folder** and **double click** the **Logos folder**.
>
> **Click**   **Flab.bmp** to enter this file name.

---

**NOTES**
Many invoices include the alpha or letter portion of the invoice number on the preprinted invoice form. You could then enter the next number from the numeric portion in the Invoices Number field. Alphanumeric invoice numbers, such as FF-399, cannot be increased automatically by the computer.

**NOTES**
If you hide the Time Slips module, the next number for time slips will not be included on the Forms screen. You can leave the field blank if you are not hiding the module.

## *Changing Default Names*

Flabuless uses the additional information fields in the journals. You can label these fields. However, you must use the same names for all journals. We will therefore enter a generic label for the Additional Field.

**Click    Names**:

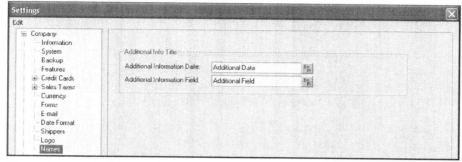

**Drag through Additional Field**.

**Type**    Ref. Number

**Click    OK** to save the new information and return to the Home window.

Many of the other settings require linked accounts. Therefore, we will create all the General Ledger accounts before entering the remaining settings.

# Preparing the General Ledger

This stage in setting up an accounting system involves preparing the General Ledger for operation. This stage involves

1. organizing all accounting reports and records (this step has been completed)
2. creating new accounts and adding opening balances
3. printing reports to check the accuracy of your records

## Creating New Accounts

The next step is to create the accounts, including the non-postable accounts. Remember to enter the correct type of account. For postable accounts you should also indicate whether you want to omit accounts with zero balances from financial statements. You need to refer to the company Chart of Accounts on page 624 to complete this step.

*Current Earnings* is the only predefined account, and you do not need to edit it.

Refer to Format of Financial Statements (page 90) for a review of these topics if needed. Refer to the instructions in the Toss for Tots application, page 98, if you need help with creating accounts.

**Click**    the **Accounts icon**  to open the Accounts window.

Maximize the Accounts window.

If the accounts are not displayed by name or by type, you should change the view. Click the Display By Type tool or choose the View menu and click Type.

**Click**    the **Create tool**  in the Accounts window or **choose** the **File menu** and **click Create**.

**NOTES**
Remember that you can finish your session any time. To continue, just open the file, accept the session date and start again from where you left off.

**NOTES**
You can also press `ctrl` + N to open a New Account ledger window and create a new account.

Drag the Ledger window so that both the Accounts window and Ledger window are visible. This will make it easier to monitor your progress.

**Type**    the **account number**. **Press** ⌈tab⌋ and **type** the **account name**.

**Click**    the correct **account type**. Remember subgroup accounts (A) must be followed by a subgroup total (S).

**Click**    **Omit From Financial Statements If Balance Is Zero** to select this option.

Allow Project Allocations will be selected by default for all postable revenue and expense accounts, so you do not need to change this option.

You will enter the account balances in the next stage.

When all the information is correct, you must save your account.

**Click**    **Create Another** [ 🗇 Create Another ] to save the new account and advance to a blank ledger account window.

**Create**    the **other accounts** by repeating these procedures.

**Close**    the **General Ledger window** when you have entered all the accounts on page 624, or when you want to end your session.

After entering all the accounts, you should check for mistakes in account number, name, type, order and account class (for expense accounts).

**Display** or **print** your updated **Chart of Accounts** at this stage to check for accuracy of account names and numbers. **Choose** the **Reports menu** and **click Chart of Accounts.**

**Click**    [ ✔ ] or **choose** the **File menu** and **click Check The Validity Of Accounts** to check for errors in account sequence such as missing subgroup totals, headings or totals. The first error is reported.

**Correct** the **error** and **check** the **validity** again. Repeat this step until the accounts are in logical order.

## Entering Historical Account Balances

The opening historical balances for Flabuless Fitness can be found in the Post-Closing Trial Balance dated March 31, 2009 (page 626). All Income Statement accounts have zero balances because the books were closed at the end of the first quarter. Headings, totals and subgroup totals (i.e., the non-postable accounts) do not have balances. Remember to put any forced balance amounts into the *Test Balance Account*.

**Open**    the account information window for **1060 Bank: Hamilton Trust Chequing**, the first account requiring a balance.

**Click**    the **Opening Balance field**.

**Type**    the **balance**.

**Correct** the **information** if necessary by repeating the above steps.

**Click**    the **Next button** [ ▶ ] to advance to the next ledger account window.

**Enter**    **negative numbers for accounts that decrease the total** in a group or section (e.g., *Allowance for Doubtful Accounts, Accum Deprec, GST Paid on Purchases*). These account balances are indicated with a minus sign (–) in the Balance Sheet.

**NOTES**
    For account 1140 Bank: USD Chequing, enter $9 500, the balance in Canadian dollars. The USD balance will be added after we set up currencies.

**Repeat** these **procedures** to **enter** the **balances** for the remaining accounts in the Post-Closing Trial Balance on page 626. *Test Balance Account* should have a zero balance.

**Close** the **Ledger window**.

After entering all account balances, you should display the Trial Balance to check the account balances. You can do this from the Accounts window.

**Choose** the **Reports menu click Trial Balance. Click** the **Print tool**.

**Close** the **display** when finished. Leave the Accounts window open.

**Check** all **accounts** and **amounts** and **make corrections** if necessary.

## Defining Account Classes

Defining bank accounts involves changing the account class to Bank and indicating the currency for the accounts and the cheque and deposit number sequences. If you use online banking, you must also enter the bank name, account numbers and Web site. We must also change the class for *Undeposited Cash and Cheques* to either Bank or Cash to use it as the linked account for receipts. Cash is the appropriate selection. Remember that the bank account class changes must be saved before we can enter the next cheque numbers. Changes are saved automatically when we open the next ledger record.

We must also define the account class for the credit card asset and the credit card payable accounts. We will make all these changes before continuing the setup.

**Double click** **1030 Undeposited Cash and Cheques** to open the ledger.

**Click** the **Class Options tab**.

**Choose** **Bank** from the drop-down list of account classes.

**Click** the **Next Account button** ▸ to open the ledger for account **1060**.

**Choose** **Bank** from the list of account classes.

**Click** the **Next Deposit Number field**.

**Type** 14

**Click** the **Next Account button** ▸.

**Choose** **Bank** as the account class for *1080 Bank: Hamilton Trust Savings*.

**Click** **Chequing** (Account Type field). **Click Savings** from the list.

**Click** the **Next Account button** ▸ to **open** the ledger for **1120 Bank: Visa and Interac**.

**Choose** **Credit Card Receivable** as the account class.

**Click** the **Next Account button** ▸ to **open** the ledger for **1140 Bank: USD Chequing**.

**Choose** **Bank** as the account class.

**Click** the **Select Account list arrow** again.

**Click** **2250 Credit Card Payable** to open its ledger screen at the Class Options tab screen.

**Choose** **Credit Card Payable** as the account class. Notice that Credit Card Receivable is not available as a class option for the liability account.

**NOTES**
Refer to the chart on page 623 for bank information and to page 227 for review of Bank class accounts.

**NOTES**
We must define 1030 Undeposited Cash and Cheques as a Bank or Cash class account so that we can enter it as the linked bank account for Receivables. Cash is the most appropriate selection.
Both Bank and Cash class accounts are available in the Deposit To field for cash sales and receipts.

**NOTES**
To open the ledger for Credit Card Payable, you can click the Next Account button repeatedly or choose the account from the Select Account list arrow.

<br>

**Click** the **Select Account list arrow** again and **choose 5010 Advertising and Promotion**.

**Select** **Operating Expense** or **Expense** as the account class.

**Click** the **Next Account button** ▶. **Select Operating Expense** or **Expense** as the account class for the remaining postable expense accounts.

**Close** the **General Ledger window** and the **Accounts window**.

# Entering Company Default Settings

## Setting Up Credit Cards

Flabuless Fitness accepts Visa credit card payments from customers as well as debit cards (Interac). The store also uses a Visa card to pay for some purchases. Setting up credit cards includes naming them, identifying the linked accounts and entering fees associated with the cards.

You should be in the Home window.

**Choose** the **Setup menu**, then **choose Settings** and **click Credit Cards** under Company. Click Company first if necessary.

**Click** **Used** to open the Credit Card Information screen for the cards that the business uses.

**Click** the **Credit Card Name field**.

**Type** Visa **Press** (tab) to move to the Payable Account field.

**Press** (enter) to see the list of available accounts.

**Double click 2250** to add the account and move to the Expense Account field.

**Press** (enter) to see the account list.

**Double click 5030**.

**Click** **Accepted** to open the Credit Card Information screen for the cards that the business accepts from customers.

**Click** the **Credit Card Name field**.

**Type** Visa **Press** (tab) to advance to the Discount Fee % field.

**Type** 2.5 **Press** (tab) to advance to the Expense Account field.

**Press** (enter) to see the list of accounts available for linking.

**Double click 5030** to choose and enter the account. The cursor advances to the Asset Account field.

**Press** (enter) to see the list of accounts available for linking.

**Double click 1120** to choose and add the credit card bank account.

**Enter** Interac as the name, **0** as the %, **5030** as the Expense account and **1120** as the Asset account to set up the debit card.

## Setting Up Sales Taxes

Flabuless Fitness charges and pays GST and PST, so we need to set up default codes for these two taxes. The business wants to generate reports on both taxes.

**NOTES** Remember that you can finish your session at any time. To continue, just open the file, accept the session date and start again from where you left off.

**NOTES** Refer to the Business Information Chart on page 623 for credit card details. To review credit card setup, refer to page 230 for additional information.

**NOTES** You must choose a Credit Card Payable or Bank class account as the Payable Account for cards used.

**WARNING!** Although accounts in other classes appear on the Select Account list, selecting them will generate an error message when you save the entries.

**NOTES** You must choose a Credit Card Receivable or Bank class account as the Asset Account for cards accepted.

**NOTES** Refer to the Business Information Chart on page 623 for sales tax information. Refer to page 232 for a review of sales taxes.

**Click**    **Sales Taxes** under Company. There are settings for tax names and codes.

**Click**    **Taxes** to access the Sales Tax Information screen:

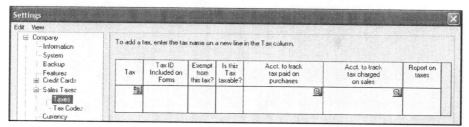

The cursor is in the Tax field on the Taxes screen where you should enter the name of the tax. We will enter the information for GST first.

**Type**    GST   **Press** (tab) to advance to the Tax ID field where we enter the business number.

**Type**    245 138 121   **Press** (tab) to advance to the **Exempt From This Tax?** column.

Flabuless Fitness is not tax exempt for GST, so the default, No, is correct. GST is not taxable in Ontario (no other tax is charged on GST as it is in PEI and Quebec).

**Click**    [icon], the **List icon for Acct To Track Tax Paid On Purchases**.

**Choose**    **2670 GST Paid on Purchases**. The cursor advances to the field for the Account To Track Taxes Charged On Sales.

**Choose**    **2650 GST Charged on Sales** from the List icon [icon] list of accounts. The cursor advances to the Report On Taxes field.

**Click**    **No** to change the default entry to Yes.

**Press**    (tab) so you can enter the information for PST.

**Type**    PST

Flabuless Fitness is not exempt for PST, the ID number is not required, PST is not taxable and the tax is not refundable, so PST paid on purchases is not tracked.

**Click**    [icon], the **List icon for Acct To Track Tax Charged On Sales**.

**Double click**  **2640 PST Payable**.

**Click**    **No** in the Report On Taxes column to change the entry to Yes.

## Entering Tax Codes

**Click**    **Tax Codes** to open the next information screen:

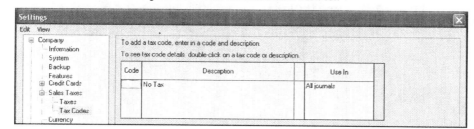

A single code, No Tax, is created as a default.

We need to create tax codes for sales and purchases when GST alone is charged and when both PST and GST apply. There are currently no situations where Flabuless Fitness charges or pays only PST, but there are purchases with both taxes included, so we need a code for this situation as well (e.g., gasoline is priced with all taxes included).

**NOTES**

For PEI in the Tesses Tresses application (Chapter 15), and for Quebec in the Village Galleries application (Chapter 14), we entered Yes for GST for Is This Tax Taxable? because PST is charged on GST in those provinces. (GST is taxable.) When you click Yes in the Is This Tax Taxable? column for GST, a list of taxes opens, and you can select the taxes that are to be charged on GST.

**NOTES**

Flabuless Fitness is exempt from PST on purchases of inventory items for sale in the store. These exemptions are handled through the vendor tax codes.

| **Click** | the **Code column** below the blank on the first line. |

| **Type** | G **Press** (tab) to move to the Description field. |

| **Press** | (enter) or **double click** to open the Tax Code Details screen: |

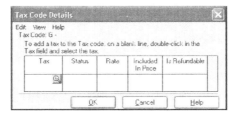

| **Click** | the **Tax field List icon** to see the list of taxes entered. |

Both taxes from the Taxes screen appear on the list.

| **Click** | **Select** because GST is already selected and return to the Details. |

Defaults are entered for the remaining fields. The **Status** is **Taxable** and the tax is **not included** — these are correct — tax is calculated and charged and is not included in the price.

| **Click** | the **Rate field**. |

| **Type** | 6 |

| **Click** | **No** in the Is Refundable column to change the entry to Yes. |

| **Click** | **OK** to return to the Tax Codes screen for additional codes. |

The description GST @ 6% appears beside the code G and the tax is used in all journals. You can edit the description if you want. If the tax were not refundable, non-refundable would be added to the description automatically. We are ready to enter the second code, to apply both GST and PST.

| **Press** | (tab) until you advance to the next line in the Code column. |

| **Type** | GP **Press** (tab) to move to the Description field. |

| **Press** | (enter) to open the Tax Code Details screen. |

| **Click** | the **Tax field List icon**. |

| **Select** | **GST**. Taxable and not included are correct. |

| **Type** | 6 in the **Rate field**. |

| **Click** | **No** in the Is Refundable column to change the entry to Yes. |

| **Press** | (tab) to return to the Tax field again. |

| **Press** | (enter) and then **select PST**. **Type** 8 in the **Rate field**. |

PST is taxable, not refundable, not included in the price and the tax is used in all journals so the remaining defaults are correct.

| **Click** | **OK** to return to the Tax Codes screen. The description GST @ 6%; PST @ 8%, non-refundable has been added. |

| **Press** | (tab) until you advance to the next line in the Code column, below GP. |

| **Type** | IN **Press** (tab) to move to the Description field. |

| **Press** | (enter) or **double click** to open the Tax Code Details screen. |

| **Enter** | **GST** as the tax, **6%** as the rate. Taxable status is correct. |

**Click**    **No** in the Included In Price column to change the entry to Yes.

**Click**    **No** in the Is Refundable column to change the entry to Yes.

**Press**    `tab` to return to the Tax field again. PST at 8% is taxable, included in the price and not refundable.

**Enter**    **PST** as the tax and **8%** as the rate.

**Click**    **No** in the Included In Price column to change the entry to Yes.

**Click**    **OK** to return to the Tax Codes screen.

No description appears beside the code IN so we must add it. The cursor is in the Description field beside IN.

**Type**    `GST @ 6%, included; PST @ 8%, included`

# Adding a Foreign Currency

Flabuless Fitness purchases some inventory items from vendors in the United States and must set up the company files to allow transactions in USD, United States dollars. We will set up the foreign currency now because we need this information for bank account and vendor settings.

**Click**    **Currency** under Company to see the Currency Information window:

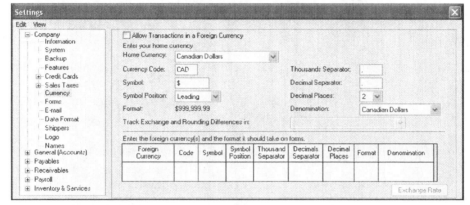

Canadian Dollars is the default in the Home Currency field, and its code, symbol, format and so on are added. You enter the currencies in the columns in the lower half of the screen. First you must turn on the option for other currencies.

**Click**    **Allow Transactions In A Foreign Currency**.

Exchange rates vary from day to day and even within the day. When purchases and payments are made at different times, they are subject to different exchange rates. We have seen these differences in the Maple Leaf Rags application (Chapter 12). Exchange rate differences may result in a gain — if the exchange rate drops before a payment is made or if the rate increases before a payment is received from a customer — or a loss — if the rate increases before a payment is made or if the rate drops before a customer makes a payment. These differences are tracked in the linked account designated on this screen. Rounding differences may also result in gains and losses because the amounts are recorded with two decimal places and exchange rates usually have several significant digits. The account for these differences may be an expense account or a revenue account. Flabuless Fitness uses a revenue account.

**Click**    the **list arrow** for **Track Exchange And Rounding Differences In**.

Both revenue and expense accounts are available for linking.

**Click**    **4120 Exchange Rate Differences** to enter the linked account.

The next step is to identify the foreign currency or currencies.

**Click**    the **Foreign Currency field**.

**Click**    the **List icon**  for the field to open the list of currencies:

**Type**    U    (We want to advance to currencies beginning with U in the list.)

**Scroll down**    and **double click United States Dollars** to add it to the Currency
Information screen. The currency code, symbol and format are
added for the selected currency. Accept the defaults.

**Click**    the **Exchange Rate button**:

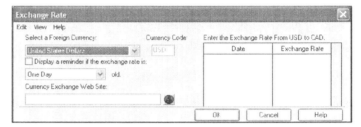

On this screen, we enter the exchange rates for various dates for each currency.
The selected currency is listed in the Select A Foreign Currency field. All currencies
you created will be listed in the drop-down list for this field.

**Click**    the **Date field**.

**Type**    04 01 **Press** (tab) to advance to the Exchange Rate field.

**Type**    1.195

If you know the rates for other dates, you can enter them as well. Otherwise, you
can enter current rates in the journals as we did in the previous chapters. These rates
will be added to the list on this screen.

To ensure that you do not use an old exchange rate that is no longer accurate, you
should turn on the reminder that warns if the rate is out of date. A one-day period for
updating should be sufficient.

**Click**    **Display A Reminder If The Exchange Rate Is**.

**Accept** **One Day Old** as the time interval.

Now every time you change the transaction date to one day past the rate previously
used, the program will warn you and give you an opportunity to change the rate. If the
rate has not changed, you can accept the old rate.

**Click**    **OK** to return to the Currency Settings screen.

Currency settings affect other settings — they require additional linked accounts —
so they must be saved before continuing. And, now that we have added the foreign
currency, we can identify the currency for the USD bank account. We must complete

this step before we can choose it as the linked bank account for United States dollar transactions. At the same time we will add cheque numbers.

**Click**  **OK** to return to the Home window.

# Updating Bank Account Settings

## Adding Currency to a Bank Account

We need to complete one more step for bank accounts — identifying the currency for the account. By default the home currency is selected so we need to change this setting for the USD chequing account.

**Click**  the **Search tool** 🔍. Accounts should be selected.

**Click**  **1140 Bank: USD Chequing**. **Click OK** to open the ledger.

**Click**  the **Class Options tab** to see the current class setting — Bank.

**Click**  the **Currency list arrow**:

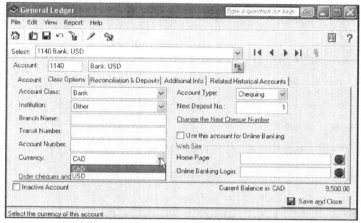

Once we identify an account as a bank account and allow foreign currency transactions, we identify the currency for the account on the Class Options tab screen.

**Click**  **USD**. Zero now appears as the balance amount for the USD currency.

**Click**  **Change The Next Cheque Number**:

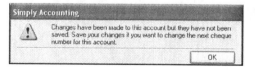

**Click**  **OK** to return to the ledger window so we can save the changes.

**Click**  the **Save tool** 💾 or **choose** the **File menu** and **click Save**:

Because we have entered the balance in only the Home currency, we are asked to confirm that this is correct. It is not.

**Click**  **No** to return to the ledger window so we can add the USD balance.

**Click**  the **Account tab** to return to the Opening Balance fields. A second field has been added for the balance in USD.

> **Click**    the **Opening Balance In USD field**. **Type**  8020
>
> **Click**    the **Save tool** 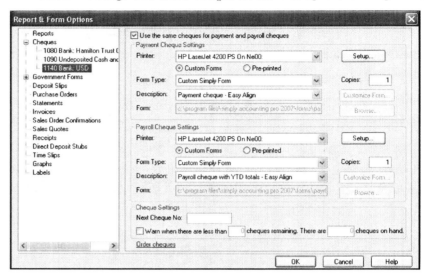.


### Adding Cheque Numbers

> **Click**    the **Class Options tab**.
>
> **Click**    **Change The Next Cheque Number** to open the cheque Form settings:

The account we started from is selected, so the cheque number field is available.

> **Click**    the **Next Cheque No. field**. **Type**  346
>
> **Click**    **1060 Bank: Hamilton Trust Chequing** in the left panel under Cheques.
>
> **Click**    the **Next Cheque No. field**. **Type**  101

We will make additional printer setting changes before proceeding, while the Reports & Forms window is open.

### Changing Other Printer Settings

Reports and forms settings apply only to the data file that you are using. They must be set for each data file separately and the settings are saved with each file.

> Click Reports or click the form for which you want to enter settings.
>
> Choose the printer you will be using for reports. Change the margins if necessary. Choose fonts and type sizes for the report from the lists.
>
> Click Setup to set the options for your particular printer if you need to change the paper size and location.
>
> Click OK to save your settings and return to the previous Printer setting screen.

Each type of form — cheques, invoices and so on — has its own setup.

> **Click**    **Invoices** to see the settings for printing invoices.
>
> **Check**    that the **file locations** for the forms are correct or dimmed.

As you did for reports, select the printer, set the margins, font and type size to match the forms you are using. Preprinted forms were included as part of the program installation and are located in the Forms folder.  You should Show Subtotals In Invoices.

---

**NOTES**
You can change other printer settings at this stage if you want, or you can change them at any time as needed.

**NOTES**
From the Home window, choose the Setup menu and click Reports & Forms. The printer setting options for reports are given.

For **E-mail Forms** you may want to choose generic forms such as Invoice and Purchase Order to avoid a file location error message from an incorrect file path in the Form File field. The file name field will be dimmed when you change the selection.

> To preview invoices, you must select the **Custom Form** and **Custom Simply Form** options.
>
> If you want to customize and preview the invoice form, choose **User-Defined Form** as the Printed Form Description and then click Customize Form.
>
> To print labels, click Labels and enter the size of the labels and the number that are placed across the page.
>
> To set the printer options for cheques or other forms, click the form you want and make the necessary changes.
>
> **Click**    **OK** to save the information when all the settings are correct. You can change printer settings at any time.
>
> **Close**    the **Ledger window** to return to the Home window.

# Entering Ledger Default Settings

## General Ledger Settings

Most of the settings for the General Ledger are already correct. Flabuless is not setting up budgets or departments yet, and it does not use the additional ledger record fields. Using and showing numbers for accounts, the default setting, is also correct. We need to add linked accounts.

> **Choose** the **Setup menu** and **click Settings** to continue entering the settings.

### *Defining Linked Accounts*

Linked accounts are General Ledger accounts that are affected by entries in other journals. For example, recording an inventory purchase will update the Inventory Ledger, several General Ledger accounts and the balance owing to the vendor. Refer to page 235 for a review of linked accounts. Refer to page 92 for a review of the Current Earnings Account. Linked accounts are also needed for other features.

> You can access the linked accounts screens for any journal directly from the Home window. Right-click a journal icon for the ledger you want and then click the Setup tool. For example, to access General Linked Accounts,
>
> Right-click  or ![Reconciliation & Deposits] (the General Journal or the Reconciliation and Deposits icon) to select it.
>
> Then click the Setup tool ![Setup tool icon] or choose the Setup menu, then Settings. The General linked accounts screen opens.
>
> If a journal icon is selected in the Home window, clicking the Setup tool will display the Linked Accounts window for the corresponding ledger.
>
> If no icon is highlighted, click the Setup tool and click General — the journal from the drop-down list — and click Select to display the ledger's linked accounts.
>
> Follow the same steps for the other ledgers. Start with the Sales or Receipts icon to open the linked accounts screen for the Receivables ledger, and so on.

**WARNING!**
Simply Accounting will not allow you to remove an account while it is being used as a linked account. When you try to remove an account, click OK in the Warning window to return to the Accounts window. First, turn the linking function off by deleting the account in the Linked Accounts window. Then remove the account in the Accounts window. You cannot remove an account if it has a balance or if journal entries have been posted to it.

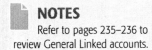
### *Identifying General Linked Accounts*

The *Current Earnings* capital account records the changes in net income resulting from sales and expenses. At the end of the fiscal period, the net income, the balance from *Current Earnings*, is transferred to the Retained Earnings capital account — *S. Reeves, Capital* is the Retained Earnings account for Flabuless Fitness — and income and expense accounts are reset to zero to prepare for the new fiscal period.

> **Click**    **General (Accounts)**.

If you have not yet saved the Currency settings you will see a warning message:

> **Click**    **Yes** to continue if you see this message.

> **Click**    **Linked Accounts under General (Accounts)**.

The General Ledger has two linked accounts. Both must be capital accounts.

| GENERAL LINKED ACCOUNTS | | |
|---|---|---|
| Retained Earnings | 3560 | S. Reeves, Capital |
| Current Earnings | 3600 | Current Earnings |

> **Type**    the **account number** or **select** the **account** from the drop-down list.

## Payables Ledger Settings

> **Click**    **Payables** and then **click Options**.

You should change the intervals for the aging of accounts. Some vendors offer discounts for payment within 5, 10 or 15 days. Discounts from one-time vendors are calculated on before-tax amounts.

> **Set**    the **aging** intervals at **15**, **30** and **60** days.

> **Click**    **Calculate Discounts Before Tax For One-Time Vendors**.

### *Setting Up Import Duties*

Although most goods imported from the United States are not subject to tariffs or import duties because of NAFTA (the North American Free Trade Agreement), you should know how to set up this feature. We will set up the program to charge duty but set the rates at zero so that no duty will be applied on purchases. You must activate the Duty option before creating vendor records so that you can indicate in the vendor records those vendors that supply goods on which duty is charged. Without these two steps, the duty fields in the Purchases Journal will be unavailable.

> **Click**    **Duty** to access the settings we need:

> **Click**    **Track Duty On Imported Items** to use the feature and open the linked account field.

A Payables account is linked to import duties for the liability to the Receiver General.

> **Click**    **2220 Import Duty Payable** from the Import Duty Account drop-down list.

## Identifying the Payables Linked Accounts

Flabuless Fitness uses *Bank: Hamilton Trust Chequing* as its principal linked bank account for the subsidiary Payables and Payroll ledgers — for all home currency cheque transactions.

| PAYABLES | | |
|---|---|---|
| Bank Account to use for Canadian Dollars | 1060 | Bank: Hamilton Trust Chequing |
| Bank Account to use for United States Dollars | 1140 | Bank: USD Chequing |
| Accounts Payable | 2200 | Accounts Payable |
| Freight Expense | 5080 | Freight Expense |
| Purchase Discount | 5090 | Purchase Discounts |
| Prepayments and Prepaid Orders | 1250 | Purchase Prepayments |

To enter the Payables Ledger linked accounts,

> **Click**    **Linked Accounts** to display the Linked Accounts window:

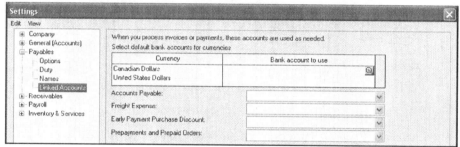

We need to identify the default General Ledger bank accounts used to make payments to vendors. Cash transactions in the Payments Journal will be posted to the bank account you select in the journal window. All Bank class accounts are available in the journals, and the principal linked account defined here will be selected as the default.

You can see the list of accounts available for linking by clicking the drop-down list arrow for any linked account field. Only Bank and Cash class accounts may be used in the bank fields. That is why we needed to classify the bank accounts first.

Flabuless has two bank accounts for payments. The chequing account is the principal bank account for Canadian currency transactions, and the USD account is used for transactions in United States dollars.

You can choose a separate linked account for each currency, or you may use the Canadian dollar account for more than one currency. You can select a Home currency bank as the linked account for foreign currency transactions, but you cannot select a foreign currency account as the linked account for Home currency transactions.

> **Click**    the **List icon** in the Bank Account To Use column for Canadian Dollars.
>
> **Click**    **1060 Bank: Hamilton Trust Chequing** and **click Select**.
>
> **Click**    List icon in the Bank Account To Use column for United States Dollars.
>
> **Click**    **1140 Bank: USD Chequing** and **click Select**.
>
> **Enter**    the **remaining linked accounts** in the chart at the top of this page. **Type** the **account number** or **select** the **account** from the drop-down list.

**NOTES**
To add the Payables Ledger linked accounts from the Home window, right-click the Purchases or the Payments Journal icon in the Home window to select it.

Click the Setup tool or choose the Setup menu, then choose Settings, Payables and Linked Accounts.

**NOTES**
Notice that this screen is different from the one on page 238 for Dorfmann Design that uses only one currency.

**WARNING!**
You cannot change the currency for an account when it is used as a linked account. You can choose home currency accounts as the the linked account to use with a foreign currency. If you had not yet changed the currency for 1140 Bank: USD Chequing, you could still choose it as the linked account but you would then be unable to change the currency to USD.

**NOTES**
The remaining Payables accounts were introduced in Chapter 7. Refer to page 238 if you need to review these accounts.

Check the linked accounts carefully. To delete a linked account, click it to highlight it and press ⌐del⌐. You must complete this step of deleting the linked account before you can remove the account in the General Ledger from the Accounts window.

# Receivables Ledger Settings

**NOTES**
Refer to page 239 if you need to review Receivables Ledger settings.

**Click**    **Receivables** and then **click Options** to display the ledger's defaults.

Flabuless Fitness prints the salesperson's name on all customer forms for the customer's reference in case a follow-up is required. Most customers use the tax code GP, so we will use this as the default for new customers. The default tax code will be selected when we enter the customer records.

Flabuless charges 1.5 percent interest on overdue accounts after 30 days, includes paid invoices on customer statements for 31 days — this is appropriate for the monthly statements — and uses the payment terms to set the aging intervals.

**Enter**    **10**, **30** and **60** days as the **aging** periods.

**Click**    **Interest Charges** to turn on the calculation.

**Click**    the **% field** for **Interest Charges**.

**Type**    1.5 **Press** ⌐tab⌐.

**Type**    30

**Click**    the **Tax Code For New Customers field** to see the list of tax codes.

**Click**    **GP GST @ 6%; PST @ 8%, non-refundable**.

**Click**    **Print Salesperson On Invoices Orders & Quotes**.

## *Entering Discount Settings*

Flabuless Fitness offers its account customers a 2 percent after-tax discount for 10 days; full payment is due in 30 days. Flabuless does not use the line discount feature at this time.

**Click**    **Discount** to open the next Receivables settings screen.

**Click**    the **% field** of the **Early Payment Terms** section.

**Type**    2 **Press** ⌐tab⌐.

**Type**    10 **Press** ⌐tab⌐.

**Type**    30

**Click**    **Calculate Line Discounts On Invoices** ... to turn off the feature. You will see the warning:

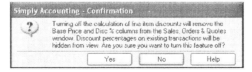

**Click**    **Yes** to confirm your selection.

## *Changing Default Comments*

**Click**    **Comments**.

You may add a comment or notice to all your invoices, quotes and order confirmations. You could use this feature to include payment terms, a company motto or notice of an upcoming sale. Remember that you can change the default message any time you want. You can also edit it for a particular sale or quote when you are completing the invoice. The cursor is in the Sales Invoices field.

**Type**    Interest @ 1.5% per month on accounts over 30 days.

Repeat this procedure to enter comments for the other forms.

## Defining the Receivables Linked Accounts

The Receivables Ledger linked accounts parallel those for the Payables Ledger.

**Click**    **Linked Accounts** under Receivables:

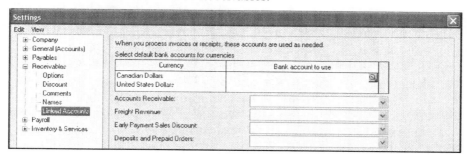

**NOTES**
To add the Receivables Ledger linked accounts from the Home window, right-click the Sales or the Receipts Journal icon in the Home window to select it.

Click the Setup tool or choose the Setup menu, then choose Settings, Receivables and Linked Accounts.

**NOTES**
Notice that this screen has changed because of the second currency. You can compare it with the one on page 241 for Dorfmann Design.

We need to identify the default General Ledger bank account used to receive payments from customers. Cash transactions in the Sales and Receipts journals will be posted to the bank account you select in the journals. The linked account will be the default account but any Bank or Cash class account may be selected.

Flabuless has several bank accounts. Cheques and cash receipts are held in the *Undeposited Cash and Cheques* account and then deposited weekly to the *Bank: Hamilton Trust Chequing* account. Therefore, the default principal Canadian bank account is *Undeposited Cash and Cheques. Bank: USD Chequing* is the default account for foreign currency customer transactions. Although most linked accounts may be used only once, one bank account can be linked to the Payables, Receivables and Payroll ledgers.

The following accounts are required as linked accounts for the Receivables Ledger.

| RECEIVABLES LINKED ACCOUNTS | | |
|---|---|---|
| Bank Account to use for Canadian Dollars | 1030 | Undeposited Cash and Cheques |
| Bank Account to use for United States Dollars | 1140 | Bank: USD Chequing |
| Accounts Receivable | 1200 | Accounts Receivable |
| Freight Revenue | 4200 | Freight Revenue |
| Sales Discount | 4060 | Sales Discounts |
| Deposits and Prepaid Orders | 2210 | Prepaid Sales and Deposits |

**Click**    the **List icon** in the Bank Account To Use column for Canadian Dollars.

**Click**    **1030 Undeposited Cash and Cheques** and **click Select**.

**Click**    List icon in the Bank Account To Use column for United States Dollars.

**Click**    **1140 Bank: USD Chequing** and **click Select**.

**Enter**    the **remaining linked accounts** from the chart on this page. **Type** the **account number** or **select** the **account** from the drop-down list.

**NOTES**
The remaining accounts were introduced in Chapter 7. Refer to page 241 if you need to review these accounts.

# Payroll Ledger Settings

At this stage, we will change the settings for Payroll Names, Income, Deductions, Taxes and Entitlements. After creating vendor and employee records, we can change the Remittance and Job Category settings.

## *Entering Payroll Names*

Because the names we use will appear on the remaining payroll setting screen, we will define them first.

<table>
<tr><td>**Click**</td><td>**Payroll** and then **click Names** under Payroll.</td></tr>
<tr><td>**Click**</td><td>**Incomes & Deductions** to access the first group of payroll names.</td></tr>
</table>

Many of the standard income types are mandatory and cannot be changed. These fields are shown in colour on a shaded background. Some of the other default names are also correct so you do not need to redefine them. You can leave Income 1 and Income 2, labelled "Salary" and "Commission," unchanged because Flabuless Fitness has two salaried employees and pays a sales commission to one employee. There is allowance for 20 different kinds of income in addition to the compulsory fields and 20 different payroll deductions. Each income and deduction label may have up to 12 characters.

Flabuless Fitness uses the additional income fields for bonuses, piece rate pay and taxable benefits (tuition fee payments) so that these incomes can be identified by name on the paycheque. The piece rate pay is based on completed favourable client surveys for the employees. Travel expenses repaid directly to employees are also entered as income but they will not be taxed.

Flabuless also has three payroll deductions at this time: RRSP — the Registered Retirement Savings Plan; CSB Plan — the Canada Savings Bond plan; and Garnishee — the wages that are withheld and submitted to the Receiver General for prior years' taxes.

<table>
<tr><td>**Click**</td><td>**Income 3 in the Name Column** to highlight the contents.</td></tr>
<tr><td>**Type**</td><td>No. Clients **Press** (tab) to advance to the Income 4 field.</td></tr>
<tr><td>**Type**</td><td>Bonus **Press** (tab) to advance to the Income 5 field.</td></tr>
<tr><td>**Type**</td><td>Tuition **Press** (tab) to advance to the Income 6 field.</td></tr>
<tr><td>**Type**</td><td>Travel Exp. **Press** (tab) to advance to the Income 7 field.</td></tr>
<tr><td>**Press**</td><td>(del) to remove the entry. **Press** (tab) to select the next field.</td></tr>
<tr><td>**Delete**</td><td>the **remaining Income names** until they are all removed.</td></tr>
<tr><td>**Press**</td><td>(tab) after deleting Income 20 to select Deduction 1 in the Deductions column.</td></tr>
<tr><td>**Press**</td><td>(tab) again if necessary to select Deduction 1 in the Name column.</td></tr>
<tr><td>**Type**</td><td>RRSP **Press** (tab) to advance to the second deduction Name field.</td></tr>
<tr><td>**Type**</td><td>CSB Plan **Press** (tab) to highlight the next field.</td></tr>
<tr><td>**Type**</td><td>Garnishee **Press** (tab) to highlight the next field.</td></tr>
<tr><td>**Press**</td><td>(del). Flabuless Fitness does not have other payroll deductions.</td></tr>
<tr><td>**Press**</td><td>(tab) to select the next field. **Delete** the **remaining deductions**.</td></tr>
</table>

---

**NOTES**
Refer to pages 324–330 to review payroll settings if necessary.

**NOTES**
If clicking does not highlight the field contents, drag through an entry to select it. Double clicking will select only one word, either Income or 3.

**NOTES**
In Chapter 9, we created Travel Expenses as a user-defined expense and issued separate cheques to the employee for them.

**NOTES**
For Lime Light Laundry, we used the generic Benefits field to enter all employee benefits.

**NOTES**
You can add names to any of these fields later if you need to.

## *Entering Additional Payroll Names*

Flabuless Fitness keeps an emergency contact name and phone number for each employee in the personnel files. We will name these extra fields for the Payroll Ledger.

On this next screen, we also name the additional payroll expenses for Flabuless and the entitlements for employees. Flabuless has group insurance as a user-defined expense and offers sick leave and personal leave days for all employees as well as vacation days for salaried employees.

We will briefly review income, benefits and user-defined expenses.

Group insurance is classified as a benefit for employees because the premiums are paid to a third party rather than to the employee. The employer's expense for the benefit is entered as a user-defined expense. Tuition is classified as an income because it is paid to the employee through regular paycheques. The employer's expense for this benefit is recorded in the expense account linked to the income, just like wage expenses. Reimbursements may also be entered as income or as user-defined expenses, depending on how the payment is made. If we entered travel expenses as a user-defined expense, we would create a linked payable account and then issue a separate cheque to the employee to provide the reimbursement. If we repay the expense on the payroll cheque, we defined it as an income — reimbursement — income that is not taxable.

**Click**　　**Additional Payroll**.

**Double click**　**Field1**.

**Type**　　Emergency Contact **Press** (tab) **twice** to highlight the next field.

**Type**　　Contact Number

**Delete**　the **names for fields 3 to 5**.

**Drag through**　**User Exp 1**, the Expense 1 field to highlight the contents.

**Type**　　Gp Insurance

**Delete**　the **remaining expenses**.

**Drag through**　**Days 1**, the Entitlement 1 field to highlight the contents.

**Type**　　Vacation **Press** (tab) **twice** to highlight the next entitlement name.

**Type**　　Sick Leave **Press** (tab) **twice** to highlight the next name.

**Type**　　PersonalDays

**Delete**　the **remaining entitlement names**.

The Prov. Tax field is used for Quebec payroll taxes. Since we will not choose Quebec as the employees' province of taxation, the program will automatically skip the related payroll fields. WSIB is entered as the name for WCB (Workers' Compensation Board) because we selected Ontario as the business province. The field has a drop-down list of alternative names.

## *Entering Settings for Incomes*

**Click**　　**Incomes** under Payroll.

This screen designates the types of income and the taxes that apply. By deleting the names we did not need, this list is easier to work with. As we did for Lime Light (Chapter 9), we can modify this screen by deleting the columns that apply to Quebec so that only the columns we need are on-screen at the same time.

---

**NOTES**
Reimbursements are added to net pay (the amount of the paycheque) but are not added to gross pay to calculate taxes.
For Lime Light Laundry, travel expenses were set up as a user-defined expense — separate cheques were issued to the employee.

**NOTES**
On this screen, you need to press (tab) twice to skip the Fr/Eng language button. On the Incomes & Deductions screen, the language button was automatically skipped.

**NOTES**
You can use up to 12 characters for User-Defined Expense and Entitlement names including spaces — that is why we omitted the space for the Personal Days entitlement name.
You can use the language button to enter labels in the second language.

**NOTES**
If necessary, scroll to the right to see the column margin you need.

**NOTES**
When you close and re-open the Payroll Settings screen, the hidden and resized columns will be restored.

QPIP (Quebec Parental Insurance Plan) provides parental leave benefits to EI-insurable employees. Both employers and employees pay into the plan.

**NOTES**
Tuition is defined as an "Income" rather than a benefit because it is paid directly to the employee. It is not a reimbursement because it is taxable.

An alternative approach for tuition fees is to set them up as a user-defined expense, enter the amount in the Benefits field on the paycheque and then issue a cheque to the employee for the Tuition Payable amount.

In Lime Light Laundry (Chapter 9), tuition was set up as a user-defined expense; the amount was paid directly to the college and entered as a benefit for the employee.

**Point to**     the **right column heading margin for Calc. Tax (Que.)** until the pointer changes to a two-sided arrow ⊹ .

**Drag**     the **margin to the left** until the column is hidden.

**Point to**     the **right column heading margin for Calc. QHSF** until the pointer changes to a two-sided arrow. **Drag** the **margin to the left** until the column is hidden.

**Point to**     the **right column heading margin for Calc. QPIP** until the pointer changes to a two-sided arrow. **Drag** the **margin to the left**.

For each type of income, you must indicate what taxes are applied and whether vacation pay is calculated on the income. Most of the information is correct. Regular and overtime hours are paid on an hourly basis, while salary and commissions are paid at designated income amounts per period. All taxes apply to these types of income at Flabuless Fitness, so these default settings are correct. Vacation pay and EI, however, are not calculated on all incomes so some of these checkmarks should be removed. In addition, we should designate the type of income for the income names that we created and the taxes that apply to them. First, we should choose the type of income because that will change the defaults that are applied.

**Click**     **No. Clients** to place the cursor on the correct line.

**Press**     ⟨tab⟩ to move to the Type column. A List icon is added.

**Click**     the **List icon** 🔍 to see the income types.

By default, all new incomes are assigned to the Income type. This assignment is correct for Bonus, the extra annual holiday payment. The tuition fee payment is a taxable benefit paid directly to the employee, so it is classified as income. The Benefit type is used only for items such as medical or life insurance premiums that the employer pays directly to a third party on behalf of the employee. The monetary value of the premiums is added as a benefit to the employee's gross wages to determine taxes and then subtracted again to determine the net pay. The employee does not receive the actual dollar amount. If a benefit is added to net pay, it should be classified as an Income. Therefore, tuition is an Income.

Travel Expenses are **Reimbursements** and No. Clients is the name for the **Piece Rate** basis of paying bonuses. **Differential Rates** apply to different hourly rates paid at different times and are not used by Flabuless.

**Click**     **Piece Rate** to select this type for No. Clients.

**Click**     **Select** to add the Type to the Settings screen. **Press** ⟨tab⟩.

The cursor advances to the Unit of Measure field and the entry has changed to Item. The amount paid to employees is based on the number of completed surveys. Notice that the Insurable Hours checkmark was removed when we changed the type.

**Type**     Surveys

**Click**     **Travel Exp** to select this income line. **Press** ⟨tab⟩.

**Click**     the **List icon** to see the types we can select.

**Double click**  **Reimbursement** to enter this type on the Settings screen. All taxes are removed because this type of payment is not taxable.

We need to make some other modifications. Insurable Hours, the number of work hours, is used to determine eligibility for Employment Insurance benefits. Regular, overtime and salary paid hours are entered but commissions, bonuses and benefits are not. No work time can be reasonably attached to commissions and bonuses so they are not counted. EI is not calculated on taxable benefit income. The checkmarks for these should be removed.

**Click**   **Commission** to select this income line.

**Press**   (tab) **repeatedly** until the cursor is in the **Calc. Ins. Hours field**.

**Click**   to remove the ✓, or **press** the **space bar**.

**Press**   (↓) **twice** to place the cursor in the **Calc. Ins. Hours field for Bonus**.

**Click**   to remove the ✓, or **press** the **space bar**.

**Press**   (↓) to place the cursor in the **Calc. Ins. Hours field for Tuition**.

**Click**   to remove the ✓, or **press** the **space bar**.

**Press**   (shift) and (tab) together to return to the Calc. EI field for Tuition.

**Click**   to remove the ✓, or **press** the **space bar**.

We still need to modify the entries for vacation pay. In Ontario, vacation pay is calculated on all performance-based wages. This includes the regular wages, overtime wages and piece rate pay. We need to remove the remaining ✓. The ✓ for Travel Exp has already been removed. Salaried workers receive paid time off rather than a percentage of their wages as vacation pay. We do not need to remove the ✓ for Overtime 2. If it is used later, vacation pay will be calculated on it as well.

**Click**   **Salary** in the Income column.

**Press**   (tab) **repeatedly** until the cursor is in the **Calc. Vac. column**.

**Click**   to remove the ✓, or **press** the **space bar**.

**Press**   (↓) to place the cursor in the **Calc. Vac. field for Commission**.

**Click**   to remove the ✓, or **press** the **space bar**.

**Press**   (↓) to place the cursor in the **Calc. Vac. field for No. Clients**.

**Press**   (↓) to place the cursor in the **Calc. Vac. field for Bonus**.

**Click**   to remove the ✓, or **press** the **space bar**.

**Press**   (↓) to place the cursor in the **Calc. Vac. field for Tuition**.

**Click**   to remove the ✓, or **press** the **space bar**.

We do not need to change the Quebec tax settings. They will not be applied when we select Ontario as the province for employees. The option to **track tips** applies to payroll in Quebec, so we do not need to choose this option.

The completed Income Settings screen is shown below:

> **NOTES**
> Vacation pay is calculated on all wages. This calculation includes the piece rate pay — number of client evaluations — because it is a performance-based wage or income. Bonuses are not based on measurable performance; therefore, vacation pay is not applied to these amounts or to the other benefits.
> The regulations governing vacation pay are set provincially.

| Income | Type | Unit of Measure | Calc. Tax | Calc. EI | Calc. Ins. Hours | Calc. CPP/QPP | Calc. EHT | Calc. Vac. |
|---|---|---|---|---|---|---|---|---|
| Advance | System | Period | | | | | | |
| Benefits | System | Period | ✓ | | | ✓ | ✓ | |
| Benef. (Que) | System | Period | | | | ✓ | | ✓ |
| Vac. Earned | System | Period | | | | | | |
| Vac. Paid | System | Period | ✓ | ✓ | | ✓ | ✓ | |
| Regular | Hourly Rate | Hour | ✓ | ✓ | ✓ | ✓ | ✓ | ✓ |
| Overtime 1 | Hourly Rate | Hour | ✓ | ✓ | ✓ | ✓ | ✓ | ✓ |
| Overtime 2 | Hourly Rate | Hour | ✓ | ✓ | ✓ | ✓ | ✓ | ✓ |
| Salary | Income | Period | ✓ | ✓ | ✓ | ✓ | ✓ | |
| Commission | Income | Period | ✓ | ✓ | | ✓ | ✓ | |
| No. Clients | Piece Rate | Surveys | ✓ | ✓ | | ✓ | ✓ | ✓ |
| Bonus | Income | Period | ✓ | ✓ | | ✓ | ✓ | |
| Tuition | Income | Period | ✓ | | | ✓ | ✓ | |
| Travel Exp. | Reimbursement | Period | | | | | | |

☐ Track Quebec Tips

## Entering Tax Settings for Deductions

> **Click**    **Deductions** under Payroll.

Only the deduction names you entered earlier appear on this screen. You can calculate deductions as a percentage of the gross pay or as a fixed amount. Some deductions, like union dues, are usually calculated as a percentage of income. The Amount settings are correct for Flabuless Fitness.

All deductions are set by default to be calculated after all taxes (Deduct After Tax is checked). For CSB Plan and Garnishee, this is correct — they are subtracted from income after income tax and other payroll taxes have been deducted. However, RRSP contributions qualify as tax deductions and will be subtracted from gross income before income tax is calculated, but not before EI, CPP and so on, so you must change this setting.

> **Click**    the **Deduct After Tax column** for RRSP to remove the ✓ and change the setting to before tax.

The remaining settings are correct. RRSP is deducted after the other payroll taxes and vacation pay because these deductions are based on gross wages.

## Defining Default Tax Rates

> **Click**    **Taxes** under Payroll.

This group of fields refers to the rate at which employer tax obligations are calculated. The factor for Employment Insurance (**EI Factor**) is correct at 1.4. The employer's contribution is set at 1.4 times the employee's contribution. In the next field, you can set the employer's rate for **WSIB** (Workplace Safety and Insurance Board) premiums. On this screen, you can enter 1.29, the rate that applies to the majority of employees. You can modify rates for individual employees in the ledger records.

The next field, **EHT Factor**, shows the percentage of payroll costs that the employer contributes to the provincial health plan. The rate is based on the total payroll costs per year; the percentage for Flabuless Fitness is 0.98 percent.

The **QHSF Factor** (Quebec Health Services Fund) applies to Quebec employees so we do not need to enter a rate for it. QHSF is similar to EHT.

> **Click**    the **WSIB Rate field**.
>
> **Type**    1.29
>
> **Press**    ⌧tab⌧ to advance to the EHT Factor field.
>
> **Type**    .98

We do not need to change the Quebec tax settings. They will not be applied when we select Ontario as the province for employees.

## Defining Entitlements

> **Click**    **Entitlements** under Payroll.

On this screen you can enter the rules for entitlements that apply to all or most employees. These will be added to new employee records as defaults.

Entitlements are linked to the number of hours worked. Employees at Flabuless Fitness are not entitled to take vacation time until they have worked for a certain period of time, or to take paid sick leave immediately after being hired. The **Track Using % Hours Worked** determines how quickly entitlements accumulate. For example, 5 percent of hours worked yields about one day per month or 12 days of leave per year. Flabuless Fitness has **Maximums** for the number of Days per year that an employee can take or accumulate. And finally, the days unused are not **cleared at the end of a year**. The number of days carried forward is still limited by the Maximum number of days available. The calculations are based on an eight-hour day.

Flabuless Fitness gives salaried workers three weeks of vacation (8 percent) and allows a maximum of 25 days. Sick leave at 10 days per year is earned at the rate of 5 percent to the maximum of 15 days. Personal leave days (5 days) accrue at the rate of 2.5 percent for a maximum of 5 days per year. Flabuless Fitness allows two of the three weeks of vacation time and five of the ten days of sick leave to be carried over to the following year; that is, they are not cleared at the end of the year. Personal leave days cannot be carried forward — the maximum is the same as the yearly allotment.

**Click** the **Track Using % Hours Worked field for Vacation**.

**Type** 8 **Press** ⌑tab⌑ to advance to the Maximum Days field.

**Type** 25 **Press** ⌑tab⌑.

**Click** the **Track Using % Hours Worked field for Sick Leave**.

**Type** 5 **Press** ⌑tab⌑ to advance to the Maximum Days field.

**Type** 15 **Press** ⌑tab⌑.

**Click** the **Track Using % Hours Worked field for PersonalDays**.

**Type** 2.5 **Press** ⌑tab⌑ to advance to the Maximum Days field.

**Type** 5 **Press** ⌑tab⌑.

## *Entering Payroll Linked Accounts*

There are many linked accounts for payroll because each type of income, tax, deduction and expense that is used must be linked to a General Ledger account. The following linked accounts are used by Flabuless Fitness for the Payroll Ledger.

**NOTES**
Refer to page 331 to review payroll linked accounts if necessary.

**WARNING!**
Simply Accounting will not allow you to remove an account while it is being used as a linked account. When you try to remove an account, click OK in the Warning window to return to the Accounts window. First, turn the linking function off by deleting the account in the Linked Accounts window. Then remove the account in the Accounts window. You cannot remove an account if it has a balance or if journal entries have been posted to it.

---

**PAYROLL LINKED ACCOUNTS**

**INCOMES**

| | | | | |
|---|---|---|---|---|
| Principal Bank | 1060 Bank: Hamilton Trust Chequing | | | |
| Vac. Owed | 2300 Vacation Payable | Advances | 1220 | Advances Receivable |

**Income**

| | | | | |
|---|---|---|---|---|
| Vac. Earned | 5300 Wages | Commission | 5310 | Commissions & Bonuses |
| Regular | 5300 Wages | No. Clients | 5310 | Commissions & Bonuses |
| Overtime 1 | 5300 Wages | Bonus | 5310 | Commissions & Bonuses |
| Overtime 2 | Not used | Tuition | 5380 | Employee Benefits |
| Salary | 5305 Salaries | Travel Exp. | 5320 | Travel Expenses |

**DEDUCTIONS**

| | | | | |
|---|---|---|---|---|
| RRSP | 2400 RRSP Payable | Garnishee | 2430 | Garnisheed Wages Payable |
| CSB Plan | 2410 CSB Plan Payable | | | |

**TAXES**

**Payables**      **Expenses**

| Payables | | | Expenses | | |
|---|---|---|---|---|---|
| EI | 2310 | EI Payable | EI | 5310 | EI Expense |
| CPP | 2320 | CPP Payable | CPP | 5320 | CPP Expense |
| Tax | 2330 | Income Tax Payable | WSIB | 5330 | WSIB Expense |
| WSIB | 2460 | WSIB Payable | EHT | 5360 | EHT Expense |
| EHT | 2380 | EHT Payable | | | |
| **Not used** | Tax (Que.), QPP, QHSF, QPIP | | **Not used** | QPP, QHSF, QPIP | |

**USER-DEFINED EXPENSES**

**Payables**      **Expenses**

| Payables | | | Expenses | | |
|---|---|---|---|---|---|
| Gp Insurance | 2420 | Group Insurance Payable | Gp Insurance | 5370 | Gp Insurance Expense |

**NOTES**
To add the Payroll Ledger linked accounts from the Home window, right-click the Paycheques or the Payroll Cheque Run Journal icon in the Home window to select it.
Click the Setup tool or choose the Setup menu, and then choose Settings, Payroll and Linked Accounts.
If no Home window icon is selected, you can use the Setup tool icon pop-up list, choose Paycheques and click Select.

**NOTES**
The deleted income and deduction names do not appear on the screens for linked accounts.

**NOTES**
You can add accounts from the Linked Accounts windows. Type a new number, press (enter) and choose to add the account.

**NOTES**
If you can use an account for more than one link, the account will be available in the drop-down list. Otherwise, once an account is selected as a linked account, it is removed from the list.

**Click**    **Linked Accounts** under Payroll then **click Incomes**.

The names here are the ones you entered in the Names windows. If you deleted a name, it will not appear here.

The linked accounts for all types of income appear together on this first screen. You must identify a wage account for each type of employee payment used by the company, even if the same account is used for all of them. Once the Payroll bank account is identified as the same one used for Payables, the program will apply a single sequence of cheque numbers for all cheques prepared from the Payables and Payroll journals.

**Type**    the **account number** or **select** the **account** from the drop-down list.

**Choose**  **1060 Bank: Hamilton Trust Chequing** for the Principal Bank field.

**Press**   (tab) to advance to the next linked account field.

**Choose**  **2300 Vacation Payable** for the Vac. Owed field.

**Choose**  **1220 Advances Receivable** for the Advances field.

**Choose**  **5300 Wages** for Vacation Earned, Regular and Overtime 1.

**Choose**  **5305 Salaries** for Salaries.

**Choose**  **5310 Commissions & Bonuses** for Commission, No. Clients and Bonus.

**Choose**  **5380 Employee Benefits** for Tuition.

**Choose**  **5320 Travel Expenses** for Travel Exp.

**Click**   **Deductions** to see the next set of Payroll accounts.

**Enter**   the **linked** payable **accounts** for **RRSP**, **CSB Plan** and **Garnishee** from the chart on page 661.

**Click**   **Taxes** to see the next set of Payroll linked accounts.

**Enter**   the **linked payables accounts** for **EI**, **CPP**, **Tax**, **WSIB** and **EHT** in the Payables section and the **linked expense accounts** for **EI**, **CPP**, **WSIB** and **EHT** in the Expenses section from the chart on page 661.

**Click**   **User-Defined Expenses** to see the final Payroll accounts.

**Enter**   the **linked** payable **accounts** for **Gp Insurance Payable** and **Gp Insurance Expense** from the chart on page 661.

**Check**   the **linked** payroll **accounts** against the chart on page 661.

## Inventory & Services Ledger Settings

**Click**   **Inventory & Services** to see the options for this ledger:

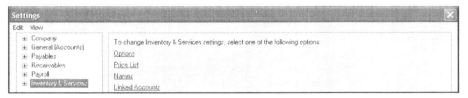

**Click**   **Options**:

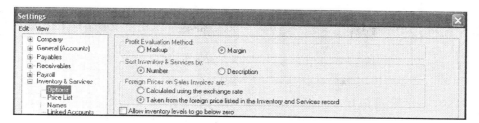

Profits may be calculated on the basis of margin or markup. You can change the setting at any time, so you can prepare reports using both evaluation methods. The formulas for profit evaluation by Margin and Markup are as follows:

Margin = (Selling Price – Cost Price) x 100%/Selling Price

Markup = (Selling Price – Cost Price) x 100%/Cost Price

Flabuless Fitness uses the markup method of evaluating the profit on inventory sales, so we need to change the default setting.

**Click**  **Markup** to change the calculation method.

If you choose to sort Inventory Ledger items by description, the product name field will appear before the product number in the Inventory Ledger input forms, and inventory selection lists will be sorted alphabetically by name. When item numbers are not used, sorting by description will make it easier to find the item you want.

Because we added a foreign currency, the option to take foreign prices for sales from the Inventory Ledger or from the exchange rate is added. The default setting to use the foreign price in the Inventory Ledger Record is correct for Flabuless Fitness. With this option, you can switch pricing methods for individual items. If you choose the exchange rate method, you cannot choose different methods for different items.

The final option is to Allow Inventory Levels To Go Below Zero. Flabuless Fitness will choose this option to permit customer sales for inventory that is backordered.

**Click**  **Allow Inventory Levels To Go Below Zero** to select the option.

In the Pro version, you can create additional price lists and modify price lists from this settings screen. For example, by increasing prices in one price list by a fixed percentage or setting one price list relative to another. We will examine price lists later.

## *Inventory Items Linked Accounts*

Flabuless Fitness currently uses only one linked account for inventory, the one for inventory adjustments or damaged merchandise. The linked accounts for the Inventory Ledger are listed here:

| INVENTORY | |
|---|---|
| Item Assembly Costs | Not used |
| Adjustment Write-off | 5040   Damaged Inventory |

**Click**  the **Linked Accounts** under Inventory & Services:

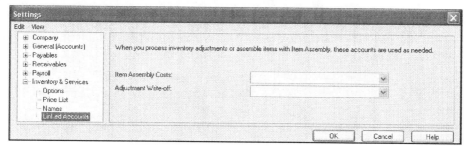

**basic BASIC VERSION**
The Price List option is not available in the Basic version.

**NOTES**
Price lists are used in Chapter 18 to update prices.

**NOTES**
To add the Inventory and Services Ledger linked accounts from the Home window, right-click the Item Assembly or the Inventory Adjustments Journal icon in the Home window to select it.

Click the Setup tool or choose the Setup menu, and then choose Settings, Inventory & Services and Linked Accounts.

**WARNING!**
Check your work carefully. Although you can change the designated linked accounts at any time, journal entries will be posted incorrectly if you do not have the correct linked accounts.

**NOTES**
To see the Project module options, refer to page 527.

> **Type** the **account number** or **select** the **account** from the drop-down list.
>
> **Choose 5040 Damaged Inventory** as the Adjustment Write-off linked account.

Settings options for the hidden Project module are also hidden. Time and Billing, introduced in Chapter 18, has no settings options.

> **Click** **OK** to save the new settings.

You will see several warnings. Because we deleted some payroll names, we are being warned that any accounts linked to these deleted fields will also be removed. The next message refers to the additional payroll names and we are again being warned that their linked accounts will also be removed. Refer to Chapter 9, page 333.

A second group of three warnings relates to required account class changes for linked accounts. Refer to Chapter 7, page 242.

> **Read** each message **carefully** and **click Yes** in response to return to the Home window.

## Entering Users and Security Passwords

Simply Accounting allows you to set up passwords for different users. The password for the system administrator (sysadmin) controls access to the system or program. Passwords for other users control viewing and editing privileges for different ledgers, journals and reports. For example, if different employees work with different accounting records, they should use different passwords.

We strongly advise you not to set passwords for applications used for tutorial purposes. If you set them and forget them, you will be locked out of your data files.

If you want to set passwords, refer to Appendix G on the Student CD-ROM and your Simply Accounting manuals before you begin.

# Preparing the Subsidiary Ledgers

We have now completed the General Ledger setup including:

1. organizing all accounting reports and records
2. creating new accounts
3. identifying linked accounts for all ledgers
4. activating additional features and entering their linked accounts

The remaining steps involve setting up the records in the subsidiary ledgers:

5. inserting vendor, customer, employee and inventory information
6. entering historical startup information
7. printing reports to check the accuracy of your records

## Preparing the Payables Ledger

Use Flabuless Fitness' Vendor Information on pages 626–627 to create the vendor records and add the outstanding historical invoices. If any information is missing for a vendor, leave that field blank.

### *Entering Vendor Accounts*

**NOTES**
For a review of the Payables Ledger setup, refer to page 242.

> **Click** the **Vendors icon** 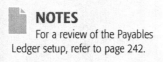 in the Home window to open the Vendors window.

**Click**     the **Create button** [🗐 Create] or **choose** the **File menu** and **click Create**
           or **press** (ctrl) + **N**. The cursor is in the Vendor field.

**Enter**     the vendor's **name**. On the Address tab screen, enter the **contact**,
           **address**, **phone**, **fax** and **tax ID** numbers, and the **e-mail** and **Web site**
           addresses from pages 626–627.

**Click**     the **Options tab**.

**Enter**     the **discounts**, if there are any, in the Terms fields, and the number of
           days in which the net amount is due. **Click Calculate Discounts Before**
           **Tax** if the discounts are before tax. Otherwise, leave the box unchecked.

You can print the contact on cheques if this is appropriate for the vendor.

**Enter**     the **default expense account** for the vendor if there is one.

**Click**     the **Taxes tab** to open the tax information screen for the vendor.

**Click**     the **Tax Code field list arrow** to see the codes.

For Ancaster Insurance, the selection No Tax is correct because some transactions
are taxable and others are not. GST is not applied to insurance.

**Click**     **No** in the Tax Exempt column for GST to change the setting to Yes.

Do not change the tax exempt setting for PST because PST is charged on
insurance in Ontario.

It is not necessary to change Tax Exempt entries. Leaving the setting at No will
make all tax codes available for a vendor. As long as the tax code in the journal is
correct, taxes will be calculated correctly. You can change the tax settings at any time.

**Correct**   any **errors** by returning to the field with the mistake, highlighting the
           errors and entering the correct information.

**Enter**     **historical transactions** using the keystroke instructions in the
           following section if the vendor has historical transactions.

**Click**     **Create Another** [🗐 Create Another] to save the record and open a blank
           Payables Ledger window.

**Click**     the **Address tab** to begin entering the next vendor record.

## *Entering Historical Vendor Transactions*

The chart on page 627 provides the information you need to complete this stage.

**Enter**     the vendor's **name**, **address tab information**, **options** and **taxes**.

**Click**     the **Historical Transactions tab**.

**Click**     **Save Now**.

**Click**     **Invoices**.

**Enter**     the **Invoice Number**, **Date**, **Pre-Tax Amount** and **Tax** for the first
           invoice. The default terms should be correct.

**Press**     (tab) to advance to the next field after entering each piece of
           information.

When all the information is entered correctly, you must save your vendor invoice.

**NOTES**
Leaving the code as No Tax and leaving the exempt status set at No will permit you to charge taxes if needed. PST is applied to insurance in Ontario.
   If taxes are not calculated correctly for a vendor or customer, check that the Ledger entries for Tax Exempt are No.

**NOTES**
Feelyte Gym Accessories is the first vendor with historical invoices.

**⚠ WARNING!**
If you save an incorrect invoice amount, you must pay the invoice, clear paid invoices for the vendor (Home window, Maintenance menu), reset the payments for the year to zero (vendor's ledger, Statistics tab) and re-enter the outstanding invoices. Refer to page 258.

> **Click**    **Record** to save the invoice and to display another blank invoice for this vendor.
>
> **Repeat**   these steps to **enter other invoices** for this vendor.
>
> **Click**    **Close** to return to the Payables Ledger when you have recorded all outstanding invoices for the vendor.

## *Historical Payments*

> **Click**    **Payments**.
>
> **Click**    the **Number field**.
>
> **Enter**    the **cheque number** for the first payment.
>
> **Press**    ( *tab* ) and **enter** the **payment date** for the first payment. Skip the Discount fields because discounts are taken only when the early payment is a full payment.
>
> **Click**    the **Amount Paid column** (on the line for the invoice being paid).
>
> **Enter**    the **payment amount**.
>
> **Press**    ( *tab* ) to advance to the next invoice if there is one. Delete any amounts or discounts that are not included in the payment.
>
> **Click**    **Record** to save the information and to display an updated statement for this vendor.
>
> **Repeat**   these steps to **enter other payments** to this vendor.

When you have recorded all outstanding payments for a vendor,

> **Click**    **Close** to return to the Payables Ledger for the vendor. Notice that the payments you have just entered have been added to the Balance field.
>
> **Click**    the **Create tool**  to display a new blank Payables Ledger screen.
>
> **Click**    the **Address tab**.
>
> **Repeat**   these procedures to **enter** the **remaining vendors** and their **historical transactions**.

## *Identifying Foreign Vendors*

In order to identify Prolife Exercisers Inc. and Redux Home Gym Wholesalers as foreign vendors, the Options tab screen requires additional information.

> **Enter**    the vendor's **name** and **address tab information**.
>
> **Click**    the **Options tab**:

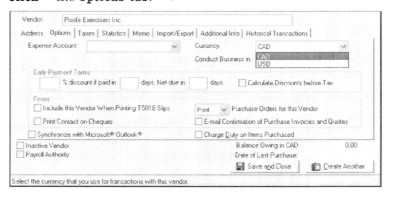

---

**⚠ WARNING!**
Remember not to include any discounts taken in the historical payments. If you do include them, the Payables Ledger will not be balanced and you will be unable to finish the history.

**📄 NOTES**
The historical invoices and payments will be entered on the Statistics tab screen as Last Year's Purchases and Payments because we are starting a new fiscal period.

**📄 NOTES**
Prolife Exercisers Inc. is the first foreign vendor you will enter, so we show the screens for this vendor.

**Enter**    **2**% in **10** days, net **30** days as the Early Payment Terms for the vendor.

**Click**    **Calculate Discounts Before Tax**.

**Click**    the **Currency field list arrow**.

**Click**    **USD**.

**Click**    **Charge Duty On Items Purchased**.

You must change this Duty setting to access the duty fields in the Purchases Journal for this vendor.

Do not enter a default expense account for inventory purchases — the linked asset account from the Inventory Ledger record is selected automatically by the program. You do not need to enter any details on the Statistics, Memo and Import/Export tab screens. The Balance Owing will be entered automatically by the program once you have entered historical invoices.

**Click**    the **Taxes tab** and **choose code G** for the foreign vendor.

**Correct**  any **errors** by returning to the field with the mistake, highlighting the errors and entering the correct information.

**Click**    the **Historical Transactions tab** and **click Save Now** if the vendor has historical transactions. (Proceed to the next keystroke section.)

**Click**    **Create Another**  to save the record and open a blank Payables Ledger window.

**Click**    the **Address tab** to begin entering the next vendor record.

## Invoices for Foreign Vendors

**Enter**    the vendor's **name, address tab information, options** and **taxes**.

**Click**    the **Historical Transactions tab**. **Click Save Now**.

**Click**    **Invoices** on the Historical Transactions tab screen for Redux Home Gym Wholesalers:

The Historical Invoices input screen for foreign vendors has additional fields for the second currency information.

You can edit the payment terms for individual invoices if needed.

Because Redux discounts are calculated before taxes, there are separate fields for pretax and tax invoice amounts.

**Enter**    **R-914** as the **Invoice Number** and **Mar 28** as the invoice **Date**.

**Press**    (tab) to see the Exchange Rate screen.

---

**⚠ WARNING!**

You cannot change the currency for a vendor or customer after entering historical invoices, so you must set up the currencies first. After you enter historical invoices for a foreign vendor or customer, you cannot change the currency setting for the company. You must pay the invoices, clear paid transactions, remove the vendor and then re-create the vendor record from scratch.

You cannot access the duty fields in the Purchases Journal unless Charge Duty On Items Purchased is checked in the vendor's ledger.

**NOTES**

The Exchange Rate screen opens as soon as you enter the date. If you press (tab) after entering the date, it will open immediately. If you do not press (tab) and click the USD Amount field, it will open at that point. Click Cancel when it appears.

**Click**   **Cancel**. We will enter the amounts in both currencies and allow the program to calculate the exchange rate.

**Click**   the **Pretax Amount field for USD**.

**Type**   5910   **Press** (tab) to advance to the Tax amount field for USD.

**Type**   354.60

**Click**   the **Home Amount field for CAD**.

**Type**   7420   **Press** (tab).

The exchange rate is determined automatically from these amounts.

**Click**   **Record**.

When you have recorded all outstanding invoices for a vendor,

**Click**   **Close** to save the invoice and return to the Historical Transactions tab screen.

The invoices you entered have been added to the Balance fields. Balances are displayed in both currencies. Continue by entering historical payments to this vendor if there are any, or proceed to enter the next vendor.

**Click**   the **Create tool** 🔲. **Click** the **Address tab**. **Enter** the remaining **vendors**.

**Click**   **Save and Close** 💾 Save and Close after adding the last vendor and then **close** the **Vendors window**.

**Display** or **print** the **Vendor List** and the **Vendor Aged Detail Report**, including terms and historical differences, to check the accuracy of your work.

## Preparing the Receivables Ledger

Use Flabuless Fitness' Customer Information on pages 627–628 to create the customer records and add the outstanding historical invoices. Revenue accounts are added from the inventory records so they are not needed in the customers' records. If any information is missing for a customer, leave that field blank.

### *Entering Customer Accounts*

**Click**   the **Customers icon**  in the Home window to open the Customers window.

**Click**   the **Create button** 🔲 Create or **choose** the **File menu** and then **click Create**. The cursor is in the Customer field.

**Enter**   the customer's **name**. On the Address tab screen, enter the **contact**, **address**, **phone** and **fax numbers**, and the **e-mail** and **Web site addresses** according to pages 627–628.

You can edit the default payment terms for individual customers or for individual historical invoices if necessary.

**Click**   the **Ship-To Address tab**.

The Mailing Address is already selected as the default ship-to address, so the same address will apply to both fields on invoices, orders and quotes.

**Click**    the **Options tab**.

Most entries on the Options tab screen are correct. Terms are entered from the default Receivables settings. Customer statements should be printed. Buffalo Health Clinic and Lockport Gymnasium are USD customers. All other customers are Canadian and use the Home currency (CAD).

**Choose**    **USD** from the Currency list for Buffalo Health Clinic (and for Lockport Gymnasium).

**Choose**    **Preferred** from the Price List field list for **Buffalo Health Clinic** and for other preferred customers (the ones marked with * in the customer information chart) to change the price list for these customers.

**Change**    the payment **terms** to **net 1** for **Cash and Interac**, and **Visa Sales customers**.

**Click**    the **Taxes tab**. For most customers, the default code GP is correct.

Buffalo Health Clinic and Lockport Gymnasium, the foreign currency customers, do not pay taxes.

**Select**    **No Tax** as the **tax code** from the drop down list for the US customers.

**Click**    the **Statistics tab**.

**Enter**    the **credit limit**. Enter the credit limit in both currencies for USD customers.

This is the amount that the customer can purchase on account before payments are required. If the customer goes beyond the credit limit, the program will issue a warning before posting an invoice.

The balance owing will be included automatically once you have provided the outstanding invoice information. If the customer has outstanding transactions, proceed to the next section on historical information. Otherwise,

**Click**    **Create Another**  to save the information and advance to the next new Receivables Ledger input screen.

**Click**    the **Address tab**.

## *Entering Historical Customer Information*

The chart on page 628 provides the information you need to complete this stage.

**Enter**    the customer's **name**, **address**, **options**, **taxes** and **credit limit**.

**Click**    the **Historical Transactions tab**. **Click Save Now**.

**Click**    **Invoices**.

**Enter**    the **invoice number**, **date** and **amount** for the first invoice. The default terms should be correct.

**Press**    [tab] to advance to the next field after entering each piece of information.

When all the information is entered correctly, you must save the customer invoice.

**Click**    **Record** to save the information and to display another blank invoice for this customer.

**Repeat**    these procedures to **enter** the **remaining invoices** for the customer, if there are any.

**NOTES**
The preferred customers are:
Buffalo Health Clinic
Chedoke Health Care
McMaster University
Mohawk College
Stelco Health Club

 **WARNING!**
Do not forget to remove the discount for cash and credit card customer sales. Changing the ledger records will make the sales invoice terms correct automatically.

**WARNING!**
If you save an incorrect invoice amount, you must pay the incorrect invoice, clear paid transactions for the customer, then re-enter the customer's outstanding invoices. Refer to page 258.

When you have recorded all outstanding invoices for a customer,

**Click**    **Close** to return to the Historical Transactions window for the customer.

The invoices you entered have been added to the Balance field. Continue by entering payments received from this customer, if there are any, or proceed to enter the next customer.

**Click**    **Payments**.

**Click**    the **Number field**.

**Enter**    the **cheque number** for the first payment.

**Press**    ( tab ) and **enter** the **payment date** for the first payment. Again, discounts apply only to full payments made before the due dates, so you should skip the Discount fields.

**Click**    the **Amount Paid column** (on the line for the invoice being paid).

**Enter**    the **payment amount**.

**Press**    ( tab ) to advance to the next amount if other invoices are being paid. Delete any amounts or discounts that are not included in the payment.

**Click**    **Record** to save the information and to display an updated statement for this customer.

**Repeat**   these procedures to **enter** the **remaining payments** from the customer.

When you have recorded all outstanding receipts from a customer,

**Click**    **Close** to return to the Receivables Ledger window for the customer.

The payments you entered have been added to the customer's Balance field.

**Click**    **Create tool** 🗗 to open another new Receivables Ledger input screen.

**Click**    the **Address tab** to prepare for entering other customers. After entering all customer records and historical data,

**Click**    **Save and Close** 🖫 Save and Close (or ☒) after adding the last customer. **Close** the **Customers window** to return to the Home window.

**Display** or **print** the **Customer List** and the **Customer Aged Detail Report**, including terms and historical differences, to check your work.

## Preparing the Payroll Ledger

**NOTES**
For a review of the Payroll Ledger setup, refer to page 333.

Use the Flabuless Fitness Employee Information Sheet, Employee Profiles and Additional Payroll Information on pages 628–630 to create the employee records and add historical information.

We will enter the information for Flabuless Fitness employee George Schwinn.

**Click**    the **Employees icon** 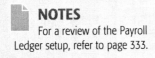 in the Home window.

**Click**    the **Create button** 🗐 Create or **choose** the **File menu** and **click Create**.

### *Entering Personal Details for Employees*

The Payroll Ledger new employee information form will open at the Personal information tab screen so you can begin to enter the employee record.

**WARNING!**
Remember not to include any discounts taken in the historical payments. If you do include them, the Receivables Ledger will not be balanced and you will be unable to finish the history.

The Payroll Ledger has a large number of tabs for the different kinds of payroll information. The cursor is in the Employee field. By entering the surname first, your employee lists will be in correct alphabetic order.

**Type**    Schwinn, George **Press** ⏎ tab ⏎.

**Type**    55 Carter St.  to enter the Street address.

The default city, province and province code, those for the store, are correct.

**Click**    the **Postal Code field**.

**Type**    l8b2v7 **Press** ⏎ tab ⏎.

The program corrects the postal code format and advances the cursor to the Phone 1 field.

**Type**    9054261817

The default **Language Preference** is correctly set as English.

**Click**    the **Social Insurance Number (SIN) field**. You must use a valid SIN. The program has corrected the telephone number format.

**Type**    532548625 **Press** ⏎ tab ⏎.

The cursor advances to the Birth Date field. Enter the month, day and year using any accepted date format.

**Type**    9-18-69 **Press** ⏎ tab ⏎ **twice**.

The cursor moves to the Hire Date field, which should contain the date when the employee began working for Flabuless Fitness.

**Type**    1-6-03

The next two fields will be used when the employee leaves the job — the date of termination and the reason for leaving that you can select from the drop-down list. The final option designates employees as active or inactive. All employees at Flabuless Fitness are active, so the default selection is correct.

We have not yet created Job Categories to identify salespersons, so we will assign employees to them later. The Date Last Paid will be entered automatically by the program.

## Entering Employee Tax Information

**Click**    the **Taxes tab** to advance to the next set of employee details.

This screen allows you to enter income tax–related information for an employee, including the historical amounts for the year to date.

**Click**    the **Tax Table list arrow** to see the list of provinces and territories.

**Click**    **Ontario**, the province of taxation for Flabuless Fitness employees.

**Press**    ⏎ tab ⏎ to advance to the **Federal Claim** field.

**Type**    8929 **Press** ⏎ tab ⏎ to advance to the **Federal Claim Subject To Indexing**. This is the amount of personal claim minus pension and tuition/education exemption amounts.

**Type**    8929 **Press** ⏎ tab ⏎ to advance to the Provincial Claim field.

Since 2001, provincial personal income taxes have not been linked to the rates for federal income taxes, so separate **provincial claim** amounts are needed.

**NOTES**
The program will allow you to omit the Social Insurance Number but you must enter the employee's birth date.

**NOTES**
For all Flabuless Fitness employees, the total federal and provincial claim amounts are subject to indexing. Governments raise these claim amounts based on inflation and budget decisions.

**Type**    8533    **Press** (*tab*).

**Type**    8533    **Press** (*tab*) to enter the Provincial Claim Amount Subject To Indexing.

The cursor advances to the **Additional Federal Tax** field. Prekor is the only employee with other income who chooses to have additional taxes withheld.

For **Prekor**, click the **Additional Fed. Tax** field and type **50**.

If an employee is insurable by EI, you must leave the box for **Deduct EI** checked. The default EI contribution factor, 1.4, for Flabuless Fitness is correct. We entered it in the Payroll Taxes Settings window (page 660).

All employees at Flabuless make CPP contributions so this check box should remain selected.

We will enter the historical income tax amounts next.

**Click**    the **Historical Amount field** for **Income Tax**.

**Type**    1562.21    **Press** (*tab*) to advance to the EI Premiums Historical Amount field. Enter the amount of EI paid to date.

**Type**    217.54    **Press** (*tab*) to move to the CPP Contributions Historical Amount field.

**Type**    375.20

### *Entering Income Amounts for Employees*

We defined all the types of income for Flabuless Fitness in the Names, Incomes & Deductions setup (page 656). All employees use the following types of income, although not all will have regular amounts and not all will be used on all paycheques:

- Advances
- Benefits
- No. Clients
- Bonus
- Tuition
- Travel Exp.

For Schwinn the following incomes are also used: Vacation (Vac.) Owed, Vacation (Vac.) Paid, Regular and Overtime 1.

For Kisangel and Prekor the following incomes are used: Salary and Commission. Because Quebec is not selected as the province of taxation, Benefits (Que) is not preselected. Advance, Benefits and Vacation checkmarks cannot be removed.

All the details you need to complete the Income tab chart are on page 629.

**Click**    the **Income tab**.

On the Income chart you can indicate the types of income that each employee receives (the **Use** column), the usual rate of pay for that type of income (**Amount Per Unit**), the usual number of hours worked (**Hours Per Period**), the usual number of pieces for a piece rate pay base (**Pieces Per Period**) and the amounts received this year before the earliest transaction date or the date used for the first paycheque (**Historical Amount**). The **Year-To-Date (YTD) Amount** is added automatically by the program based on the historical amounts you enter and the paycheques entered in the program.

Checkmarks should be entered in the Use column so that the fields will be available in the payroll journals, even if they will not be used on all paycheques.

**Click**    **Regular** in the Income column to select the line.

### ! WARNING!

Enter employee historical payroll details carefully. You will be unable to edit these fields after finishing the history or after making Payroll Journal entries for the employee.

They must also be correct because they are used to create T4s for tax reporting.

### NOTES

The program skips the Quebec tax fields because Ontario was selected as the province of taxation.

### NOTES

In the chart on page 629, the incomes that are used by an employee have ✓ or an amount in the employee's column.

### NOTES

Checkmarks are added by default for all incomes, deductions and expenses that have linked accounts entered for them.

### ! WARNING!

Do not click the Use column beside Regular as that will remove the checkmark.

**Press** (tab) to advance to the Amount Per Unit field where we need to enter the regular hourly wage rate.

**Type** 16

**Press** (tab) to advance the Hours Per Period field.

The usual number of work hours in the bi-weekly pay period is 80. You can change the default amount in the Payroll journals. Salaried workers normally work 150 hours each month.

**Type** 80 **Press** (tab) to advance to the Historical Amount field.

Historical income and deduction amounts for the year to date are necessary so that taxes and deductions can be calculated correctly and T4 statements will be accurate.

**Type** 8960 **Press** (tab).

The amount is entered automatically in the YTD column and the cursor advances to the Use column for Overtime 1.

**Press** (tab) so you can enter the overtime hourly rate.

**Type** 24

**Press** (tab) **twice** to advance to the Historical Amount field. There is no regular number of overtime hours.

**Type** 336

The next three income types do not apply to Schwinn, so they should not be checked. The next income that applies is No. Clients, the piece rate method of pay. There is no historical amount, but we need to enter the rate or amount per unit (survey). The remaining incomes (No. Clients, Bonus and Travel Exp.) are correctly checked. There is no fixed amount per unit or period and there are no historical amounts.

Pressing the space bar when you are in the Use column will also add a ✓ or remove one if it is there. Pressing ⊕ will move you to the next line in the same column.

**Click** the **Use column beside Salary** to remove the ✓.

**Click** the **Use column beside Commission** to remove the ✓.

**Click** **No. Clients** in the Income column to select the line. **Press** (tab).

**Type** 10 to enter the amount received for each completed survey.

If employees have received vacation pay, enter this amount in the **Vac. Paid** field. Vacation pay not yet received is entered in the **Vac. Owed** field. Any advances paid to the employees and not yet repaid are recorded in the **Advances Paid** field. There is no record of advance amounts recovered.

We need to add the historical advances, benefits and vacation amounts for Schwinn. Schwinn has $100 in advances not yet repaid, and he has not used all the vacation pay he has earned this year.

**Scroll** **to the top** of the list so that the information for Advance is available.

**Click** the **Historical Amount column beside Advance** to move the cursor.

**Type** 100

**Press** (tab) to move to the Amount Per Period column for Benefits. The group insurance premiums paid by the employer are employee benefits.

**NOTES**
If you added a linked account for Overtime 2, it will have a ✓ in the Use column and you should remove it for all employees.

**NOTES**
Remember that commissions must be calculated manually and entered in the Payroll journals. The Commission field in the Payroll Ledger allows only a fixed amount, not a percentage of sales, as the entry.

**WARNING!**
The totals for all employees for advances paid and vacation pay owing must match the corresponding General Ledger account balances before you can finish entering the history.

**Type**    5    **Press** `tab` to move to the Historical Amount for Benefits.

**Type**    35    **Press** `tab` to advance to the Historical Amount for Vac. Owed.

**Type**    371.84    **Press** `tab` to advance to the Historical Vac. Paid Amount.

**Type**    385.92

For **Prekor**, click the Use column for Regular, Overtime 1 and Commission to remove the ✓. Enter the monthly salary and press `tab`. Enter 150 as the number of hours worked in the pay period. Press `tab` and enter the historical amount. For No. Clients, enter 10 as the amount per unit. For Travel Exp., enter 120 as the historical amount. You cannot remove the ✓ for Vac. Owed and Vac. Paid, even if they are not used.

For **Kisangel**, repeat these steps but leave Commission checked and enter the historical amount. For Tuition, enter 440 as the historical amount.

**Pay Periods Per Year** refers to the number of times the employee is paid, or the pay cycle. Schwinn is paid every two weeks, 26 times per year.

**Click**    the **list arrow** beside the field **for Pay Periods Per Year**.

**Click**    **26**.

**Retaining Vacation** pay is normal for full-time hourly paid employees. Part-time and casual workers often receive their vacation pay with each paycheque because their work schedule is irregular. You will turn the option to retain vacation off when an employee receives the vacation pay, either when taking a vacation or when leaving the company (see page 290). If the employee is salaried and does not receive vacation pay, the option should also be turned off. For Schwinn, or any employee who receives vacation pay, leave the option to Retain Vacation checked and type the vacation pay rate in the % field.

**Double click**    the **% field beside Retain Vacation**.

**Type**    6

For **Prekor** and **Kisangel**, click Retain Vacation to remove the ✓.

Employee wages may be linked to the default expense account or to another account. Wage expenses for all Flabuless Fitness employees are linked to the default accounts entered on page 661.

## Entering Default Payroll Deduction Amounts

**Click**    the **Deductions tab** to open the screen for payroll deductions.

On this screen, you can indicate which deductions apply to the employee, the amount normally deducted and the historical amount — the amount deducted to date this year. All deductions are selected in the Use column. These are the deductions you entered previously (page 656).

By entering deductions here, they will be included automatically on the Payroll Journal input forms. Otherwise, you must enter them manually in the Journal for each pay period. Since all three employees have chosen to participate in these plans, you can enter the information here so that the deductions are made automatically. You should make permanent changes by editing the employee ledger record.

If you choose to calculate deductions as a percentage of gross pay in the Payroll Settings, the Percentage Per Pay Period fields will be available.

For one-time changes, you can edit deduction amounts in the Payroll journals on the Deductions tab or the Deductions Details screen.

**NOTES**
Employees may be paid yearly (1), semi-annually (2), monthly for 10 months (10), monthly (12), every four weeks (13), every two weeks for a 10-month year (22), twice a month (24), every two weeks (26) or weekly (52).

**NOTES**
When you select a specific account, all payroll expenses for that employee will be linked to the same account — the one you identify in this field. If you want to use different accounts for different wage expenses, you must use the linked accounts.

**Click**    RRSP in the Deduction column to select the line.

**Press**    `tab`. You should enter the amount that is withheld in each pay period.

**Type**    50 **Press** `tab` to advance the cursor to the Historical Amount field.

**Type**    350 **Press** `tab` to advance the cursor to the Use column for CSB Plan.

**Press**    `tab`. Enter the amount that is to be withheld in each pay period.

**Type**    50 **Press** `tab` to advance the cursor to the Historical Amount field.

**Type**    350

**Press**    `tab` to update the YTD Amount and advance to the Use column for Garnishee. Schwinn does not have wages withheld.

**Click**    the **Use column for Garnishee** to remove the ✓.

The remaining deductions are not used by Flabuless Fitness. The names were deleted (page 656) so they do not appear on the chart.

## Entering WSIB and Other Expenses

**Click**    the **WSIB & Other Expenses tab**.

The user-defined expenses we created in the Additional Payroll Names screen (page 657) and the default WSIB rate (page 660) are entered on this screen.

In Ontario, WSIB (Workplace Safety and Insurance Board) is the name for Workers' Compensation Board, so the tab is labelled WSIB. In other provinces, the tab label will be WCB & Other Expenses.

The default WSIB rate is entered from our setup information, but you can enter a different rate for an individual employee in this field. The rate is correct for Schwinn.

For **Kisangel**, enter 1.02 as the WSIB rate.

Other user-defined expenses are also added on this screen. Flabuless Fitness has only group insurance as a user-defined expense.

**Click**    the **Gp Insurance Amt. Per Period**. Enter the amount that the employer contributes in each pay period.

**Type**    5 **Press** `tab` to advance to the Historical Amount field.

**Type**    35

The remaining expenses are not used by Flabuless Fitness.

## Entering Employee Entitlements

We entered the default rates and amounts for entitlements as Payroll Settings (page 660), but they can be modified in the ledger records for individual employees.

We must also enter the historical information for entitlements. This historical number will include any days carried forward from the previous periods. The number of days accrued cannot be greater than the maximum number of days defined for the entitlement for an employee. The number of Net Days Accrued, the amount unused and available for carrying forward, is updated automatically from the historical information and current payroll journal entries.

**Click**    the **Entitlements tab**.

You cannot enter information directly in the Net Days Accrued fields on the Entitlements tab screen.

**NOTES**
The Ontario name was changed to emphasize safety rather than compensation for accidents. WSIB (or WCB) pays workers when they have been injured on the job and are unable to work.

**NOTES**

If employees take days before the sufficient number of hours worked have been accrued, the program will warn you. Then you can allow the entry for entitlements or not. This entry is similar to allowing customers to exceed their credit limits.

Schwinn receives vacation pay instead of paid time off so the vacation entitlements details should be removed. The defaults for sick leave and personal days are correct.

| | |
|---|---|
| **Click** | **8.00** in the **Track Using % Hours Worked field for Vacation**. |
| **Press** | del to remove the entry. |
| **Press** | tab to advance to the Maximum Days field. |
| **Press** | del to remove the entry. |
| **Click** | the **Historical Days field for Sick Leave**. |
| **Type** | 12 |
| **Press** | ↓ to advance to the Historical Days field for PersonalDays. The number of days is added to the Net Days Accrued. |
| **Type** | 4 **Press** tab to enter the amount. |

For Kisangel and Prekor, the default entries for tracking and maximum days are correct, but you must enter the Historical Days for each entitlement.

### *Entering Direct Deposit Information*

**NOTES**

All banks in Canada are assigned a three-digit bank number and each branch has a unique five-digit transit number. Account numbers may range from five to twelve digits.

| | |
|---|---|
| **Click** | the **Direct Deposit tab**. |

All three employees have elected to have their paycheques deposited directly to their bank accounts. On this screen, we need to enter the bank account details. For each employee who has elected the Direct Deposit option, you must turn on the selection in the Direct Deposit Paycheques For This Employee check box. Then you must add the three-digit **Bank Number**, five-digit **Transit Number**, the bank Account Number and finally the amount that is deposited, or the percentage of the cheque.

**NOTES**

The paycheque deposit may be split among multiple bank accounts by entering different percentages for the accounts.

To delete bank account details, change the status to Inactive and then delete the bank information.

| | |
|---|---|
| **Click** | the **Direct Deposit Paycheques For This Employee check box** to add a ✓. |
| **Click** | the **Bank Number** field. |
| **Type** | 102 **Press** tab to advance to the Transit Number field. |
| **Type** | 89008 **Press** tab to advance to the Account Number field. |
| **Type** | 2998187 **Press** tab **twice** to advance to the Percentage field. |
| **Type** | 100 |

The Memo tab will not be used at this time. You could enter a note with a reminder date to appear in the Daily Business Manager, for example, a reminder to issue vacation paycheques on a specific date or to recover advances.

### *Entering Additional Information*

**NOTES**

Additional information for other ledgers may also be displayed or hidden in journal transactions.

Flabuless Fitness has chosen to enter the name and phone number of the person to be contacted in case of an emergency involving the employee at work. We added the names for these fields in the Payroll Settings (page 657).

| | |
|---|---|
| **Click** | the **Additional Info tab** to access the fields we added for the ledger when we entered Names. |

You can indicate whether you want to display any of the additional information when the employee is selected in a transaction. We do not need to display the contact information in the Payroll Journal.

| | |
|---|---|
| **Click** | the **Emergency Contact field**. |

**Type**    Adrian Ingles

**Press**   ( *tab* ) **twice** to move to the Contact Number field.

**Type**    (905) 722-0301

## Entering T4 and RL-1 Reporting Amounts

The next information screen allows you to enter the year-to-date EI insurable and pensionable earnings. By adding the historical amounts, the T4 slips prepared for income taxes at the end of the year and the record of employment termination reports will also be correct.

Because there are yearly maximum amounts for CPP and EI contributions, these historical details are also needed. Totals for optional deductions are also retained in the employee record.

**Click**    the **T4 and RL-1 Reporting tab** to open the next screen we need to complete.

In the **Historical EI Ins. Earnings** field, you should enter the total earned income received to date that is EI insurable. The program will update this total every time you make payroll entries until the maximum salary on which EI is calculated has been reached. At that time, no further EI premiums will be deducted.

Pensionable Earnings are also tracked by the program. This amount determines the total income that is eligible for Canada Pension Plan. The Pension Adjustment amount is used when the employee has a workplace pension program that will affect the allowable contributions for personal registered pension plans and will be linked with the Canada Pension Plan. Workplace pension income is reduced when the employee also has income from the Canada Pension Plan. Since Flabuless Fitness has no company pension plan, the Pension Adjustment amount is zero.

The T4 Employee Code applies to a small number of job types that have special income tax rules.

**Click**    the **Historical Amounts field for EI Ins. Earnings**.

**Type**    9681.92

**Click**    the **Historical Amounts field for Pensionable Earnings field**.

**Type**    9716.92

**Correct** any employee information **errors** by returning to the field with the error. **Highlight** the **error** and **enter** the **correct information**. **Click each tab** in turn so that you can check all the information.

When all the information is entered correctly, you must save the employee record.

**Click**    **Create Another**  [🗐 Create Another]  to save the record and to open a new blank employee information form.

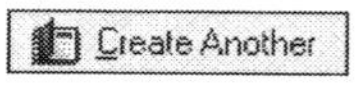

**Click**    the **Personal tab** so that you can enter address information.

**Repeat** these procedures to **enter** other employee **records**.

**Click**    **Save And Close**  [🖫 Save and Close]  after entering the last record to save the record and close the Payroll Ledger.

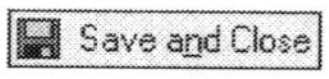

**Display** or **print** the **Employee List** and the **Employee Summary Report** to check the accuracy of your work.

**Close**    the **Employees window** to return to the Home window.

# Entering Job Categories

**NOTES**
Refer to page 344 if you want to review the setup for job categories.

Now that we have entered all the employees, we can set up job categories and indicate which employees are in each category.

> **Choose** the **Setup menu** and **click Settings.** Then **click Payroll** and **Job Categories**.

On the Job Categories screen, you enter the names of the categories and indicate whether the employees in each category submit time slips and whether they are salespersons. Categories may be active or inactive. We need a new category called Sales.

Notice that if you do not create categories, the employees in the default selection <None> are salespersons so they can be selected in the Sales Journal.

> **Click** the **Job Category field below <None>**.
>
> **Type** Sales **Press** (tab) to add checkmarks to the next two columns and set the status to Active.
>
> **Click** **Assign Job Categories** to change the screen.

The Sales category is selected and the screen is updated with employee names. Initially, all are Employees Not In This Job Category.

> You can add employee names to the category by choosing an employee and clicking **Select** or by choosing **Select All**. Once employees are in a category (the column on the right), you can remove them by selecting an employee and clicking **Remove** or clicking **Remove All** to move all names at the same time.
>
> **Click** **Select All** to place all employees in the Sales category.
>
> **Click** **OK** to save the information and return to the Home window.

# Setting Up Payroll Remittances

**NOTES**
Refer to page 345 if you want to review payroll remittance setup.

**NOTES**
Refer to the Company Information on page 623 and the Trial Balance on page 626 to complete the remittance setup.

Because we have entered all payroll settings and all vendors, we can set up the payroll remittances information. This process has three steps: identifying the vendors who receive payroll remittance amounts, linking the vendors to the taxes or deductions they receive, and entering opening dates and balances. First we should designate the payroll authorities. Refer to the chart on page 623 for the Payroll remittance settings.

The vendors to which we remit payroll taxes or other deductions are Ancaster Insurance, Minister of Finance, Mt. Hope Investment Corp., Receiver General for Canada and Workplace Safety & Insurance Board.

> **Right-click** the **Vendors icon** to select it.
>
> **Click** the **Search tool** to open the Search window for vendors.
>
> **Click** **Ancaster Insurance** and then **click OK** to open the vendor's record.
>
> **Click** **Payroll Authority** to add the ✓ and change the vendor's payroll status.
>
> **Click** the **Next Vendor tool** **repeatedly** to access the record for the Minister of Finance, the next payroll authority.
>
> **Click** **Payroll Authority** to add the ✓ and change the vendor's payroll status.
>
> **Repeat** these **steps** for the remaining payroll authorities: **Mt. Hope Investment Corp., Receiver General for Canada** and **Workplace Safety & Insurance Board**.

**NOTES**
You can also double click the vendor's name to add it to the Settings screen.

If you type the first few letters of the name and then press (tab), the Select Vendor list will have the vendor you need selected. Press (enter) to add the name to the Settings screen.

To open the next vendor record, you can also click the Select list arrow and click Minister of Finance.

**Close**  the **Payables Ledger window** to return to the Home window.

**Choose**  the **Setup menu** and **click Settings** to open the Settings screen.

**Click**  **Payroll** to display the payroll settings options.

**Click**  **Remittance** to open the screen we need next.

All the payroll items that are linked to liability (remittance) accounts are listed: taxes, deductions and user-defined expenses. For each liability, we can select a vendor and enter the balance forward date and amount.

**Click**  the **List icon** 🔍 in the Payroll Authority column on the line for EI to see the list of vendors we marked as Payroll Authorities.

**Click**  **Receiver General for Canada**.

**Click**  **Select** or **press** ⏎ to return to the Remittance Settings screen.

The Receiver General for Canada appears beside EI. The cursor advances to the Balance Forward Date field for EI. We need to enter the balances owing at the time we are converting the data to Simply Accounting and the pay period covered by those amounts. These balances are in the Trial Balance on page 626. The effective date is April 1 for all liabilities.

**Type**  Apr 1 **Press** (tab) to advance to the Balance Forward field.

**Type**  563.28 **Press** (tab) to advance to the Payroll Authority field for CPP.

**Enter**  the remaining **Payroll Authorities**, **dates** and **balances**.

**Click**  **OK** to save the settings.

# Preparing the Inventory Ledger

Use the Flabuless Fitness Inventory Information and chart on pages 630–631 to record details about the inventory items on hand.

## *Entering Inventory Records*

The following keystrokes will enter the information for Flabuless Fitness's first inventory item, Body Fat Scale.

**Click**  the **Inventory & Services icon** in the Home window. Again, with no inventory items on file, the icon window is empty.

**Click**  the **Create button** or **choose** the **File menu** and **click Create**:

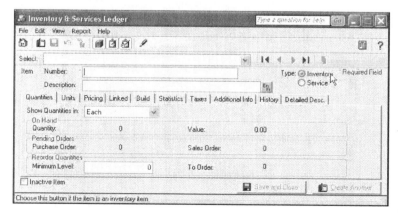

*basic* **BASIC VERSION**

The Inventory & Services icon in the Basic version does not include the clock part of the image.

*basic* **BASIC VERSION**

There isn't a Build tab in the Basic version, and only two show icons will be included in the tool bar. The Show Activities tool applies only to Pro features, and the Refresh tool is used in the multi-user option in Pro.

**NOTES**

If you skip the Inventory icon window (Setup menu, User Preferences, View), you will see this Inventory Ledger immediately when you click the Inventory icon.

The cursor is in the Item Number field. Use this field for the code or number for the first item. When you sort inventory by description, the two item fields shown here will be reversed — the Description field will appear first.

> **Type**   A010   **Press** ⌨tab to advance to the Item Description field, the field for the name of the inventory item.
>
> **Type**   Body Fat Scale

The Type is set correctly for this item as Inventory rather than Service.

The Show Quantities In field allows you to select the units displayed in the ledger. If you have entered different units for stocking, selling and buying, these will be available from the drop-down list. The Quantity On Hand and Value fields are updated by the program as are the Purchase Orders and Sales Orders Pending.

> **Click**   the **Minimum Level field**. Here you should enter the minimum stock level or re-order point for this inventory item.
>
> **Type**   2
>
> **Click**   the **Units tab** to see the next information screen:

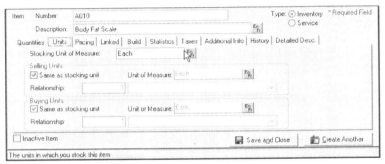

You can enter different units for items when the units for buying, stocking and selling differ. Flabuless Fitness uses the same units for stocking and selling but some buying units are different. For example, if items are purchased in dozens and stocked individually, the relationship is 12 to 1. The Stocking Unit must be changed. Body Fat Scales are purchased in cartons of 12 scales and stocked and sold individually (unit).

> **Double click**   the default entry **Each** for the Stocking Unit Of Measure.
>
> **Type**   Unit
>
> **Click**   **Same As Stocking Unit** for the **Buying Units** section to remove the ✓.

The relationship fields open so that you can indicate how many stocking units are in each buying unit.

> **Press**   ⌨tab to advance to the Unit Of Measure field.
>
> **Type**   Carton **Press** ⌨tab **twice** to advance to the Relationship field.
>
> **Type**   12   **Press** ⌨tab.

Check that the entry is 12 Unit Per Carton. If it is not, click the drop-down list and choose this relationship.

> **Click**   the **Pricing tab** to open the next group of inventory record fields:

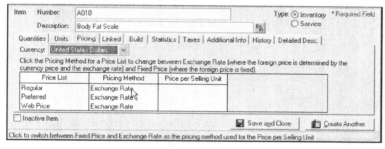

The Currency field and foreign price fields are available only if you indicated that inventory prices should be taken from the Inventory Ledger and not calculated using the exchange rate. The pricing option appears on the Inventory Settings screen only after you enter foreign currency information. Therefore, you must add and save currency information first. Taking prices from the Ledger is the default setting.

On the Pricing tab screen, you can enter regular, preferred and Web prices in the currencies that you have set up. If you created additional price lists, their names will also appear on this screen. The home currency (Canadian Dollars) is selected first.

> **Click**    the **Regular Price Per Selling Unit field**. Here you should enter the selling price for this inventory item.
>
> **Type**    100 **Press** (tab) to advance to the Preferred Selling Price field.

The regular price is also entered as the default Preferred and Web Price. We do not have Web sales so we can accept the default entry for Web prices. Preferred selling prices are shown in brackets in the Inventory Information chart on pages 630–631.

> **Type**    90 to replace the default entry.
>
> **Choose United States Dollars** from the Currency list to open USD price fields:

The pricing method is entered separately for each price. You can choose either Exchange Rate or Fixed Price for Regular and Preferred prices.

> **Click**    **Exchange Rate** beside Regular to change the entry to Fixed Price.
>
> **Press**    (tab) to advance to the Regular Price Per Selling Unit field.
>
> **Type**    85 **Press** (tab) to advance to the Pricing Method field.
>
> **Click**    **Exchange Rate** to change the entry to Fixed Price.
>
> **Press**    (tab) to advance to the Preferred Price Per Selling Unit field.
>
> **Type**    77 **Press** (tab).

**NOTES**
To see the Inventory Ledger Settings, refer to page 663. You cannot change these settings while the Inventory Ledger is open.

**NOTES**
By working from the Inventory Ledger Settings, Price Lists screen, you can create new price lists and update all prices from one location. In Chapter 18, we update inventory prices using this approach.

*basic* **BASIC VERSION**
You cannot create additional price lists or update them globally in the Basic version.

**Click**   the **Linked tab** to open the linked accounts screen for the item:

**Click**   the **Asset field list arrow**.

Here you must enter the **asset** account associated with the sale or purchase of this inventory item. The Inventory chart on pages 630–631 shows that all accessories use account *1520*. All fitness equipment items use *1540* as the asset account. All available asset accounts are in the displayed list.

Enter the account by clicking the list arrow and choosing from the drop-down account list, or

**Type**   1520   **Press** [tab].

The program asks you to confirm the account class change for account 1520:

**Click**   **Yes** to accept the change.

The cursor advances to the **Revenue** field. Here you must enter the revenue account that will be credited with the sale of this inventory item. Again, you can display the list of revenue accounts by clicking the list arrow. Or,

**Type**   4020   **Press** [tab].

The cursor advances to the **C.O.G.S.** field. Here you must enter the expense account to be debited with the sale of this inventory item, normally the *Cost of Goods Sold* account. Flabuless Fitness keeps track of each inventory category separately and has different expense accounts for each category. The appropriate expense account is updated automatically when an inventory item is sold.

Click the list arrow beside the field to display the list of available expense accounts. Or,

**Type**   5050   **Press** [tab] to advance to the Variance field.

**Click**   **Yes** to accept the account class change.

Simply Accounting uses the **Variance** linked account when sales are made of items that are not in stock. If there is a difference between the historical average cost of goods remaining in stock and the actual cost when the new merchandise is received, the price difference is charged to the variance expense account at the time of the purchase. If you have not indicated a variance account, the program will ask you to identify one when you are entering the purchase.

**Type**   5070   or click the list arrow and choose the account.

**Click**   the **Build tab**.

**Click**   **Yes** to accept the account class change and access the Build screen:

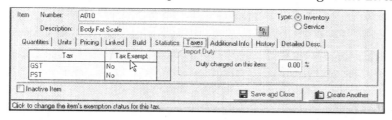

The Build feature is available in Pro but not in the Basic version of Simply Accounting. You can use this screen to define how this item is made or built from other inventory items. Then, in the journal, you can build the item by choosing it from the available list and entering the number of units you want to build. This screen holds the components portion of the Item Assembly Journal.

**Click**   the **Statistics tab** to open the next tab information screen:

On this screen, you can enter historical information about the sale of the product. It would then be added to the inventory tracking information for reports.

The first activity field, the Date Of Last Sale, refers to the last date on which the item was sold. The next two sections contain information for the Year To Date and the previous year. Since Flabuless Fitness has not kept this information, you can skip these fields. Refer to the description of new inventory items on page 388 in the Adrienne Aesthetics application (Chapter 10) for a more detailed description of these historical fields.

**Click**   the **Taxes tab** to input the sales taxes relating to the inventory item:

You can indicate whether the item is taxable for all the taxes you set up, provincial and federal sales taxes in this case. Both PST and GST are charged on sales of all inventory items, so the default entry No for **Tax Exempt** is correct.

For service items, you must change the PST entry to Yes because PST is not charged on services offered by Flabuless Fitness.

**Duty** is also entered on this screen. You must activate the duty tracking option before the duty rate field becomes available. Since no duty is charged on the imported inventory, you can leave the duty rate at 0%.

We have not added fields to the ledger record as we did for Payroll so we can skip the **Additional Info** screen.

The next step is to add the opening historical balances for the inventory items.

**basic BASIC VERSION**
The Build tab screen is not included in the Basic version. Click the Statistics tab as the next step.

**NOTES**
To open the Duty fields in the Purchases Journal, you must activate tracking of duty information and indicate in the vendor record that duty is charged on purchases from the vendor. Rates entered in the Inventory Ledger records will appear automatically in the Purchases Journal for those items. Duty rates can also be entered in the journal if you have not entered them in the ledger records.

**Click**    the **History tab**:

This screen has information about the starting quantities for the item at the time of conversion to Simply Accounting. The opening quantities and values are added to the quantity on hand and value on the Quantities tab screen. History is entered in stocking unit quantities (the same as selling units for Flabuless Fitness).

**Click**    the **Opening Quantity field** to enter the opening level of inventory — the actual number of items available for sale.

**Type**    10   **Press** `tab` .

The cursor advances to the Opening Value field, where you should enter the actual total cost of the inventory on hand.

**Type**    400

The remaining tab allows you to enter further descriptive information.

**Click**    the **Detailed Desc. tab**:

This optional information provides a detailed description of the inventory item (about 500 characters) as well as a picture in image file format.

Type the detailed item description in the Long Description text box.

**Click**    **Browse** beside Picture. **Click** the **Up One Level tool** 🔼 . **Double click** **Setup** and then **Logos** and **scale.bmp** to add the file name and picture.

**Correct** any **errors** by returning to the field with the mistake. **Highlight** the **error** and **enter** the **correct information**. **Click** the different **tabs** to see all the information that you entered.

When all the information is entered correctly, you must save your inventory record.

**Click**    **Create Another**  `Create Another`  to save the record and advance to a new input screen.

**Click**    the **Quantities tab** to prepare for entering the next item.

**Repeat** these procedures to **enter other** inventory **records**.

## Entering Inventory Services

The final items on the inventory chart are services that Flabuless Fitness provides. Entering service items is similar to entering inventory, but there are fewer details.

You should have a blank Inventory & Services Ledger window open at the Quantities tab screen.

---

**WARNING!**
The total opening value amounts for all items in an asset group must match the General Ledger asset account balance before you can finish entering the history.

**NOTES**
A picture file for the Body Fat Scale has been added to the Setup\Logos folder with your other data files. We have not provided picture files for the remaining inventory items.

**NOTES**
If you add a .bmp format picture file, you will see the picture in the box beside the Long Description field. Other file formats may be used, but the pictures will not be displayed.

**Click**    **Service** to change the Type in the upper right section of the screen:

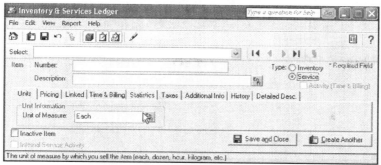

There are fewer tabs and fields for services because some item details do not apply. The Unit Of Measure and Selling Price have the same meaning for services as they do for inventory items. Because service items are not kept in stock or purchased, only the selling unit is applicable, there is no minimum quantity and the History tab fields are removed. Flabuless Fitness' services are not exported, so you do not need to enter foreign prices. Only expense and revenue accounts are linked for services. The other two linked account fields do not apply and are removed for services. Remember to use *Revenue from Services* and *Cost of Services* as the linked accounts for inventory services.

**Enter**    the **Item Number** and **Description** and the **Unit Of Measure**.

**Click**    the **Pricing tab** and add **Regular** and **Preferred prices** in Canadian dollars. Select Canadian Dollars as the currency if necessary.

**Click**    the **Linked tab. Enter** the linked accounts for **Revenue (4040)** and **Expense (5065)**. Accept the account class change.

Most services in Canada are subject to GST. Some services are subject to Provincial Sales Taxes but others are not. These rules also vary from one province to another. Therefore, you should indicate in the Ledger record whether the service is exempt from the tax. By indicating in the Ledger that the service is exempt, PST will not be calculated on sales of the services. All services offered by Flabuless Fitness are exempt from PST, so you should change the Tax Exempt setting in the Taxes tab screen to Yes for PST.

**Click**    the **Taxes tab**.

**Click**    **PST. Press** ⌞tab⌟ to advance to the Tax Exempt column.

**Click**    **No** to change the entry to Yes.

**Click**    **Create Another** 🗋 Create Another

**Click**    the **Units tab. Repeat** these procedures to **enter other service records**.

**Click**    **Save And Close** 🖫 Save and Close after entering the last service record.

**Close**    **Inventory & Services window** to return to the Home window.

**Display** or **print** the **Inventory List**, **Synopsis**, **Quantity** and **Price Lists** reports to check them for accuracy.

# Finishing the History

The last stage in setting up the accounting system involves finishing the history for each ledger. Before proceeding, you should check the data integrity (Home window, Maintenance menu) to see whether there are any out-of-balance ledgers that will prevent you from proceeding. Correct these errors and then make a backup copy of the files.

**basic BASIC VERSION**
The Time & Billing tab screen is used to set up Time & Billing, a feature that is not available in the Basic version. The Activity setting and Internal Customer also apply to the Time & Billing feature, so they do not appear on the Basic version screen.

**NOTES**
In Ontario, some services, such as repairs to tangible property — cars, machinery, etc. — are PST taxable. Personal services are generally not taxed with PST in Ontario.

**NOTES**
The tax code in the Sales Journal for services may show as GP, the code for the customer. However, as we have seen in earlier applications, the tax calculations will be correct if the service record information is correct.

**WARNING!**
Before you finish entering the history, make a backup copy of Flabuless Fitness company files. This is necessary if you find later that you need to correct some of the historical information. Remember, once you finish entering the history, you cannot add information for any period before the earliest transaction date.

# Making a Backup of the Company Files

With the Flabuless Fitness files open, use the File menu Backup command to create a backup. You may also want to create a complete working copy of the not-finished files.

**Choose** the **File menu** and **click Save A Copy**.

**Choose** the **data folder you want** for the not-finished version of the data file. If you are using a different location for your files, substitute the file name and path for your setup.

**Click** the **New Folder tool** 🗔 to create a new folder.

**Type** NF-FLAB to rename the folder.

**Double click** **NF-FLAB** to **open** the new folder.

**Double click** the **File name field**.

**Type** nf-flab

**Click** **Save** to create a copy of all the files for Flabuless Fitness.

The "NF" designates files as not finished to distinguish them from the ones you will work with to enter journal transactions. You will return to your working copy of the file so you can finish the history.

# Changing the History Status of Ledgers to Finished

Refer to page 101 and page 258 for assistance with finishing the history and correcting history errors.

**Choose** the **History menu** and **click Finish Entering History**.

If your amounts, account types and linked accounts are correct, you will see the warning about this step not being reversible and advising you to back up the file first.

**Click** **Proceed** when there are no errors and you have backed up your files.

If you have made errors, you will not see the warning message. Instead you will see a list of errors.

**Click** **Print** so that you can refer to the list for making corrections.

**Click** **OK** to return to the Home window. **Make** the **corrections**, and then **try again**.

**Click** **Proceed**.

The Flabuless Fitness files are now ready for you to enter transactions. Notice that all the Home window icons appear without the open history icons.

Only unhidden modules are set as finished. For Flabuless Fitness, all not-finished symbols are removed. All the ledgers are ready for transactions.

Congratulations on reaching this stage! This is a good time to take a break.

**Finish** your **session**. This will give you an opportunity to read the next section and the instructions before starting the source document transactions.

# Exporting Reports

Simply Accounting allows you to export reports to a specified drive and path. The files created by the program may then be used by spreadsheet or wordprocessing programs.

Exporting files will allow you to perform additional calculations and interpret data for reporting purposes. This process of integrating Simply Accounting files with other software is an important step in making the accounting process meaningful.

The following keystrokes will export the opening Balance Sheet for Flabuless Fitness to a Lotus Version 2 file.

**Display** the **Balance Sheet** or the report you want to export.

**Click** the **Export Report tool** ⬆ or **choose** the **File menu** and **click Export** to display the following screen:

**Click** the **Save As Type list arrow** to see the types of files you can create:

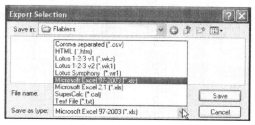

File formats available for export purposes include HTML for Web pages, Text for a wordprocessing format file, Lotus 1-2-3 Versions 1 and 2, Lotus Symphony, Microsoft Excel Versions 97–2003 and 2.1, Supercalc and Comma separated.

**Click** **Lotus 1-2-3 v2** as the type for the Balance Sheet in the Save As Type field. Use the field list arrow to display the file type options if needed.

**Choose** the **location** for your exported file. By default your working folder is selected, or the folder you used for the previous exported report.

**Click** the **list arrow** for the **Save In field** to access the drive and folder you want.

For example, click 3fi Floppy (A:) from the Save In field list to select Drive A. (Be sure that you have a formatted disk in Drive A.) Then double click the folder you want to use to store your file or create a new folder.

**Accept** the default **file name**, or **type** the **name** you want for your file. The program assigns an extension to the file name so that Lotus will recognize the new file as a Lotus file.

**Click** **Save**.

To create an Excel spreadsheet, click Microsoft Excel 97–2003 (or 2.1 if your version is older than Excel 97). To generate a file that you can use with wordprocessing software, click Text.

**NOTES**
Depending on your previous export selection, your default format and folder may be different from the ones we show here.

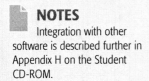

**NOTES**
    Integration with other software is described further in Appendix H on the Student CD-ROM.

# Using Simply Files and Reports with Other Software

Any Simply Accounting report that you have on display can be opened as a Microsoft Excel spreadsheet. Formulas for totals, and so on, are retained and you can then use the spreadsheet file immediately.

> **Display** the **Simply Accounting report** you want to use in Excel.
>
> **Click**   the **Open In Excel tool** 🔲 or **choose** the **File menu** and **click Open In Excel** to see the file name window:

> **Choose** a **location** for your spreadsheet data file.
>
> **Click**   **Save** to open the spreadsheet. Your Simply Accounting data file will remain open. (Save the Excel file if you want to work with it later.)
>
> **Close**   the **Excel file** when finished.

You can now work with a report that you have exported.

> Finish the session using Simply Accounting. Start the software program you want to use with the exported file, referring to the program manuals if necessary. When the blank document or spreadsheet screen appears,
>
> Choose the File menu and click Open if this is a Windows program. Change folders if necessary to locate and then select the exported file. Be sure that the selected file type also matches the format of your exported file (e.g., .txt for a text file, or .xls for Excel).

Some spreadsheet programs can open and convert a file that was saved in the format of a different program. For example, Microsoft Excel can open (or save) text files or Lotus 1-2-3 files. Simply choose the alternative file type in your Open File (or Save File) window. Click OK. Your exported file should replace the blank document screen.

Once you have exported a financial statement as a text file, you can include it in a written report prepared with any wordprocessing program. You can then use the features of the wordprocessing software to enhance the appearance of the statement using format styles that are consistent with the remainder of the report. If you have exported a spreadsheet file, you can use the spreadsheet program to perform additional calculations. Then you can save the modified report as a text file or copy the cells you want to be incorporated in a wordprocessing report. We used exported spreadsheets to create the bank statements for this text.

When working with a spreadsheet program such as Lotus 1-2-3 or Microsoft Excel, you can use the calculation capabilities of the spreadsheet program to make comparisons between statements from different financial periods. You might also want to use the charting or graphing features to prepare presentation materials.

Exporting reports offers advantages over re-creating the statements. Not only do you save the time of retyping, but you also ensure greater accuracy by avoiding errors made while retyping the numbers and accounts.

**NOTES**
    The bank statements for Chapter 15 and for Chapter 16 – Case 6 in Appendix E on the Student CD-ROM – were created by exporting the General Ledger reports to a spreadsheet, modifying the data and then copying the results to a wordprocessing file.

# SOURCE DOCUMENT INSTRUCTIONS

## Instructions for April

1. **Enter** the **transactions** for April using all the information provided.

2. **Print** the following **reports**:
   a. Journal Entries (All Journals) for April, including foreign amounts, corrections and additional transaction details
   b. Customer Aged Detail Report for all customers for April
   c. General Ledger account reports for
      - Bank: Hamilton Trust Chequing
      - Revenue from Sales
      - Sales Returns and Allowances
   d. Vendor Purchases Summary for Footlink Corporation, all categories, for April

3. **Export** the **Balance Sheet** as at April 30, 2009, to a spreadsheet application. **Calculate** the following **key ratios** in your spreadsheet and compare them with the ratios in the Daily Business Manager Business Performance indicators:

   a. current ratio     b. quick ratio

4. **Set up** a **budget** for use in May and June and **enter amounts** based on expenses and revenues for April and for the first quarter.

## Instructions for May

1. **Enter** the **transactions** for May using all the information provided.

2. **Print** the following **reports**:
   a. Journal Entries (All Journals) for May, including foreign amounts, corrections and additional transaction details
   b. Vendor Aged Detail Report for all vendors for May
   c. Employee Summary Report for all employees for the pay period ending May 31, 2009
   d. Inventory Synopsis Report (observe and report items that have not sold well over the two-month period)
   e. Customer Sales Summary (all customers, items and categories) for May

3. **Export** the **Comparative Balance Sheet** for April 30 and May 31, 2009, to a spreadsheet application. You will use these at the end of the quarter for three-month comparisons.

4. **Compare** May's **performance against** April's budget **forecast**.

## Instructions for June

1. **Enter** the **transactions** for June using all the information provided.

2. **Print** the following **reports**:
   a. Journal Entries (All Journals) for June, including foreign amounts, corrections and additional transaction details
   b. Trial Balance, Balance Sheet and Income Statement on June 30
   c. Inventory Activity Report for Fitness Equipment (All Journals) for June
   d. Bank Transaction Report for all bank accounts from April 1 to June 30

**NOTES**
You can use the data file setup\flab\flab-apr to complete the transactions for April.

**NOTES**
You can use the data file setup\flab\flab-may to complete the transactions for May. This file does not include budget amounts.

**NOTES**
You can use the data file setup\flab\flab-jun to complete the transactions for June. This file does not include budget amounts.

***basic* BASIC VERSION**
Print the General Ledger Report for the bank accounts instead of the Bank Transaction Report.

3. **Export** the **Balance Sheet** and **Income Statement** to a spreadsheet application. Combine the Balance Sheet with the comparative one for April and May. **Compare** first- and second-quarter figures, item by item, to assess the performance of Flabuless Fitness.

4. **Make** a **backup copy** of your data files. **Advance** the **session date** to July 1, 2009.

5. **Print** the **Trial Balance**, **Balance Sheet** and **Income Statement** for July 1. **Compare** the end of June and the first of July **statements** and note the changes that result from Simply Accounting closing the books for the new fiscal period.

# SOURCE DOCUMENTS

## SESSION DATE – APRIL 15, 2009

☑️ **Cash Receipt #39**                          Dated April 1, 2009

From Stoney Creek Sports Arena, cheque #147 for $4 468.80 in payment on account including $91.20 discount for early payment. Reference invoice #2191.

☒ **Sales Order #41-DRC**                        Dated April 2, 2009

Shipping date April 6, 2009
To Dundas Recreation Centre

| | | | | |
|---|---|---|---|---|
| 2 | A080 | Heart Rate Monitor | $ 75/ unit |
| 40 | A130 | Weight Plates | 1.20/ kg |
| 1 | E020 | Elliptical Exerciser: AE-200 | 1 700/ unit |
| 1 | E040 | Elliptical Exerciser: LE-400 | 2 200/ unit |
| 2 | E140 | Ski Exerciser: Skitrek SE-680 | 400/ unit |
| 1 | E190 | Treadmill: Basic T-800B | 1 200/ unit |
| 5 | S010 | Personal Trainer: 1 hour | 75/ hour |
| 2 | S040 | Yoga Instructor: 1 hour | 100/ hour |
| | | Freight (tax code G) | 50 |
| | | GST | 6% |
| | | PST | 8% |

Terms: 2/10, n/30.
Received cheque #96 for $1 000 as down payment (deposit #15) to confirm sales order.

☒ **Cheque Copy #101**                           Dated April 3, 2009

To Footlink Corporation, $8 380 in payment of account including $100 discount for early payment. Reference invoice #FC-618.

☒ **Purchase Order #25**                          Dated April 3, 2009

Shipping date April 8, 2009
From Footlink Corporation

| | | | |
|---|---|---|---|
| 2 | E190 | Treadmill: Basic T-800B | $ 960.00 |
| 2 | E200 | Treadmill: Basic Plus T-910P | 1 280.00 |
| | | Freight | 40.00 |
| | | GST | 136.80 |
| | | Total | $2 416.80 |

Terms: 1/15, n/30.

☒ **Cash Receipt #40**                            Dated April 4, 2009

From Mohawk College, cheque #73 for $5 586 in payment of account including $114 discount for early payment. Reference invoice #2194.

**Cheque Copy #346**                             **Dated April 5, 2009**

To Redux Home Gym Wholesalers, $6 146.40 USD in payment of account including $118.20 discount for early payment. Reference invoice #R-914. The exchange rate is 1.181.

**Sales Invoice #3000**                          **Dated April 5, 2009**

To Dundas Recreational Centre, to fill sales order #41-DRC

| | | | |
|---|---|---|---|
| 2 | A080 | Heart Rate Monitor | $   75/ unit |
| 40 | A130 | Weight Plates | 1.20/ kg |
| 1 | E020 | Elliptical Exerciser: AE-200 | 1 700/ unit |
| 1 | E040 | Elliptical Exerciser: LE-400 | 2 200/ unit |
| 2 | E140 | Ski Exerciser: Skitrek SE-680 | 400/ unit |
| 1 | E190 | Treadmill: Basic T-800B | 1 200/ unit |
| 5 | S010 | Personal Trainer: 1 hour | 75/ hour |
| 2 | S040 | Yoga Instructor: 1 hour | 100/ hour |
| | | Freight | 50 |
| | | GST | 6% |
| | | PST | 8% |

Terms: 2/10, n/30.

**Credit Card Purchase Invoice #HS-114**        **Dated April 6, 2009**

From Hamilton Spectator, $500 plus $30 GST and $40 PST for prepaid advertisement to run over the next 12 weeks. Purchase invoice total $570 paid in full by Visa.

**Credit Card Purchase Invoice #W-1149**        **Dated April 6, 2009**

From Westdale Office Supplies, $150 plus $9.00 GST and $12.00 PST for stationery and other office supplies for store. Purchase invoice total $171 paid in full by Visa.

**Purchase Invoice #FC-691**                     **Dated April 6, 2009**

From Footlink Corporation, to fill purchase order #25

| | | | |
|---|---|---|---|
| 2 | E190 | Treadmill: Basic T-800B | $   960.00 |
| 2 | E200 | Treadmill: Basic Plus T-910P | 1 280.00 |
| | | Freight | 40.00 |
| | | GST | 136.80 |
| | | Total | $2 416.80 |

Terms: 1/15, n/30.

**Deposit Slip #14**                             **Dated April 7, 2009**

Prepare deposit slip for all receipts for April 1 to April 7 to deposit the funds to Bank: Hamilton Trust Chequing from Undeposited Cash and Cheques. The total deposit for the three cheques is $11 054.80.

**Memo #4-1**                                    **Dated April 8, 2009**

Re: Damaged Inventory
Two (2) stability balls, item A110, were torn and damaged beyond repair. Adjust the inventory to recognize the loss.

**Cheque Copy #102**                             **Dated April 9, 2009**

To Feelyte Gym Accessories, $1 040 in payment of account including $20 discount for early payment. Reference invoice #FG-1611.

**Memo #4-2**                                    **Dated April 9, 2009**

From Visa, received monthly credit card statement for $240 including $220 for purchases up to and including April 3 and $20 annual renewal fee. Submitted cheque #103 for $240 in full payment of the balance owing.

**NOTES**
Remember to change the payment method to Pay Later for the sales invoice that fills the order.

If you want, you can enter Kisangel as the salesperson for all sales that include service revenue. Then you can use the Sales By Salesperson Report to determine her commission.

**NOTES**
All deposits are made to Bank: Hamilton Trust Chequing from Undeposited Cheques and Cash.

**Cash Receipt #41**                          **Dated April 9, 2009**

From Chedoke Health Care, cheque #472 for $6 837.60 in payment of account including $182.40 discount for early payment. Reference invoice #2199.

**Sales Invoice #3001**                       **Dated April 12, 2009**

To Hamilton District Bd of Education

| | | | | |
|---|---|---|---|---|
| 8 | A070 | Glide Slidetrak | $ | 50 each |
| 5 | A110 | Stability Balls | | 10 each |
| 1 | E030 | Elliptical Exerciser: DE-300 | | 2 000/ unit |
| 1 | E060 | Bicycle: Dual Action DA-70 | | 600/ unit |
| 2 | E070 | Bicycle: Recumbent R-80 | | 750/ unit |
| | | Freight | | 50 |
| | | GST | | 6% |
| | | PST | | 8% |

Terms: 2/10, n/30.

**Credit Card Purchase Invoice #WS-6112**     **Dated April 14, 2009**

From Waterdown Sunoco, $92 including GST and PST for gasoline purchase for delivery vehicle. Invoice paid in full by Visa. (Use tax code IN.)

**Memo #4-3**                                 **Dated April 14, 2009**

Record payment for GST for March to the Receiver General for Canada. Issue cheque #104 in full payment.
Record payment for PST Payable for March to the Minister of Finance. Remember to collect 5% of the amount owing as the sales tax compensation. Issue cheque #105 in full payment.

**Memo #4-4**                                 **Dated April 14, 2009**

Payroll Remittances: Use April 1 as the End of Remitting Period date to make the following payroll remittances in the Payments Journal.

Record payment for EI, CPP and Income Tax Payable up to April 1 to the Receiver General for Canada. Issue cheque #106 in full payment.

Record payment for Garnisheed Wages Payable up to April 1 to the Receiver General for Canada. Issue cheque #107 in full payment.

Record payment for EHT Payable up to April 1 to the Minister of Finance. Issue cheque #108 in full payment.

Record payment for RRSP Payable up to April 1 to Ancaster Insurance. Issue cheque #109 in full payment.

Record payment for CSB Payable up to April 1 to Mt. Hope Investment Corporation. Issue cheque #110 in full payment.

Record payment for Group Insurance Payable up to April 1 to Ancaster Insurance. Issue cheque #111 in full payment.

Record payment for WSIB Payable up to April 1 to Workplace Safety and Insurance Board. Issue cheque #112 in full payment.

**Purchase Order #26**                        **Dated April 14, 2009**

Shipping date April 23, 2009
From Prolife Exercisers Inc.

| | | | | |
|---|---|---|---|---|
| 1 | E020 | Elliptical Exerciser: AE-200 | $ 550.00 | USD |
| 1 | E030 | Elliptical Exerciser: DE-300 | 670.00 | USD |
| 1 | E040 | Elliptical Exerciser: LE-400 | 740.00 | USD |
| | | Freight | 110.00 | USD |
| | | GST | 124.20 | USD |
| | | Total | $2 194.20 | USD |

Terms: 2/10, n/30. The exchange rate is 1.179.

**Credit Card Sales Invoice #3002**      **Dated April 14, 2009**

To Visa customers (sales summary)

| | | | | |
|---|---|---|---|---|
| 2 | A010 | Body Fat Scale | $ 100/ unit | $ 200.00 |
| 8 | A040 | Dumbbells: 5kg set | 15/ set | 120.00 |
| 2 | A100 | Power Blocks up to 200 kg | 300/ set | 600.00 |
| 8 | A110 | Stability Balls | 10 each | 80.00 |
| 80 | A130 | Weight Plates | 1.20/ kg | 96.00 |
| 2 | A160 | Weights: Olympic 125 kg | 250/ set | 500.00 |
| 6 | A180 | Workout Gloves: all sizes | 10/ pair | 60.00 |
| 2 | E130 | Rowing Machine: RM-1000 | 480/ unit | 960.00 |
| 1 | E210 | Treadmill: Deluxe T-1100D | 2 400/ unit | 2 400.00 |
| 3 | S020 | Personal Trainer: 1/2 day | 200/ 1/2 day | 600.00 |
| 2 | S030 | Personal Trainer: full day | 400/ day | 800.00 |
| 4 | S050 | Yoga Instructor: 1/2 day | 200/ 1/2 day | 800.00 |
| | GST | | 6% | 432.96 |
| | PST | | 8% | 401.28 |
| | Total paid by Visa | | | $8 050.24 |

**Deposit Slip #15**      **Dated April 14, 2009**

Prepare deposit slip for all receipts for April 8 to April 14 to deposit the funds. One cheque for $6 837.60 is being deposited.

**Employee Time Summary Sheet #14**      **Dated April 14, 2009**

For the Pay Period ending April 14, 2009
George Schwinn worked 80 regular hours and 2 hours of overtime in the period. Recover $50 advance. Issue payroll deposit slip DD19.

**Cash Receipt #42**      **Dated April 15, 2009**

From Dundas Recreational Centre, cheque #195 for $6 461.94 in payment of account including $152.88 discount for early payment. Reference invoice #3000 and deposit #15.

## SESSION DATE – APRIL 30, 2009

**Cash Purchase Invoice #ES-64329**      **Dated April 21, 2009**

From Energy Source, $120 plus $7.20 GST paid for hydro service. Purchase invoice total $127.20. Terms: cash on receipt of invoice. Issue cheque #113 in full payment.

**Cheque Copy #114**      **Dated April 21, 2009**

To Footlink Corporation, $2 394.00 in payment of account including $22.80 discount for early payment. Reference invoice #FC-691.

**Deposit Slip #16**      **Dated April 22, 2009**

Prepare deposit slip for all receipts for April 15 to April 22 to deposit the funds. The total deposit for the single cheque is $6 461.94.

**Sales Invoice #3003**      **Dated April 22, 2009**

To Stelco Health Club (preferred customer)

| | | | |
|---|---|---|---|
| 1 | A140 | Weights: Olympic 75 kg | $ 135/ set |
| 1 | E030 | Elliptical Exerciser: DE-300 | 1 875/ unit |
| 1 | E070 | Bicycle: Recumbent R-80 | 680/ unit |
| 2 | E140 | Ski Exerciser: Skitrek SE-680 | 360/ unit |
| 2 | E190 | Treadmill: Basic T-800B | 1 100/ unit |
| | GST | | 6% |
| | PST | | 8% |

Terms: 2/10, n/30.

**NOTES**
Use H-2009-2 and H-2009-3 as the Invoice numbers for the postdated payments for property taxes.

**Cash Purchase Invoice #BC-59113**      **Dated April 22, 2009**

From Bell Canada, $80 plus $4.80 GST paid and $6.40 PST for phone service. Purchase invoice total $91.20. Terms: cash on receipt of invoice. Issue cheque #115 in full payment.

**Cash Purchase Invoice #H-2009-1**      **Dated April 23, 2009**

From City of Hamilton Treasurer, $900 in full payment of first instalment of quarterly property tax assessment. Terms: EOM. Issued cheque #116 in full payment. Store as monthly recurring entry. Recall the stored transaction to issue cheques #117 and #118 as postdated cheques for the next two instalments, dated May 23 and June 23.

**Purchase Invoice #PE-364**      **Dated April 23, 2009**

From Prolife Exercisers Inc. to fill purchase order #26

| | | | | |
|---|---|---|---|---|
| 1 | E020 | Elliptical Exerciser: AE-200 | $ 550.00 | USD |
| 1 | E030 | Elliptical Exerciser: DE-300 | 670.00 | USD |
| 1 | E040 | Elliptical Exerciser: LE-400 | 740.00 | USD |
| | | Freight | 110.00 | USD |
| | | GST | 124.20 | USD |
| | | Total | $2 194.20 | USD |

Terms: 2/10, n/30. The exchange rate is 1.177.

**Credit Card Sales Invoice #3004**      **Dated April 28, 2009**

To Visa customers (sales summary)

| | | | | |
|---|---|---|---|---|
| 5 | A020 | Yoga Mats | $ 30/ unit | $ 150.00 |
| 20 | A030 | Dumbbells: pair | 1.50/ kg | 30.00 |
| 2 | A080 | Heart Rate Monitor | 75 each | 150.00 |
| 3 | A090 | Power Blocks up to 100 kg | 160/ set | 480.00 |
| 1 | A100 | Power Blocks up to 200 kg | 300/ set | 300.00 |
| 2 | A180 | Workout Gloves: all sizes | 10/ pair | 20.00 |
| 2 | E060 | Bicycle: Dual Action DA-70 | 600/ unit | 1 200.00 |
| 2 | E190 | Treadmill: Basic T-800B | 1 200/ unit | 2 400.00 |
| 1 | E220 | Treadmill: Deluxe Plus T-1200P | 2 800/ unit | 2 800.00 |
| 6 | S020 | Personal Trainer: 1/2 day | 200/ 1/2 day | 1 200.00 |
| 6 | S050 | Yoga Instructor: 1/2 day | 200/ 1/2 day | 1 200.00 |
| | | GST | 6% | 595.80 |
| | | PST | 8% | 602.40 |
| | | Total paid by Visa | | $11 128.20 |

**Employee Time Summary Sheet #15**      **Dated April 28, 2009**

For the Pay Period ending April 28, 2009
George Schwinn worked 80 regular hours and 4 hours of overtime. Recover $50 advance. Issue payroll deposit slip DD20.

**Sales Invoice #3005**      **Dated April 28, 2009**

To Stoney Creek Sports Arena

| | | | |
|---|---|---|---|
| 1 | A120 | Wavemaster | $ 150/ unit |
| 40 | A130 | Weight Plates | 1.20/ kg |
| 1 | E110 | Rider: Airwalker RA-900 | 300/ unit |
| 1 | E200 | Treadmill: Basic Plus T-910P | 1 600/ unit |
| | | Freight | 30 |
| | | GST | 6% |
| | | PST | 8% |

Terms: 2/10, n/30.

**Memo #4-5**      **Dated April 28, 2009**

Transfer $15 000 CAD to Savings account from 1120 Bank: Visa and Interac.

### Cash Purchase Invoice #DMC-55       Dated April 28, 2009

From Dundurn Maintenance Co. (use Full Add), $300 plus $18 GST paid for cleaning and maintenance of premises. Terms: cash on receipt. Issue cheque #119 for $318 in full payment. The company bills monthly for their services so store the entry as a monthly recurring transaction.

### Credit Invoice #8       Dated April 28, 2009

To Stelco Health Club, $50 allowance for scratched treadmill unit. Reference invoice #3003. There is no tax on the allowance. Enter a negative amount. Create new Subgroup Account 4070 Returns and Allowances. Change the customer terms to net 60; there is no discount. Delete or change the comment.

### Credit Card Purchase Invoice #WS-6533       Dated April 28, 2009

From Waterdown Sunoco, $69 including GST and PST for gasoline (tax code IN) and $40 plus $2.40 GST and $3.20 PST for oil change (tax code GP). Purchase invoice total $114.60 charged to Visa account.

### Cheque Copy #347       Dated April 30, 2009

To Prolife Exercisers Inc., $2 152.80 USD in payment of account including $41.40 discount taken for early payment. Reference invoice #PE-364. The exchange rate is 1.1810.

### Memo #4-6       Dated April 30, 2009

Transfer $5 000 USD to cover the cheque to Prolife Exercisers. Transfer money to Bank: USD Chequing from 1120 Bank: Visa and Interac.

### Bank Debit Memo #91431       Dated April 30, 2009

From Hamilton Trust, authorized withdrawals were made from the chequing account on our behalf for the following:

| | |
|---|---:|
| Bank service charges | $ 35 |
| Mortgage interest payment | 1 880 |
| Mortgage principal reduction | 120 |
| Bank loan interest payment | 420 |
| Bank loan principal reduction | 480 |

2935

### Memo #4-7       Dated April 30, 2009

Prepare the payroll for the two salaried employees, Nieve Prekor and Assumpta Kisangel. Add 2 percent of revenue from services for April as a commission to Kisangel's salary. Issue payroll deposit slips DD21 and DD22.

## SESSION DATE — MAY 15, 2009

### Cash Receipt #43       Dated May 1, 2009

From Stelco Health Club, cheque #434 for $6 217.49 in payment of account including $127.91 discount for early payment. Reference sales invoice #3003 and credit invoice #8.

### Purchase Order #27       Dated May 1, 2009

Delivery date May 7, 2009
From Prolife Exercisers

| | | | | |
|---|---|---|---:|---|
| 2 | E020 | Elliptical Exerciser: AE-200 | $1 100.00 | USD |
| 2 | E030 | Elliptical Exerciser: DE-300 | 1 340.00 | USD |
| 2 | E040 | Elliptical Exerciser: LE-400 | 1 480.00 | USD |
| | | Freight | 180.00 | USD |
| | | GST | 246.00 | USD |
| | | Invoice total | $4 346.00 | USD |

Terms: 2/10, n/30. The exchange rate is 1.1790.

**NOTES**

Dundurn Maintenance Co. (contact Vak Kume)
890 Dundurn St. N.
Hamilton, ON L8G 2P9
Tel: (905) 529-4187
Fax: (905) 529-3116
Terms: net 1
Tax code: G
Expense account: 5240

**NOTES**

Enter the two items purchased from Waterdown Sunoco on separate lines because you need different tax codes for them.

**NOTES**

You must calculate the amount of the commission manually and then enter the amount in the journal.

Use the Revenue from Services amount in the Income Statement for the month of April to calculate the commission.

**NOTES**

Remember to check the prices and edit them when they have changed.

**Memo #5-1**                                   **Dated May 1, 2009**

Create new tax code P for purchases that charge only PST at 8%. The status is taxable and PST is not included and not refundable.

**Sales Invoice #3006**                          **Dated May 1, 2009**

To McMaster University (preferred customer)

| | | | |
|---|---|---|---|
| 1 | E030 | Elliptical Exerciser: DE-300 | $1 875/ unit |
| 1 | E070 | Bicycle: Recumbent R-80 | 680/ unit |
| 1 | E080 | Home Gym: Basic HG-1400 | 900/ set |
| 1 | E190 | Treadmill: Basic T-800B | 1 100/ unit |
| 1 | E210 | Treadmill: Deluxe T-1100D | 2 200/ unit |
| | | Freight | 40 |
| | | GST | 6% |
| | | PST | 8% |

Terms: 2/10, n/30.

**Purchase Order #28**                           **Dated May 2, 2009**

Delivery date May 10, 2009
From Footlink Corporation

| | | | |
|---|---|---|---|
| 2 | E190 | Treadmill: Basic T-800B | $ 960.00 |
| 2 | E200 | Treadmill: Basic Plus T-910P | 1 280.00 |
| 2 | E210 | Treadmill: Deluxe T-1100D | 1 920.00 |
| 2 | E220 | Treadmill: Deluxe Plus T-1200P | 2 240.00 |
| | | Freight | 50.00 |
| | | GST | 387.00 |
| | | Invoice total | $6 837.00 |

Terms: 1/15, n/30.

**Cash Purchase Invoice #AI-6921**               **Dated May 3, 2009**

From Ancaster Insurance, $2 400 plus $192 PST for six months of insurance coverage. Invoice total $2 592. Issued cheque #120 in payment.

**Purchase Order #29**                           **Dated May 4, 2009**

Delivery date May 14, 2009
From Redux Home Gym Wholesalers

| | | | | |
|---|---|---|---|---|
| 2 | E080 | Home Gym: Basic HG-1400 | $820.00 | USD |
| | | GST | 49.20 | USD |
| | | Invoice total | $869.20 | USD |

Terms: 2/10, n/30. Free delivery. The exchange rate is 1.17905.

**Purchase Order #30**                           **Dated May 4, 2009**

Delivery date May 12, 2009
From Feelyte Gym Accessories

| | | | |
|---|---|---|---|
| 1 | A020 | Yoga Mats (1 box of 10 mats) | $ 120.00 |
| 10 | A040 | Dumbbells: 5kg set | 60.00 |
| 10 | A070 | Glide Slidetrak | 250.00 |
| 5 | A090 | Power Blocks up to 100 kg | 400.00 |
| 15 | A110 | Stability Balls | 60.00 |
| | | GST | 53.40 |
| | | Invoice total | $943.40 |

Terms: 2/10, n/30.

**Cash Receipt #44**                             **Dated May 5, 2009**

From Stoney Creek Sports Arena, cheque #198 for $2 375.05 in payment of account, including $48.47 discount for early payment. Reference invoice #3005.

**Deposit Slip #17**          **Dated May 5, 2009**

Prepare deposit slip for all receipts for April 29 to May 5 to deposit the funds. The total deposit for the two cheques is $8 592.54.

**Memo #5-2**          **Dated May 5, 2009**

Adjust the selling prices for item E080 (Home Gym: Basic HG-1400) to reflect the cost increase for the next delivery. Change the prices in the Inventory Ledger. The new selling prices are

| | |
|---|---|
| Regular Canadian dollar price | $1 100 CAD |
| Preferred Canadian dollar price | 1 000 CAD |
| Regular United States dollar price | 950 USD |
| Preferred United States dollar price | 860 USD |

**Cash Receipt #45**          **Dated May 7, 2009**

From McMaster University, cheque #1257 for $7 588.24 in payment of account, including $154.86 discount for early payment. Reference invoice #3006.

**Purchase Invoice #PE-2014**          **Dated May 7, 2009**

From Prolife Exercisers, to fill purchase order #27

| | | | | |
|---|---|---|---|---|
| 2 | E020 | Elliptical Exerciser: AE-200 | $1 100.00 | USD |
| 2 | E030 | Elliptical Exerciser: DE-300 | 1 340.00 | USD |
| 2 | E040 | Elliptical Exerciser: LE-400 | 1 480.00 | USD |
| | | Freight | 180.00 | USD |
| | | GST | 246.00 | USD |
| | | Invoice total | $4 346.00 | USD |

Terms: 2/10, n/30. The exchange rate is 1.1805.

**Credit Card Purchase Invoice #WS-6914**          **Dated May 10, 2009**

From Waterdown Sunoco, $69 including GST and PST for gasoline. Purchase invoice total $69 charged to Visa account.

**Purchase Invoice #FC-768**          **Dated May 10, 2009**

From Footlink Corporation, to fill purchase order #28

| | | | |
|---|---|---|---|
| 2 | E190 | Treadmill: Basic T-800B | $ 960.00 |
| 2 | E200 | Treadmill: Basic Plus T-910P | 1 280.00 |
| 2 | E210 | Treadmill: Deluxe T-1100D | 1 920.00 |
| 2 | E220 | Treadmill: Deluxe Plus T-1200P | 2 240.00 |
| | | Freight | 50.00 |
| | | GST | 387.00 |
| | | Invoice total | $6 837.00 |

Terms: 1/15, n/30.

**Purchase Invoice #FG-1804**          **Dated May 12, 2009**

From Feelyte Gym Accessories, to fill purchase order #30

| | | | |
|---|---|---|---|
| 1 | A020 | Yoga Mats (1 box of 10 mats) | $ 120.00 |
| 10 | A040 | Dumbbells: 5kg set | 60.00 |
| 10 | A070 | Glide Slidetrak | 250.00 |
| 5 | A090 | Power Blocks up to 100 kg | 400.00 |
| 15 | A110 | Stability Balls | 60.00 |
| | | GST | 53.40 |
| | | Invoice total | $943.40 |

Terms: 2/10, n/30.

**Memo #5-3**          **Dated May 12, 2009**

From Visa, received monthly credit card statement for $947.60 for purchases up to and including May 3. Submitted cheque #121 for $947.60 in full payment.

**Sales Order #5-1-MC**                               **Dated May 12, 2009**

Delivery date May 14, 2009
From Mohawk College (preferred customer)

| | | | |
|---|---|---|---|
| 40 | A130 | Weight Plates | $ 1.10/ kg |
| 1 | A170 | Weights: Olympic 150 kg | 270/ set |
| 1 | E050 | Bicycle: Calorie Counter CC-60 | 360/ unit |
| 1 | E060 | Bicycle: Dual Action DA-70 | 540/ unit |
| 1 | E090 | Home Gym: Deluxe HG-1401 | 1 400/ set |
| 1 | E110 | Rider: Airwalker RA-900 | 270/ unit |
| 1 | E120 | Rider: Powerglider RP-1500 | 315/ unit |
| | | Freight | 30 |
| | | GST | 6% |
| | | PST | 8% |

Terms: 2/10, n/30.

**Employee Time Summary Sheet #16**          **Dated May 12, 2009**

For the Pay Period ending May 12, 2009
George Schwinn worked 80 regular hours in the period. He will receive $200 as
an advance and have $50 recovered from each of the following four paycheques.
Issue payroll deposit slip DD23.

**Deposit Slip #18**                                   **Dated May 12, 2009**

Prepare deposit slip for all receipts for May 6 to May 12 to deposit the funds. The
total deposit for the single cheque is $7 588.24.

**Credit Card Sales Invoice #3007**             **Dated May 12, 2009**

To Visa customers (sales summary)

| | | | | |
|---|---|---|---|---|
| 11 | A020 | Yoga Mats | $ 30/ unit | $ 330.00 |
| 6 | A040 | Dumbbells: 5kg set | 15/ set | 90.00 |
| 2 | A060 | Dumbbells: 15kg set | 40/ set | 80.00 |
| 4 | A070 | Glide Slidetrak | 50 each | 200.00 |
| 2 | A080 | Heart Rate Monitor | 75/ unit | 150.00 |
| 1 | A090 | Power Blocks up to 100 kg | 160/ set | 160.00 |
| 1 | A100 | Power Blocks up to 200 kg | 300/ set | 300.00 |
| 1 | A150 | Weights: Olympic 100 kg | 200/ set | 200.00 |
| 1 | E180 | Stair Climber: Unlinked SC-U75 | 2 100/ unit | 2 100.00 |
| 1 | E220 | Treadmill: Deluxe Plus T-1200P | 2 800/ unit | 2 800.00 |
| 4 | S020 | Personal Trainer: 1/2 day | 200/ 1/2 day | 800.00 |
| | | GST | 6% | 432.60 |
| | | PST | 8% | 512.80 |
| | | Total paid by Visa | | $8 155.40 |

**Purchase Invoice #R-1031**                      **Dated May 13, 2009**

From Redux Home Gym Wholesalers, to fill purchase order #29

| | | | |
|---|---|---|---|
| 2 | E080 | Home Gym: Basic HG-1400 | $820.00  USD |
| | | GST | 49.20  USD |
| | | Invoice total | $869.20  USD |

Terms: 2/10, n/30. Free delivery. The exchange rate is 1.1820.

**Cash Receipt #46**                                   **Dated May 13, 2009**

From Mohawk College, cheque #284 for $1 000 as down payment (deposit #16)
in acceptance of sales order #5-1-MC.

**Memo #5-4**                                            **Dated May 14, 2009**

Record payment for GST for April to the Receiver General for Canada. Issue
cheque #122 in full payment. Clear the GST Report up to April 30.

**NOTES**
Enter Memo 5-4A and Memo
5-4B as the reference numbers for
the tax remittances.

Record payment for PST Payable for April to the Minister of Finance. Remember to collect 5% of the amount owing as the sales tax compensation. Issue cheque #123 in full payment. Clear the PST Report up to April 30.

**Memo #5-5**                                    **Dated May 14, 2009**

Payroll Remittances: Make the following remittances for the period ending April 30. Choose Pay Remittance for payroll remittances.

Record payment for EI, CPP and Income Tax Payable for April to the Receiver General for Canada. Issue cheque #124 in full payment.

Record payment for Garnisheed Wages Payable for April to the Receiver General for Canada. Issue cheque #125 in full payment.

Record payment for RRSP Payable to Ancaster Insurance. Issue cheque #126 in full payment.

Record payment for CSB Payable to Mt. Hope Investment Corporation. Issue cheque #127 in full payment.

Record payment for Group Insurance Payable for April to Ancaster Insurance. Issue cheque #128 in full payment.

**NOTES**
Enter Memo 5-5A, Memo 5-5B, and so on, in the Additional Information field as the reference numbers for the payroll remittances.

**Memo #5-6**                                    **Dated May 15, 2009**

Create new inventory item:

| | |
|---|---|
| Item: | E105 Home Gym: Free Weight HG-1403 |
| Selling price: | $2 200 /set Regular ($2 000 Preferred) CAD |
| Foreign currency price: | $1 850 Regular ($1 680 Preferred) USD |
| Minimum level: | 1 |

Linked accounts:

| | |
|---|---|
| Asset | 1540 Fitness Equipment |
| Revenue | 4020 Revenue from Sales |
| Expense | 5060 Cost of Goods Sold: Equipment |
| Variance | 5070 Cost Variance |

**Purchase Invoice #R-1047**                     **Dated May 15, 2009**

From Redux Home Gym Wholesalers, new inventory item purchase

| | | | | |
|---|---|---|---|---|
| 2 | E105 | Home Gym: Free Weight HG-1403 | $2 200.00 | USD |
| | GST | | 132.00 | USD |
| | Invoice total | | $2 332.00 | USD |

Terms: 2/10, n/30. Free delivery. The exchange rate is 1.1825.

**Cheque Copy #348**                             **Dated May 15, 2009**

To Prolife Exercisers, $4 264 USD in payment of account including $82 discount for early payment. Reference invoice #PE-2014. The exchange rate is 1.1825.

**Sales Invoice #3008**                          **Dated May 15, 2009**

To Mohawk College, to fill sales order #5-1-MC

| | | | | |
|---|---|---|---|---|
| 40 | A130 | Weight Plates | $ | 1.10/ kg |
| 1 | A170 | Weights: Olympic 150 kg | | 270/ set |
| 1 | E050 | Bicycle: Calorie Counter CC-60 | | 360/ unit |
| 1 | E060 | Bicycle: Dual Action DA-70 | | 540/ unit |
| 1 | E090 | Home Gym: Deluxe HG-1401 | | 1 400/ set |
| 1 | E110 | Rider: Airwalker RA-900 | | 270/ unit |
| 1 | E120 | Rider: Powerglider RP-1500 | | 315/ unit |
| | | Freight | | 30 |
| | | GST | | 6% |
| | | PST | | 8% |

Terms: 2/10, n/30.

## SESSION DATE – MAY 31, 2009

**Cheque Copy #129**                                    Dated May 18, 2009

To Footlink Corporation, $6 772.50 in payment of account including $64.50 discount for early payment. Reference invoice #FC-768.

**Deposit Slip #19**                                     Dated May 19, 2009

Prepare deposit slip for the single cheque for $1 000 for May 13 to May 19.

**Cash Purchase Invoice #ES-79123**              Dated May 20, 2009

From Energy Source, $125 plus $7.50 GST paid for hydro service. Purchase invoice total $132.50. Terms: cash on receipt of invoice. Issue cheque #130 in full payment.

**Cash Purchase Invoice #BC-71222**              Dated May 20, 2009

From Bell Canada, $80 plus $4.80 GST paid and $6.40 PST for phone service. Purchase invoice total $91.20. Terms: cash on receipt of invoice. Issue cheque #131 in full payment.

**Cheque Copy #132**                                    Dated May 21, 2009

To Feelyte Gym Accessories, $925.60 in payment of account including $17.80 discount for early payment. Reference invoice #FG-1804.

**Credit Card Purchase Invoice #M-1034**         Dated May 22, 2009

From Mountview Delivery (use Quick Add for the new vendor), $80 plus $4.80 GST paid for delivery services. Invoice total $84.80. Full amount paid by Visa. Enter tax code G in the Purchases Journal.

**Cheque Copy #349**                                    Dated May 22, 2009

To Redux Home Gym Wholesalers, $3 140.80 USD in payment of account including $60.40 discount for early payment. Reference invoices #R-1031 and #R-1047. The exchange rate is 1.1785.

**Memo #5-7**                                           Dated May 22, 2009

Transfer $4 000 USD to cover the cheque to Redux. Transfer money to Bank: USD Chequing from 1120 Bank: Visa and Interac.

**Sales Invoice #3009**                                 Dated May 22, 2009

To Chedoke Health Care (preferred customer)

| | | | |
|---|---|---|---|
| 1 | E010 | Elliptical Exerciser: ME-100 | $1 000/ unit |
| 1 | E130 | Rowing Machine: RM-1000 | 435/ unit |
| 1 | E150 | Ski Exerciser: Linked SE-780 | 410/ unit |
| 3 | S040 | Yoga Instructor: 1 hour | 95/ hour |
| 2 | S050 | Yoga Instructor: 1/2 day | 190/ 1/2 day |
| | | Freight | 30 |
| | | GST | 6% |
| | | PST | 8% |

Terms: 2/10, n/30.

**Cash Receipt #47**                                    Dated May 22, 2009

From Mohawk College, cheque #391 for $2 605.09 in payment of account including $73.57 discount for early payment. Reference invoice #3008 and deposit #16.

**Cash Receipt #48**                                    Dated May 24, 2009

From Chedoke Health Care, cheque #532 for $2 783.20 in payment of account including $56.80 discount for early payment. Reference invoice #3009.

### Memo #5-8                          Dated May 24, 2009

Add Charitable Donations as a payroll deduction. Flabuless Fitness will match employee donations so a user-defined expense is also needed.
Create new Group accounts
    2440 Charitable Donations - Employee
    2450 Charitable Donations - Employer
    5390 Charitable Donations Expense
Add Donations as new name (Setup, Settings, Payroll, Names)
    for Deduction 4 on Names, Incomes & Deductions screen
    for User-Defined Expense 2 on Names, Additional Payroll screen
Add new payroll linked accounts
    2440  for Donations (Linked Accounts, Deductions )
    2450 for Donations (Linked Accounts, User-Defined Expenses, Payables)
    5390 for Donations (Linked Accounts, User-Defined Expenses, Expenses)
Change Deduction Settings (Payroll, Deductions)
    Deduct Donations by Amount After Tax, EI, CPP, EHT And Vacation Pay
Enter amounts in Payroll Ledger for Deductions and WSIB & Other Expenses
    Kisangel: Check Use for the deduction; enter $20 as the deduction and the
    expense amount per period
    Prekor: Check Use for the deduction; enter $25 as the deduction and the
    expense amount per period

**NOTES**

To add deductions, refer to pages 656–657 for names
page 660 for payroll deductions settings
page 661 for linked accounts
page 674 for entering the employee deduction and page 675 for WSIB & other expense amounts.

### Deposit Slip #20                          Dated May 26, 2009

Prepare deposit slip for all receipts for May 20 to May 26 to deposit the funds. The total deposit for two cheques is $5 388.29.

### Employee Time Summary Sheet #17          Dated May 26, 2009

For the Pay Period ending May 26, 2009
George Schwinn worked 80 regular hours in the period and 2 hours of overtime. Recover $50 advanced and issue payroll deposit slip DD24.

### Credit Card Sales Invoice #3010          Dated May 26, 2009

To Visa customers (sales summary)

| | | | | |
|---|---|---|---|---:|
| 2 | A050 | Dumbbells: 10kg set | $ 25/ set | $ 50.00 |
| 4 | A060 | Dumbbells: 15kg set | 40/ set | 160.00 |
| 4 | A070 | Glide Slidetrak | 50 each | 200.00 |
| 1 | A080 | Heart Rate Monitor | 75/ unit | 75.00 |
| 2 | A090 | Power Blocks up to 100 kg | 160/ set | 320.00 |
| 1 | A100 | Power Blocks up to 200 kg | 300/ set | 300.00 |
| 1 | A150 | Weights: Olympic 100 kg | 200/ set | 200.00 |
| 6 | A180 | Workout Gloves: all sizes | 10/ pair | 60.00 |
| 1 | E040 | Elliptical Exerciser: LE-400 | 2 200/ unit | 2 200.00 |
| 1 | E060 | Bicycle: Dual Action DA-70 | 600/ unit | 600.00 |
| 1 | E080 | Home Gym: Basic HG-1400 | 1 100/ set | 1 100.00 |
| 1 | E100 | Home Gym: Multi HG-1402 | 2 000/ set | 2 000.00 |
| 1 | E110 | Rider: Airwalker RA-900 | 300/ unit | 300.00 |
| 1 | E200 | Treadmill: Basic Plus T-910P | 1 600/ unit | 1 600.00 |
| 4 | S020 | Personal Trainer: 1/2 day | 200/ 1/2 day | 800.00 |
| 8 | S050 | Yoga Instructor: 1/2 day | 200/ 1/2 day | 1 600.00 |
| | | GST | 6% | 693.90 |
| | | PST | 8% | 733.20 |
| | | Total paid by Visa | | $12 992.10 |

### Cash Purchase Invoice #DMC-68          Dated May 28, 2009

From Dundurn Maintenance Co., $300 plus $18 GST paid for cleaning and maintenance of premises. Terms: cash on receipt. Issue cheque #133 for $318 in full payment. Recall stored transaction.

**Debit Card Sales Invoice #3011**  Dated May 28, 2009

To Bruno Scinto (cash and Interac customer)

| | | | | |
|---|---|---|---|---|
| 1 | A020 | Yoga Mats | | $ 30.00 |
| 1 | A080 | Heart Rate Monitor | | 75.00 |
| 1 | E170 | Stair Climber: Adjustable SC-A60 | | 1 500.00 |
| 1 | E220 | Treadmill: Deluxe Plus T-1200P | | 2 800.00 |
| | | GST | 6% | 264.30 |
| | | PST | 8% | 352.40 |
| | | Invoice total paid in full | | $5 021.70 |

Debit Card #5919 7599 7543 7777. Amount deposited to Visa and Interac account.

 **Credit Card Purchase Invoice #WS-7823**  Dated May 30, 2009

From Waterdown Sunoco, $115, including GST and PST, for gasoline and $40 plus $2.40 GST and $3.20 PST for tire repairs. Purchase invoice total $160.60 paid in full by Visa. (Remember to change the tax code for the tire repairs.)

 **Memo #5-9**  Dated May 31, 2009

Prepare the payroll for Nieve Prekor and Assumpta Kisangel, the salaried employees. Kisangel took one day personal leave. Add 2 percent of service revenue for May as a commission to Kisangel's salary. Issue payroll deposit slips DD25 and DD26.

 **Memo #5-10**  Dated May 31, 2009

Print customer statements. Prepare invoice #3012 to charge Hamilton District Bd of Education $78.60 interest — 1.5% of the overdue amount. Terms: net 15.

 **Bank Debit Memo #96241**  Dated May 31, 2009

From Hamilton Trust, authorized withdrawals were made from the chequing account on our behalf for the following:

| | |
|---|---|
| Bank service charges | $ 35 |
| Mortgage interest payment | 1 870 |
| Mortgage principal reduction | 130 |
| Bank loan interest payment | 400 |
| Bank loan principal reduction | 500 |

## SESSION DATE – JUNE 15, 2009

 **Purchase Order #31**  Dated June 2, 2009

Delivery date June 7, 2009
From Footlink Corporation

| | | | |
|---|---|---|---|
| 2 | E190 | Treadmill: Basic T-800B | $ 960.00 |
| | | Freight | 30.00 |
| | | GST | 59.40 |
| | | Invoice total | $1 049.40 |

Terms: 1/15, n/30.

 **Purchase Order #32**  Dated June 3, 2009

Delivery date June 8, 2009
From Prolife Exercisers

| | | | | |
|---|---|---|---|---|
| 2 | E020 | Elliptical Exerciser: AE-200 | $1 100.00 | USD |
| 2 | E030 | Elliptical Exerciser: DE-300 | 1 340.00 | USD |
| | | Freight | 120.00 | USD |
| | | GST | 153.60 | USD |
| | | Invoice total | $2 713.60 | USD |

Terms: 2/10, n/30. The exchange rate is 1.1788.

**NOTES**

Remember that if you want to preview the customer statement, you must choose Custom Simply Form as the Form Type in the Reports and Forms settings on the Statements tab.

**Purchase Order #33**                    **Dated June 3, 2009**

Delivery date June 15, 2009
From Feelyte Gym Accessories

| | | | |
|---|---|---|---|
| 1 | A080 | Heart Rate Monitor (1 carton of 12) | $360.00 |
| 20 | A110 | Stability Balls | 80.00 |
| 2 | A180 | Workout Gloves: all sizes (2 boxes of 10) | 80.00 |
| | | GST | 31.20 |
| | | Invoice total | $551.20 |

Terms: 2/10, n/30.

**Sales Invoice #3013**                   **Dated June 5, 2009**

To Hamilton District Bd of Education

| | | | |
|---|---|---|---|
| 60 | A130 | Weight Plates | $ 1.20/ kg |
| 1 | E020 | Elliptical Exerciser: AE-200 | 1 700/ unit |
| 1 | E030 | Elliptical Exerciser: DE-300 | 2 000/ unit |
| 1 | E050 | Bicycle: Calorie Counter CC-60 | 400/ unit |
| 1 | E130 | Rowing Machine: RM-1000 | 480/ unit |
| 1 | E150 | Ski Exerciser: Linked SE-780 | 450/ unit |
| | | Freight | 30 |
| | | GST | 6% |
| | | PST | 8% |

Terms: 2/10, n/30.

**Sales Invoice #3014**                   **Dated June 5, 2009**

To Buffalo Health Clinic, New York (preferred USD customer)

| | | | |
|---|---|---|---|
| 1 | E210 | Treadmill: Deluxe T-1100D | $1 810/ unit USD |
| 1 | E220 | Treadmill: Deluxe Plus T-1200P | 2 125/ unit USD |
| | | Freight | 60 USD |

Terms: 2/10, n/30. The exchange rate is 1.1788.

**NOTES**

Taxes are not charged on freight for foreign customers.

**Purchase Invoice #TD-1127**             **Dated June 5, 2009**

From Trufit Depot

| | | | |
|---|---|---|---|
| 2 | E110 | Rider: Airwalker RA-900 | $240.00 |
| 2 | E130 | Rowing Machine: RM-1000 | 384.00 |
| | | GST | 37.44 |
| | | Invoice total | $661.44 |

Terms: 2/5, n/30. Free delivery.

**Purchase Invoice #FC-861**              **Dated June 7, 2009**

From Footlink Corporation, to fill purchase order #31

| | | | |
|---|---|---|---|
| 2 | E190 | Treadmill: Basic T-800B | $ 960.00 |
| | | Freight | 30.00 |
| | | GST | 59.40 |
| | | Invoice total | $1 049.40 |

Terms: 1/15, n/30.

**Purchase Invoice #PE-2079**             **Dated June 8, 2009**

From Prolife Exercisers, to fill purchase order #32

| | | | |
|---|---|---|---|
| 2 | E020 | Elliptical Exerciser: AE-200 | $1 100.00 USD |
| 2 | E030 | Elliptical Exerciser: DE-300 | 1 340.00 USD |
| | | Freight | 120.00 USD |
| | | GST | 153.60 USD |
| | | Invoice total | $2 713.60 USD |

Terms: 2/10, n/30. The exchange rate is 1.1815.

**Employee Time Summary Sheet #18**     **Dated June 9, 2009**

For the Pay Period ending June 9, 2009
George Schwinn worked 80 regular hours in the period (no overtime) and took one day of sick leave. Recover $50 advanced and issue payroll deposit slip DD27.

**Cheque Copy #134**     **Dated June 9, 2009**

To Trufit Depot, $648.96 in payment of account including $12.48 discount for early payment. Reference invoice #TD-1127.

**Cash Receipt #49**     **Dated June 9, 2009**

From Hamilton District Bd of Education, cheque #1431 for $11 049.72 in payment of account including $116.96 discount for early payment. Reference invoices #3001, #3012 and #3013.

**Memo #6-1**     **Dated June 9, 2009**

From Visa, received monthly credit card statement for $314.40 for purchases made before June 3, 2009. Submitted cheque #135 for $314.40 in full payment of the balance owing.

**Deposit Slip #21**     **Dated June 9, 2009**

Prepare deposit slip for the single cheque for $11 049.72 being deposited.

**Credit Card Sales Invoice #3015**     **Dated June 9, 2009**

To Visa customers (sales summary)

| | | | | |
|---|---|---|---|---|
| 10 | A030 | Dumbbells: pair | $1.50/ kg | $    15.00 |
| 4 | A040 | Dumbbells: 5kg set | 15/ set | 60.00 |
| 2 | A080 | Heart Rate Monitor | 75/ unit | 150.00 |
| 2 | A090 | Power Blocks up to 100 kg | 160/ set | 320.00 |
| 1 | A100 | Power Blocks up to 200 kg | 300/ set | 300.00 |
| 2 | A120 | Wavemaster | 150/ unit | 300.00 |
| 1 | A140 | Weights: Olympic 75 kg | 150/ set | 150.00 |
| 1 | A170 | Weights: Olympic 150 kg | 300/ set | 300.00 |
| 1 | E110 | Rider: Airwalker RA-900 | 300/ unit | 300.00 |
| 1 | E120 | Rider: Powerglider RP-1500 | 350/ unit | 350.00 |
| 1 | E170 | Stair Climber: Adjustable SC-A60 | 1 500/ unit | 1 500.00 |
| 2 | E190 | Treadmill: Basic T-800B | 1 200/ unit | 2 400.00 |
| 8 | S010 | Personal Trainer: 1 hour | 75/ hour | 600.00 |
| 4 | S020 | Personal Trainer: 1/2 day | 200/ 1/2 day | 800.00 |
| 6 | S040 | Yoga Instructor: 1 hour | 100/ hour | 600.00 |
| 2 | S050 | Yoga Instructor: 1/2 day | 200/ 1/2 day | 400.00 |
| | | GST | 6% | 512.70 |
| | | PST | 8% | 491.60 |
| | | Total paid by Visa | | $9 549.30 |

**Memo #6-2**     **Dated June 14, 2009**

Record payment for GST for May to the Receiver General for Canada. Issue cheque #136 in full payment. Clear the GST Report up to May 31.
Record payment for PST Payable for May to the Minister of Finance. Remember to collect 5% of the amount owing as the sales tax compensation. Issue cheque #137 in full payment. Clear the PST Report up to May 31.

**Memo #6-3**     **Dated June 14, 2009**

Payroll Remittances: Make the following payroll remittances for the pay period ending May 31 in the Payments Journal.
Record payment for EI, CPP and Income Tax Payable for May to the Receiver General for Canada. Issue cheque #138 in full payment.

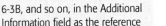

**NOTES**
Enter Memo 6-2A and Memo 6-2B as the reference numbers for the tax remittances.

**NOTES**
Enter Memo 6-3A, Memo 6-3B, and so on, in the Additional Information field as the reference numbers for the payroll remittances.

Record payment for Garnisheed Wages Payable for May to the Receiver General for Canada. Issue cheque #139 in full payment.

 Record payment for RRSP Payable to Ancaster Insurance. Issue cheque #140 in full payment.

Record payment for CSB Payable to Mt. Hope Investment Corporation. Issue cheque #141 in full payment.

Record payment for Group Insurance Payable for May to Ancaster Insurance. Issue cheque #142 in full payment.

Record payment for Charitable Donations Payable for May to Canadian Cancer Society. Create a new vendor record and select Payroll Authority for the vendor. Choose the new vendor in the Payroll Remittance Settings screen for both Donations entries. Include employee and employer contributions in remittance. Issue cheque #143 in full payment.

 **Purchase Invoice #FG-2187**      **Dated June 15, 2009**

From Feelyte Gym Accessories to fill purchase order #33

| | | | |
|---|---|---|---|
| 1 | A080 | Heart Rate Monitor (1 carton of 12) | $360.00 |
| 20 | A110 | Stability Balls | 80.00 |
| 2 | A180 | Workout Gloves: all sizes (2 boxes of 10) | 80.00 |
| | | GST | 31.20 |
| | | Invoice total | $551.20 |

Terms: 2/10, n/30.

 **Cheque Copy #350**      **Dated June 15, 2009**

To Prolife Exercisers, $2 662.40 USD in payment of account including $51.20 discount for early payment. Reference invoice #PE-2079. The exchange rate is 1.1825.

## SESSION DATE – JUNE 30, 2009

 **Cash Receipt #50**      **Dated June 16, 2009**

From Buffalo Health Clinic, cheque #638 for $3 995 USD in payment of account. Reference invoice #3013. The exchange rate is 1.1825.

 **Sales Invoice #3016**      **Dated June 16, 2009**

To Stelco Health Club (preferred customer)

| | | | |
|---|---|---|---|
| 40 | A130 | Weight Plates | $ 1.10/ kg |
| 1 | E080 | Home Gym: Basic HG-1400 | 1 000/ set |
| 1 | E100 | Home Gym: Multi HG-1402 | 1 875/ set |
| 1 | E105 | Home Gym: Free Weight HG-1403 | 2 000/ set |
| | | Freight | 30 |
| | | GST | 6% |
| | | PST | 8% |

Terms: 2/10, n/30.

 **Memo #6-4**      **Dated June 16, 2009**

Transfer $30 000 from the Visa bank account to the savings account.

 **Memo #6-5**      **Dated June 18, 2009**

Pay $5 000 to the Receiver General for Canada for quarterly instalment of business income tax. Issue cheque #144. Create new Group account 5550 Business Income Tax Expense. (Hint: Remember Business Income Tax Payable.)

 **Memo #6-6**      **Dated June 18, 2009**

Create appropriate new Heading and Total accounts around the new Group account 5550 to restore the logical order of accounts.

**NOTES**
You cannot create the new vendor from the Pay Remittance form in the Payments Journal and you must close the Remittance Journal.

Refer to page 678 for setting up payroll authorities and remittances.

**NOTES**
The next deposit, from Buffalo Health Clinic, will cover the bank overdraft.

### Cash Purchase Invoice #BC-86344          Dated June 19, 2009

From Bell Canada, $100 plus $6 GST paid and $8 PST for monthly phone service. Purchase invoice total $114. Terms: cash on receipt of invoice. Issue cheque #145 in full payment.

### Cash Purchase Invoice #ES-89886          Dated June 19, 2009

From Energy Source, $120 plus $7.20 GST paid for hydro service. Purchase invoice total $127.20. Terms: cash on receipt of invoice. Issue cheque #146 in full payment.

### Cash Sales Invoice #3017          Dated June 20, 2009

To Jim Ratter (choose Continue)

| | | | | |
|---|---|---|---|---|
| 1 | A010 | Body Fat Scale | | $100.00 |
| | | GST | 6% | 6.00 |
| | | PST | 8% | 8.00 |
| | | Invoice total | | $114.00 |

Received cheque #16 in full payment.

### Cheque Copy #147          Dated June 20, 2009

To Footlink Corporation, $1 039.50 in payment of account including $9.90 discount for early payment. Reference invoice #FC-861.

### Cheque Copy #148          Dated June 23, 2009

To Feelyte Gym Accessories, $540.80 in payment of account including $10.40 discount for early payment. Reference invoice #FG-2187.

### Cash Receipt #51          Dated June 23, 2009

From Stelco Health Club, cheque #499 for $5 526.67 in payment of account including $112.79 discount for early payment. Reference invoice #3016.

### Deposit Slip #22          Dated June 23, 2009

Prepare deposit slip for two cheques totalling $5 640.67 to deposit funds.

### Credit Card Sales Invoice #3018          Dated June 23, 2009

To Visa customers (sales summary)

| | | | | | |
|---|---|---|---|---|---|
| 10 | A020 | Yoga Mats | $ 30/ each | $ | 300.00 |
| 40 | A030 | Dumbbells: pair | 1.50/ kg | | 60.00 |
| 2 | A050 | Dumbbells: 10kg set | 25/ set | | 50.00 |
| 2 | A060 | Dumbbells: 15kg set | 40/ set | | 80.00 |
| 2 | A100 | Power Blocks up to 200 kg | 300/ set | | 600.00 |
| 10 | A110 | Stability Balls | 10 each | | 100.00 |
| 2 | A150 | Weights: Olympic 100 kg | 200/ set | | 400.00 |
| 1 | E070 | Bicycle: Recumbent R-80 | 750/ unit | | 750.00 |
| 1 | E090 | Home Gym: Deluxe HG-1401 | 1 500/ set | | 1 500.00 |
| 1 | E110 | Rider: Airwalker RA-900 | 300/ unit | | 300.00 |
| 1 | E140 | Ski Exerciser: Skitrek SE-680 | 400/ unit | | 400.00 |
| 1 | E170 | Stair Climber: Adjustable SC-A60 | 1 500/ unit | | 1 500.00 |
| 4 | S020 | Personal Trainer: 1/2 day | 200/ 1/2 day | | 800.00 |
| 8 | S040 | Yoga Instructor: 1 hour | 100/ hour | | 800.00 |
| 4 | S050 | Yoga Instructor: 1/2 day | 200/ 1/2 day | | 800.00 |
| | | GST | 6% | | 506.40 |
| | | PST | 8% | | 483.20 |
| | | Total paid by Visa | | | $9 429.60 |

### Employee Time Summary Sheet #19          Dated June 23, 2009

For the Pay Period ending June 23, 2009
George Schwinn worked 80 regular and 2 overtime hours in the period and took 1 day of sick leave. Recover $50 advanced and issue payroll deposit slip DD28.

**Memo #6-7**         **Dated June 24, 2009**

Issue a cheque to George Schwinn for vacation pay. George will be going on vacation for two weeks. A contract has been arranged with a local delivery company to complete deliveries during this period. Issue cheque #149.

**Sales Invoice #3019**        **Dated June 25, 2009**

To Lockport Gymnasium, New York

| | | | |
|---|---|---|---|
| 1 | E010 | Elliptical Exerciser: ME-100 | $  925/ unit USD |
| 1 | E040 | Elliptical Exerciser: LE-400 | 1 850/ unit USD |
| 1 | E180 | Stair Climber: Unlinked SC-U75 | 1 735/ unit USD |
| 1 | E190 | Treadmill: Basic T-800B | 1 000/ unit USD |
| | | Freight | 60 USD |

Terms: 2/10, n/30. The exchange rate is 1.1800.

**Memo #6-7**        **Dated June 25, 2009**

Received Bank Debit Memo #99142 from Hamilton Trust. Cheque #16 from Jim Ratter for $114 was returned as NSF. Prepare a sales invoice to charge Ratter for the sales amount and add $20 in service charges for the cost of processing the cheque. Create new Group account 4220 Other Revenue. Terms: net 30.

**Purchase Order #34**        **Dated June 25, 2009**

Delivery date July 1, 2009
From Scandia Weights Co.

| | | | |
|---|---|---|---|
| 1 | A130 | Weight Plates (1 order of 100 kg) | $   60.00 |
| 3 | A140 | Weights: Olympic 75 kg | 225.00 |
| 3 | A150 | Weights: Olympic 100 kg | 300.00 |
| 3 | A160 | Weights: Olympic 125 kg | 375.00 |
| 3 | A170 | Weights: Olympic 150 kg | 450.00 |
| | | GST | 84.60 |
| | | Purchase invoice total | $1 494.60 |

Terms: net 30.

**Cash Purchase Invoice #DMC-89**        **Dated June 28, 2009**

From Dundurn Maintenance Co., $300 plus $18 GST paid for cleaning and maintenance of premises. Terms: cash on receipt. Issue cheque #150 for $318 in full payment. Recall stored transaction.

**Memo #6-8**        **Dated June 29, 2009**

Write off Jim Ratter's account because attempts to locate him were unsuccessful. The outstanding amount is considered a bad debt. Improved screening of customers who pay by cheque will be implemented immediately.

**Credit Card Purchase Invoice #WS-9855**        **Dated June 30, 2009**

From Waterdown Sunoco, $98 including GST and PST paid for gasoline. Purchase invoice total $98 paid in full by Visa.

**Credit Card Sales Invoice #3020**        **Dated June 30, 2009**

To Visa customers (sales summary)

| | | | | |
|---|---|---|---|---|
| 2 | A070 | Glide Slidetrak | $  50 each | $  100.00 |
| 20 | A130 | Weight Plates | 1.20/ kg | 24.00 |
| 1 | E060 | Bicycle: Dual Action DA-70 | 600/ unit | 600.00 |
| 8 | S010 | Personal Trainer: 1 hour | 75/ hour | 600.00 |
| 2 | S030 | Personal Trainer: full day | 400/ day | 800.00 |
| 3 | S050 | Yoga Instructor: 1/2 day | 200/ 1/2 day | 600.00 |
| | | GST | 6% | 163.44 |
| | | PST | 8% | 57.92 |
| | | Total paid by Visa | | $2 945.36 |

**NOTES**
Remember to remove all wage amounts, deductions and user-defined expense amounts for the vacation paycheque.

PAYCHEQUES TO PROSORSOR AMOUNT · VAC PAY
1 280

**NOTES**
You cannot reverse this NSF cheque or enter a negative receipt for it because it was a cash sale.
Entering the Bank Account in the Sales Invoice for the amount of the NSF cheque will reverse the bank deposit and restore the accounts payable.
Use Quick Add to create a new partial record for Jim Ratter. For the Ratter invoice, credit chequing account for $114, credit Other Revenue for $20, debit Accounts Receivable for $134.

**NOTES**
Use tax code IN for $114, the sale portion of the bad debt. Use No Tax as the code for the $20 handling charge. Remember to "pay" the account. Refer to Accounting Procedures, page 634.

## NOTES

Use the Payroll Journal to enter the piece rate pay and bonuses.

- Click Enter Taxes Manually so that you can edit the income tax amounts.
- On the Income tab screen, remove all hours, wage, salary and benefit amounts. Do not remove Vacation Accrued for Schwinn.
- On the remaining tab screens, remove entitlement hours and deduction and user-defined expense amounts.
- Click the Taxes tab.
- Click Recalculate Taxes.
- Enter the income tax amount. Do not change the EI or CPP amounts.
- Click Enter Taxes Automatically after creating the bonus cheques.

 **Memo #6-9**                    **Dated June 30, 2009**

Prepare the payroll for Nieve Prekor and Assumpta Kisangel, the salaried employees. Add 2 percent of service revenue for June as a commission to Kisangel's salary. Issue payroll deposit slips DD29 and DD30.

Prepare separate payroll cheques to pay all employees for completed surveys and quarterly bonuses. Withhold 10 percent income tax. (See margin notes.)

Kisangel    $300 bonus, 20 completed client surveys, $50 income tax
Prekor      $250 bonus, 28 completed client surveys, $53 income tax
Schwinn     $250 bonus, 26 completed client surveys, $51 income tax

Issue cheques #151, #152 and #153.

 **Bank Credit Memo #7642**           **Dated June 30, 2009**

From Hamilton Trust, semi-annual interest was deposited to bank accounts. $155 was deposited to chequing account and $815 to the savings account. Remember interest receivable balance $420.

 **Bank Debit Memo #143661**           **Dated June 30, 2009**

From Hamilton Trust, authorized withdrawals were made from the chequing account on our behalf for the following:

| | |
|---|---|
| Bank service charges | $    35 |
| Mortgage interest payment | 1 850 |
| Mortgage principal reduction | 150 |
| Bank loan interest payment | 380 |
| Bank loan principal reduction | 520 |

 **Memo #6-10**                   **Dated June 30, 2009**

Prepare quarterly adjusting entries for depreciation on fixed assets using the following amounts:

| | |
|---|---|
| Cash Registers | $   300 |
| Computer Equipment | 150 |
| Furniture & Fixtures | 80 |
| Retail Premises | 2 450 |
| Van | 1 875 |

**Memo #6-11**                   **Dated June 30, 2009**

Increase the allowance for doubtful accounts by $500 in preparation for the next fiscal period.

**Memo #6-12**                   **Dated June 30, 2009**

Prepare adjusting entries for the following:

| | |
|---|---|
| Office Supplies used | $ 290 |
| Linen Supplies used | 120 |
| Prepaid Insurance expired | 2 016 |
| Prepaid Advertising expired | 620 |
| Payroll Liabilities accrued for Schwinn | 680 |

Create a new Group liability account Accrued Payroll 2260.

# REVIEW

**The Student CD-ROM with Data Files includes Review Questions and Supplementary Cases for this chapter including bank reconciliation and online banking.**

# CHAPTER SEVENTEEN

# Stratford Country Inn

## OBJECTIVES

- **plan** and **design** an accounting system for a small business
- **prepare** a conversion procedure from manual records
- **understand** the objectives of a computerized accounting system
- **create** company files
- **set up** company accounts
- **assign** appropriate account numbers and account classes
- **choose** and **enter** appropriate settings for all ledgers
- **create** vendor, customer and employee records
- **enter** historical data and account balances in all ledgers
- **finish** entering historical data to prepare for journal entries
- **enter** accounting transactions from realistic source documents

# COMPANY INFORMATION

## Company Profile

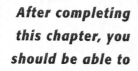

**NOTES**
Stratford Country Inn
100 Festival Road
Stratford, Ontario
N5A 3G2
Tel 1: (519) 222-6066
Tel 2: (888) 272-6000
Fax: (519) 272-7960
Business No.: 767 698 321

**S**tratford Country Inn is situated in Ontario just outside the Stratford city limits, close to Stratford Festival Theatres. The Inn has room for approximately 50 guests, with additional cots available for families who want to share rooms. In addition to the theatre, which attracts most of the guests, the Inn has facilities for rowing and canoeing on the small lake area near the Thames River, and a forested area nearby is used for lovely summer walks or cross-country skiing in winter. Boxed lunches and dinners are provided for picnics on the waterfront before theatre events or for afternoons in the woods or on the lake. Thus, many guests stay for several days at a time, and weekly rates are offered.

For an additional cost, a private consultant will pamper the guests with aromatherapy sessions. The consultant pays a rental fee to the Inn for use of her studio.

Customers come from near and far, and even a few American theatre groups have become regular visitors. The Inn prepares invoices and accepts payments in United States dollars for US accounts. For the American groups, an agency books group tours for a fixed price that includes theatre tickets and accommodation. Most individual guests pay by Visa or MasterCard. All customers pay GST and PST on the services provided by the Inn. The PST rate for accommodation is 5 percent instead of the standard 8 percent. Regular customers, corporations such as colleges, universities and schools, or agencies that reserve blocks of theatre tickets and accommodation have credit accounts. Groups place a deposit to confirm their accommodation. In the event of overbooking, guests who cannot be placed at the Inn are put up at a nearby Bed & Breakfast at the Inn's expense.

The grounds of the Inn include conference rooms for discussions and debates about theatre performances and related topics. Buses take guests to the theatre and return them to the Inn on a scheduled basis. Meals can be included for those who want an all-inclusive package. The Inn's dining room serves all full accommodation guests and also caters to the public and to guests who choose not to take a full meal package.

The owner, manager and desk attendant look after the front office. Five additional staff cater to all the other needs of the guests.

Accounts Payables have been set up for food supplies, a maintenance contract (a cleaning crew vacuums the Inn), maintenance and repairs (electrical and carpentry work), linen supplies for kitchen and guest rooms, and laundry services for towels and bedding.

By June 30, the Inn was ready to convert its accounting records to Simply Accounting and had gathered the following reports to make the conversion:

- Chart of Accounts
- Post-Closing Trial Balance
- Vendor Information
- Customer Information
- Employee Information and Profiles

## CHART OF ACCOUNTS

### STRATFORD COUNTRY INN

**ASSETS**
Bank: Stratford Trust CAD Chequing
Bank: Stratford Trust USD Chequing
Bank: Credit Card
Accounts Receivable
Advances Receivable
Purchase Prepayments
Prepaid Advertising
Prepaid Insurance
Food Inventory
Linens & Towels
Blankets & Bedding
Supplies: Computer
Supplies: Office
Supplies: Dining Room
Supplies: Washroom
Computer Equipment
Accum Deprec: Computers
Furniture & Fixtures ▶

▶Accum Deprec: Furn & Fix Vehicle
Accum Deprec: Vehicle
Country Inn & Dining Room
Accum Deprec: Inn & Dining Room
Grounds & Property

**LIABILITIES**
Bank Loan
Accounts Payable
Prepaid Sales and Deposits
Credit Card Payable
Vacation Payable
EI Payable
CPP Payable
Income Tax Payable
EHT Payable
Group Insurance Payable
Tuition Fees Payable
WSIB Payable ▶

▶PST Payable
GST Charged on Services
GST Paid on Purchases
Mortgage Payable

**EQUITY**
E. Prospero, Capital
Current Earnings

**REVENUE**
Revenue from Inn
Revenue from Dining Room
Rental Fees
Sales Tax Compensation
Other Revenue
Exchange Rate Differences

**EXPENSE**
Advertising & Promotion
Bank Charges and Card Fees
COGS: Food ▶

▶Depreciation: Computers
Depreciation: Furn & Fix
Depreciation: Vehicle
Depreciation: Inn & Dining Room
Purchase Discounts
Interest Expense: Loan
Interest Expense: Mortgage
Hydro Expenses
Maintenance & Repairs
Overflow Accommodation
Telephone Expense
Vehicle Expenses
Wages: Management
Wages: General
Wages: Dining Room
EI Expense
CPP Expense
WSIB Expense
EHT Expense
Tuition Fees Expense

**NOTES:** Use appropriate account numbers and add subgroup totals, headings and totals to organize your Chart of Accounts as necessary. Remember to add a test balance account for the setup.

# POST-CLOSING TRIAL BALANCE

## STRATFORD COUNTRY INN

June 30, 2009

| | Debits | Credits | | Debits | Credits |
|---|---|---|---|---|---|
| Bank: Stratford Trust CAD Chequing | $33 964 | | ▶ Accum Deprec: Vehicle | | 10 000 |
| Bank: Stratford Trust USD Chequing | | | Country Inn & Dining Room | 400 000 | |
| (2 540 USD) | 3 000 | | Accum Deprec: Inn & Dining Room | | 20 000 |
| Bank: Credit Card | 12 000 | | Grounds & Property | 200 000 | |
| Accounts Receivable (deposit) | | $ 1 000 | Bank Loan | | 25 000 |
| Advances Receivable | 250 | | Accounts Payable | | 7 816 |
| Prepaid Advertising | 50 | | Credit Card Payable | | 395 |
| Prepaid Insurance | 400 | | Vacation Payable | | 4 946 |
| Food Inventory | 1 650 | | EI Payable | | 1 092 |
| Linens & Towels | 2 000 | | CPP Payable | | 1 759 |
| Blankets & Bedding | 3 000 | | Income Tax Payable | | 3 109 |
| Supplies: Computer | 400 | | EHT Payable | | 577 |
| Supplies: Office | 500 | | Group Insurance Payable | | 330 |
| Supplies: Dining Room | 800 | | WSIB Payable | | 1 310 |
| Supplies: Washroom | 250 | | PST Payable | | 3 200 |
| Computer Equipment | 4 000 | | GST Charged on Services | | 3 080 |
| Accum Deprec: Computers | | 1 200 | GST Paid on Purchases | 700 | |
| Furniture & Fixtures | 38 000 | | Mortgage Payable | | 300 000 |
| Accum Deprec: Furn & Fix | | 4 200 | E. Prospero, Capital | | 361 950 |
| Vehicle | 50 000 ▶ | | | $750 964 | $750 964 |

# VENDOR INFORMATION

## STRATFORD COUNTRY INN

| Vendor Name (Contact) | Address | Phone No. Fax No. | E-mail Web Site | Terms Tax ID |
|---|---|---|---|---|
| Avon Maintenance Services (Ken Sparkles) | 66 Kleen Road Stratford, Ontario  N5A 3C3 | Tel: (519) 272-4611 Fax: (519) 272-4813 | www.avonservices.com | net 30 631 393 461 |
| Bard's Linen & Towels (Jason Bard) | 21 Venice Street Stratford, Ontario  N5A 4L2 | Tel: (519) 271-2273 Fax: (519) 271-9333 | bard@bards.com www.bards.com | 2/10, n/30 after tax 763 271 673 |
| Bell Canada (Bea Heard) | 30 Whisper Road Stratford, Ontario  N5A 4N3 | Tel: (519) 273-2355 | bheard@bell.ca www.bell.ca | net 1 634 345 373 |
| Minister of Finance | PO Box 3000, Stn A Toronto, Ontario  M5C 1M2 | | www.gov.on.ca/fin | net 1 |
| Perth County Hydro (Wynd Mills) | 66 Power Road Stratford, Ontario  N5A 4P4 | Tel: (519) 272-6121 | www.perthenergy.com | net 1 721 431 214 |
| Receiver General for Canada | PO Box 20002, Stn A Sudbury, Ontario  P3A 5C3 | Tel: (800) 959-5525 | www.cra-arc.gc.ca | net 1 |
| Stratford Service Centre (A.L.L. Ledfree) | 33 MacBeth Avenue Stratford, Ontario  N5A 4T2 | Tel: (519) 271-6679 Fax: (519) 276-8822 | ledfree@ssc.com www.ssc.com | net 1 634 214 211 |
| Tavistock Laundry Services (Martin Tavistock) | 19 Merchant Road Stratford, Ontario  N5A 4C3 | Tel: (519) 271-7479 Fax: (519) 271-7888 | www.tavistock.com | net 30 639 271 343 |
| Tempest Food Wholesalers (Vita Minns) | 35 Henry Avenue Stratford, Ontario  N5A 3N6 | Tel: (519) 272-4464 Fax: (519) 272-4600 | vita@tempest.com www.tempest.com | net 30 673 421 936 |
| Travellers' Life | | | | |
| Workplace Safety & Insurance Board | | | | |
| Zephyr Advertising Services (Tom DeZiner) | 32 Portia Blvd. Stratford, Ontario  N5A 4T2 | Tel: (519) 271-6066 Fax: (519) 271-6067 | tom@westwinds.com www.westwinds.com | net 1 391 213 919 |

## LIST OF PAYROLL AUTHORITIES

### STRATFORD COUNTRY INN

| Vendor Name | Payroll Remittance |
| --- | --- |
| Receiver General for Canada | EI, CPP and Income Tax |
| Workplace Safety & Insurance Board | WSIB |
| Minister of Finance | EHT |
| Travellers' Life | group insurance |

## OUTSTANDING VENDOR INVOICES

### STRATFORD COUNTRY INN

| Vendor Name | Terms | Date | Inv/Chq No. | Amount | Total |
| --- | --- | --- | --- | --- | --- |
| Avon Maintenance Services | net 30 | June 7/09 | AM-68 | $530 | |
| | net 30 | June 14/09 | AM-85 | 530 | |
| | net 30 | June 21/09 | AM-101 | 530 | |
| | net 30 | June 28/09 | AM-127 | 530 | |
| | | | Balance owing | | $2 120 |
| Tavistock Laundry Services | net 30 | June 8/09 | TL-693 | $848 | |
| | net 30 | June 22/09 | TL-742 | 848 | |
| | | | Balance owing | | $1 696 |
| Tempest Food Wholesalers | net 30 | June 23/09 | TF-113 | $2 000 | |
| | net 30 | June 30/09 | TF-183 | 2 000 | |
| | | | Balance owing | | $4 000 |
| | | | Grand Total | | $7 816 |

## CUSTOMER INFORMATION

### STRATFORD COUNTRY INN

| Customer Name (Contact) | Address | Phone No. Fax No. | E-mail Web Site | Terms Credit Limit |
| --- | --- | --- | --- | --- |
| Festival Club of Rosedale (Jane Birken) | 3 Rosedale Valley Rd. Toronto, Ontario  M5G 3T4 | Tel: (416) 482-6343 | janebir@conundrum.com | net 5 $6 000 |
| Hamlet Holiday Agency (Ron Doleman) | 60 Tibault Avenue Stratford, Ontario  N5A 3K3 | Tel 1: (519) 272-6461 Tel 2: (800) 777-7777 | rdoleman@hamlet.com www.hamlet.com | net 5 $6 000 |
| Metro Arts Appreciation Group (R. Downey) | 4400 Yonge St. North York, Ontario  M6L 3T4 | Tel: (416) 923-8142 | RDowney@artnet.com www.artnet.com | net 5 $6 000 |
| NY Friends of Shakespeare (J. Monte) | 33, 16th Avenue Buffalo, NY  13002 | Tel 1: (716) 755-4992 Tel 2: (888) 755-5000 | monte@aol.com | net 5 $4 000 (USD) |
| Waterloo University Literary Club (T. Fornello) | 88 College Rd. Waterloo, Ontario  N2A 3F6 | Tel: (519) 431-6343 | fornello4@uwo.ca | net 5 $6 000 |

## OUTSTANDING CUSTOMER INVOICES

### STRATFORD COUNTRY INN

| Customer Name | Terms | Date | Inv/Chq No. | Total |
| --- | --- | --- | --- | --- |
| Hamlet Holiday Agency | net 30 | June 30/09 | Deposit #40 (Chq 317; enter a negative invoice) | $1 000 |

## EMPLOYEE INFORMATION SHEET

### STRATFORD COUNTRY INN

| | Owen Othello | Clara Claudius | Mary MacBeth | Hedy Horatio | Juliet Jones | Shelley Shylock | Bud Romeo |
|---|---|---|---|---|---|---|---|
| Position | Manager | Clerk | Cook | Waiter | Concierge | Waiter | Service |
| Social Insurance No. | 691 113 724 | 873 863 211 | 284 682 556 | 294 654 421 | 177 162 930 | 891 263 634 | 254 685 829 |
| Address | 38 Falstaff St. Stratford, ON N5A 3T3 | 147 King Henry St. Mary's, ON N4X 1B2 | 3 Bard Cr. Stratford, ON N5A 6Z8 | 17 Elizabeth St. Stratford, ON N5A 4Z1 | 5 Capella Cres. Stratford, ON N5A 5M1 | 29 Avon St. Stratford, ON N5A 5N5 | 42 Hosteller St. New Hamburg, ON N0B 2G0 |
| Telephone | (519) 272-2191 | (519) 373-6495 | (519) 277-1338 | (519) 278-5343 | (519) 273-9122 | (519) 273-5335 | (519) 381-3738 |
| Date of Birth (mm-dd-yy) | 6-29-71 | 4-21-64 | 8-3-69 | 12-3-76 | 1-25-70 | 3-12-80 | 5-27-69 |
| Date of Hire (mm-dd-yy) | 3-1-98 | 5-2-91 | 6-1-01 | 6-1-03 | 1-1-02 | 1-1-06 | 12-16-00 |
| **Federal (Ontario) Tax Exemption - TD1** | | | | | | | |
| Basic Personal | $8 929 (8 533) | $8 929 (8 533) | $8 929 (8 533) | $8 929 (8 533) | $8 929 (8 533) | $8 929 (8 533) | $8 929 (8 533) |
| Spouse | – | – | $7 581 (7 262) | – | $7 581 (7 262) | – | $7 581 (7 262) |
| Other | $4 480 (4 456) | – | – | $2 570 (2 554) | $8 019 (8 031) | $9 660 (9 628) | – |
| Total Exemptions | $13 409 (12 989) | $8 929 (8 533) | $16 510 (15 795) | $11 499 (11 087) | $24 529 (23 826) | $18 589 (18 161) | $16 510 (15 795) |
| Additional Federal Tax | – | – | – | $50.00 | – | $50.00 | – |
| **Employee Taxes** | | | | | | | |
| Historical Income tax | $4 110.12 | $2 796.42 | $3 029.01 | $2 655.52 | $3 345.44 | $1 013.86 | $1 499.66 |
| Historical EI | $501.60 | $376.20 | $513.51 | $329.55 | $468.16 | $176.36 | $325.85 |
| Historical CPP | $989.34 | $721.44 | $1 014.83 | $621.80 | $917.87 | $294.49 | $613.90 |
| **Employee Income** | | | | | | | |
| Advances: Historical | – | – | – | $100.00 | – | – | $150.00 |
| Benefits: Historical | $2 800.00 | – | – | – | – | $2 470.00 | – |
| Vacation Pay Owed | – | – | $1 400.57 | $898.85 | $1 276.85 | $480.96 | $888.77 |
| Regular Wage Rate | – | – | $22.00/hr. | $14.00/hr. | $20.00/hr. | $12.00/hr. | $14.00/hr. |
| No. Hours Per Period | 160 | 160 | 80 | 80 | 80 | 80 | 80 |
| Wages: Historical | – | – | $22 880.00 | $14 560.00 | $20 800.00 | $7 872.00 | $14 560.00 |
| Overtime 1 Wage Rate | – | – | $33.00/hr | $21.00/hr | $30.00/hr | $18.00/hr | $21.00/hr |
| Overtime 1: Historical | – | – | $462.00 | $420.00 | $480.00 | $144.00 | $252.00 |
| Regular Salary | $3 800/mo. | $2 850/mo. | – | – | – | – | – |
| Salary: Historical | $22 800.00 | $17 100.00 | – | – | – | – | – |
| Commission | 1% (Sales–Returns) | – | – | – | – | – | – |
| Pay Periods | 12 | 12 | 26 | 26 | 26 | 26 | 26 |
| Vacation Rate | 4 weeks | 4 weeks | 6% retained | 6% retained | 6% retained | 6% retained | 6% retained |
| Wage Account | Management | General | Dining Room | Dining Room | General | Dining Room | General |
| **Deductions** | | | | | | | |
| Group Insurance | $30.00 | $60.00 | $30.00 | $15.00 | $30.00 | $15.00 | $30.00 |
| Insurance: Historical | $180.00 | $360.00 | $390.00 | $195.00 | $390.00 | $195.00 | $390.00 |
| **WSIB and User-Defined Expenses** | | | | | | | |
| WSIB Rate | 2.55 | 2.55 | 1.70 | 1.70 | 2.55 | 1.70 | 2.55 |
| Tuition: Historical | $2 800.00 | – | – | $1 450.00 | – | $2 470.00 | – |
| **Entitlements (Rate, Maximum Days, Clear, Days Accrued)** | | | | | | | |
| Vacation | 8%, 30, No, 20 | 8%, 30, No, 20 | – | – | – | – | – |
| Sick Leave | 5%, 15, No, 9 | 5%, 15, No, 7 | 5%, 15, No, 8 | 5%, 15, No, 9 | 5%, 15, No, 10 | 5%, 15, No, 3 | 5%, 15, No, 8 |
| **T4 and RL-1 Reporting** | | | | | | | |
| EI Insurable Earnings | $22 800.00 | $17 100.00 | $23 342.00 | $14 980.00 | $21 280.00 | $8 016.00 | $14 812.00 |
| Pensionable Earnings | $22 800.00 | $17 100.00 | $23 342.00 | $14 980.00 | $21 280.00 | $8 016.00 | $14 812.00 |
| Withheld | $5 781.06 | $4 254.06 | $4 947.35 | $3 801.87 | $5 121.47 | $1 679.71 | $2 829.41 |
| Net Pay | $17 018.94 | $12 845.94 | $18 394.65 | $11 278.13 | $16 158.53 | $6 336.29 | $12 132.59 |

# Payroll Information

**General Payroll Information**    E. Prospero, the owner, has arranged group insurance for his employees, and all employees have elected to join the plan. As entitlements, all staff may take 10 days' sick leave per year, and the vacation allowances are quite generous for the industry — four weeks of paid vacation for salaried staff after three years of service and 6 percent for all hourly paid employees. As an additional benefit, employees are reimbursed for their tuition fees on completion of eligible courses. Salaried employees are paid monthly, and hourly employees are paid every two weeks. All employees are eligible for EI and pay CPP; the EI factor is 1.4. The Inn pays 0.98 percent of payroll for EHT, the provincial health tax. WSIB rates vary for different types of work performed by the employees of the Inn.

Wage expenses for the manager, the dining room staff and the remaining general employees are tracked separately in three different payroll expense accounts.

## Employee Profiles and TD1 Information

**E. Prospero**    owns the Inn and oversees all activities. Together with family members, he fills in where needed. He does not collect a salary and is not recorded as an employee.

**Owen Othello**    is the salaried manager for the Inn. He welcomes guests, instructs other employees and discusses issues, problems and plans with the owner. He is single and studies part time in an MBA program. One night a week he commutes to Toronto. An education allowance — $140 per month federal and $138 provincial — and $2 800 for tuition increase his basic tax claim amounts. Othello is the salesperson for all sales, and beginning in July, he will receive a commission of 1 percent of sales.

**Clara Claudius**    has been with the Inn the longest and works as the desk attendant. Although her primary job is reservations clerk, she also performs the accounting for the Inn. She too is salaried. Because her husband is also fully employed, she uses only the basic single tax claim amounts. They have two young children as dependants.

**Mary MacBeth**    works as the cook in the dining room. As a single parent with dependent children, she is allowed to use the eligible dependant claim as the spousal equivalent for tax purposes. She is paid at an hourly rate of $22 per hour for the first 40 hours each week and $33 per hour after that.

**Hedy Horatio**    divides her time between waiting tables and helping the cook for her pay at the rate of $14 per hour plus $21 per hour for overtime hours. She studies part time at Conestoga College in the chef training program. The $1 450 tuition fee and the education tax claims — $140 per month federal and $138 provincial — supplement her basic single claim.

**Juliet Jones**    deals with requests from guests, working as the concierge and arranging for room service. She lives with and cares for her father and therefore has the eligible dependant claim plus a caregiver claim. She also has additional deductions transferred from her father ($4 000 federal and provincial) to supplement her basic single claim. Her hourly wage rate is $20 for the first 40 hours in the week and $30 for additional hours.

**Shelley Shylock**    waits tables in the dining room at the Inn. During the summer and festival months, she works full time for the Inn at the rate of $12 per hour and $18 for hours beyond the first 40 each week. She works part time until summer while she is a full-time student at the University of Waterloo. The education deduction of $465 ($461 provincial) per month plus tuition fees at $5 940 supplement her tax claim amounts.

> **NOTES**
> Enter entitlements as Payroll Settings and edit records for each employee as needed.
>
> Tuition is a user-defined payroll expense and taxable benefit. The benefits for Othello, Horatio and Shylock have already been paid, so only historical amounts are entered.
>
> Remember that WSIB is the name for WCB in Ontario.

> **NOTES**
> Enter the total federal and provincial amounts as claim amounts for each employee. Enter the full claim amounts as the amount subject to indexing.
>
> Education and tuition amounts are not usually subject to indexing but we are skipping this detail for this application. The amount subject to indexing is used by the program to update claim amounts when a new tax table is introduced, based on the government indexing rate.

> **NOTES**
> Federal education amounts include the monthly allowance for textbooks.

**Bud Romeo**    takes care of room service requests and also handles the baggage for the guests. He is married with two dependent children, so he has the spousal claim amount in addition to the basic single amount. He too is paid hourly at the rate of $14 per hour and $21 per hour for the time beyond 40 hours per week.

# INSTRUCTIONS

1.  Use all the information presented in this application to set up the company accounts for Stratford Country Inn in Simply Accounting using the following steps:
    a.  Create company files in a new data folder for storing the company records.
    b.  Enter the company information, starting a new fiscal period on July 1, 2009, and finishing the period on September 30, 2009.
    c.  Enter names and printer information.
    d.  Prepare the settings by changing the default settings as necessary.
    e.  Organize the Balance Sheet and Income Statement accounts.
    f.  Create accounts to correspond to your Balance Sheet and Income Statement.
    g.  Set up currency information for the USD transactions. The exchange rate on June 30 is 1.180.
    h.  Change the bank account class and set up the cheque sequence.
    i.  Enter linked accounts for the ledgers and credit cards. The fee is 2.75 percent.
    j.  Enter sales tax information and create tax codes for GST @ 6%, refundable; PST @ 8% for regular transactions and PST @ 5% for accommodation. On some items, GST alone is charged and on others PST is charged alone. GST is also sometimes charged with PST at 5 percent and sometimes with PST at 8 percent.
    k.  Enter customer, vendor and employee information.
    l.  Enter historical balances in all ledgers.
    m.  Create two Job Categories: Sales (employees are salespersons) and Other (employees in this category are not salespersons). Assign Othello to Sales and all other employees to the Other category.
    n.  Set up Payroll Authorities and Payroll Remittances. Add the balance forward amounts from the Trial Balance as at July 1, 2009.
    o.  Back up your files.
    p.  Finish entering the history for all ledgers and finish your session.

2.  Using the information provided, enter the source documents using Simply Accounting.

3.  After you have completed your entries, print the following reports:
    a.  Journal Entries (All Journals) from July 1 to July 31, 2009
    b.  Vendor Aged Detail Report for all vendors on July 31, 2009
    c.  Customer Aged Detail Report for all customers on July 31, 2009
    d.  Employee Summary (all employees) for the pay period ending July 31, 2009
    e.  Income Statement for the period ending July 31, 2009

**WARNING!**
Save your work and make backups frequently.

**WARNING!**
Remember to use a test balance account to check the trial balance before finishing the history for the General Ledger. Print the appropriate reports to check your work as you enter the company data.

**NOTES**
Set up two taxes, GST and PST. GST is refundable and PST is not refundable.
Then create tax codes for:
GST only
PST only at 8%
GST with PST at 5%
GST with PST at 8%

# SOURCE DOCUMENTS

Create new accounts or vendor and customer records as needed for the source documents that follow.

Telephone:
(519) 271-BARD (2273)
Fax:
(519) 271-9333

**ard's**
Linen & Towels

Website:
www.bards.com
E-mail:
bard@bards.com

| Invoice: | BLT-64 |
| --- | --- |

**Sold to:** Stratford Country Inn
100 Festival Road
Stratford, ON
N5A 3G2

**Date:** July 1, 2009

| STOCK NO. | QTY. | DESCRIPTION | PRICE | AMOUNT |
| --- | --- | --- | --- | --- |
| 1601 | 20 | Satin Sheets | 35.00 | 700.00 |
| 1801 | 100 | Bath Towels | 10.00 | 1000.00 |
| 2802 | 100 | Face Cloths | 3.00 | 300.00 |

| CUSTOMER COPY | Terms on Account: 2/10, N/30 | | | GROSS | 2000.00 |
| --- | --- | --- | --- | --- | --- |
| Method of payment: | On Account | C.O.D. | Credit Card | GST 6% | 120.00 |
| GST #763 271 673 | ✓ | | | PST 8% | 160.00 |
| | | | | TOTAL | 2280.00 |

**AVON**
**Maintenance**
**Services**
66 Kleen Road, Stratford, ON N5A 3C3
Telephone (519) 272-4611
Fax: (519) 272-4813
www.avonservices.com

| Invoice: | AM-148 |
| --- | --- |
| Date: | July 5, 2009 |
| Sold to: | Stratford Country Inn |
| | 100 Festival Road |
| | Stratford, ON |
| | N5A 3G2 |
| Phone: | (519) 222-6066 |

| Code | Service Description | Price |
| --- | --- | --- |
| KX-55 | Vacuum Premises | 1000.00 |
| | Floor Polishing | |
| | Washroom Cleaning | |
| | Maintenance and repairs | |
| | | |
| | Recurring bi-weekly billing | |

| Signature: |  | Terms: Net 30 days | GST | 60.00 |
| --- | --- | --- | --- | --- |
| | | GST #631 393 461 | Amount owing | 1060.00 |

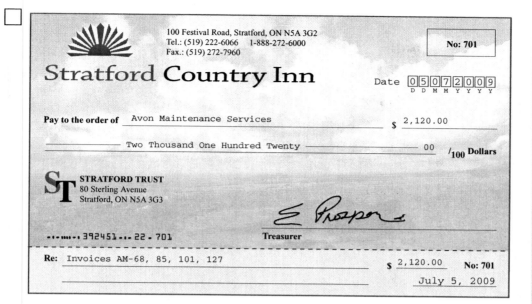

100 Festival Road, Stratford, ON N5A 3G2
Tel.: (519) 222-6066   1-888-272-6000
Fax.: (519) 272-7960

**No: 701**

# Stratford Country Inn

Date | 0 5 | 0 7 | 2 0 0 9 |
D D   M M   Y Y Y Y

**Pay to the order of**  Avon Maintenance Services

$  2,120.00

——————— Two Thousand One Hundred Twenty ———————  00 /100 **Dollars**

**S**T **STRATFORD TRUST**
80 Sterling Avenue
Stratford, ON N5A 3G3

*E Prospero*

⑈⑈⑈⑈ 392451 ⑈⑈ 22 ⑈ 701

**Treasurer**

- - - - - - - - - - - - - - - - - - - - - - - - - - - - - - - - - - - - - - - -

**Re:** Invoices AM-68, 85, 101, 127

$ 2,120.00   **No: 701**

July 5, 2009

---

100 Festival Road, Stratford, ON N5A 3G2
Tel.: (519) 222-6066   1-888-272-6000
Fax.: (519) 272-7960
prospero@stratfordinns.com

**No: 701**

# Stratford Country Inn

*The comfort of Home*  www.stratfordinns.com

### GUEST STATEMENT

**To:** Hamlet Holiday Agency,
60 Tibault Avenue,
Stratford, ON
N5A 3K3

**Check in:** July 1/09
**Check out:** July 6/09
**Room(s):**

| Date | Transaction | Daily Rate | | Price | |
|------|-------------|------------|--|-------|--|
| July 6/09 | Accommodation and Room Services | | | 2600 | 00 |
| | Restaurant Services | | | 400 | 00 |
| |    contractual prices | | | | |
| GST # 767 698 321 | | | | | |

| Signature: | **Terms:** Net 5 days | | **GST** | 180 | 00 |
|------------|-----------------------|--|---------|-----|----|
| *Ron Doleman* | **Clerk** CC | **Payment Method:** CASH ☐ CHEQUE ☐ ON ACCOUNT ☑ | **PST 1** <br> **PST 2** <br> **BALANCE** | 130 <br> 32 <br> $3342 | 00 <br> 00 <br> 00 |

📄 **NOTES**
PST1 is the tax at 5 percent on room accommodation and PST2 is the tax at 8 percent on restaurant services.

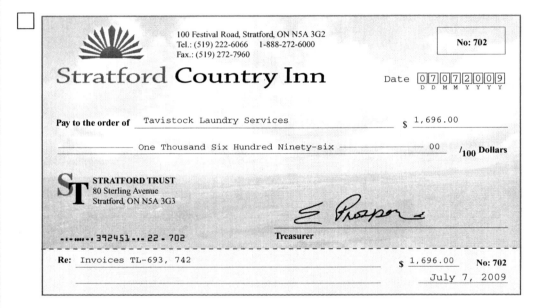

**Waterloo University Literary Club**
88 College Road
Waterloo, ON N2A 3F6

No: 413

Date 0 6 0 7 2 0 0 9
D D M M Y Y Y Y

**Pay to the order of**   Stratford Country Inn                         $ 1,000.00

——————————— One Thousand ———————————————————— 00/100 **Dollars**

**W T** **Waterloo Trust**
550 King Street
Waterloo, ON N2A 3F8

Chair

‑‑‑‑‑‑‑ 60431 ‑‑ 105 ‑‑ 413

**Re:**  Deposit #41 — booking rooms in Inn

No: 413

$1,000.00     July 6, 2009

---

100 Festival Road, Stratford, ON N5A 3G2
Tel.: (519) 222-6066   1-888-272-6000
Fax.: (519) 272-7960

No: 702

**Stratford Country Inn**

Date 0 7 0 7 2 0 0 9
D D M M Y Y Y Y

**Pay to the order of**   Tavistock Laundry Services                    $ 1,696.00

——————— One Thousand Six Hundred Ninety-six ——————— 00 /100 **Dollars**

**S T** **STRATFORD TRUST**
80 Sterling Avenue
Stratford, ON N5A 3G3

**Treasurer**

‑‑‑‑‑‑‑ 392451 ‑‑‑ 22 ‑ 702

**Re:**  Invoices TL-693, 742                         $ 1,696.00   No: 702

July 7, 2009

## Stratford Country Inn
*The comfort of Home*   www. stratfordinns.com

100 Festival Road, Stratford, ON N5A 3G2
Tel.: (519) 222-6066    1-888-272-6000
Fax.: (519) 272-7960
prospero@stratfordinns.com

**VISA**                        No: 27 V

SALES SUMMARY
STATEMENT

Week ___July 7, 2009___

Accommodation ☑

Restaurant ☑

| Transaction | Amount | |
|---|---|---|
| Accommodation and Room Services | 5,250 | 00 |
| Restaurant Services | 1,750 | 00 |
| | | |

| | | |
|---|---|---|
| GST # 767 698 321 | **Goods and Services Tax** | 420 | 00 |
| **Approved:** | **Provincial Sales Tax 1** | 262 | 50 |
| | **Provincial Sales Tax 2** | 140 | 00 |
| *E Prospero* | **V I S A  Receipts** | 7,822 | 50 |

---

| Sold to: | Stratford Country Inn |
|---|---|

Sold to:   Stratford Country Inn
100 Festival Road
Stratford, ON
N5A 3G2

**Billing Date:**  July 8, 2009

**Invoice No:**  TF-284

**Customer No.:**  3423

**Customer Copy**

**TEMPEST**
*Food Wholesalers*

35 Henry Avenue
Stratford, ON N5A 3N6

**Telephone:**
**(519) 272-4464**
**Fax:**
**(519) 272-4600**
**Website:**
**www.tempest.com**

| Date | Description | Charges | Payments | Amount |
|---|---|---|---|---|
| July 8/09 | Fish and Meats | 1000.00 | | 1000.00 |
| | Fresh Fruits | 200.00 | | 200.00 |
| | Fresh Vegetables | 200.00 | | 200.00 |
| | Dry Goods | 200.00 | | 200.00 |
| | Dairy Products | 200.00 | | 200.00 |
| | Baking Goods | 200.00 | | 200.00 |
| | Recurring bi-weekly billing | | | |

| | | |
|---|---|---|
| **Terms:** Net 30 days | **Subtotal** | 2000.00 |
| GST #673 421 936 | **GST  6%** | exempt |
| **Signature:** *E Prospero* | **PST  8%** | exempt |
| Overdue accounts are subject to 16% interest per year | **Owing** | 2000.00 |

**Invoice No:** TL-798

**Date:** July 8, 2009

**Customer:** Stratford Country Inn
100 Festival Road
Stratford, ON
N5A 3G2

**Phone:** (519) 222-6066

19 Merchant Road    Phone: (519) 271-7479
Stratford, ON       Fax: (519) 271-7888
N5A 4C3             www.tavistock.com

**GST #639 271 343**

| Code | Description | Price | Amount |
|------|-------------|-------|--------|
| C-11 | 10 Loads Sheets | 40.00 | 400.00 |
| C-14 | 5 Loads Pillow Covers | 20.00 | 100.00 |
| C-20 | 15 Loads Towels | 20.00 | 300.00 |
| | Recurring bi-weekly billing | | |

| | | |
|---|---|---|
| Overdue accounts are subject to a 2% interest penalty per month | **Sub-total** | 800.00 |
| **Terms:** Net 30 days | **GST** | 48.00 |
| **Signature:** *E Prosper* | **Total** | 848.00 |

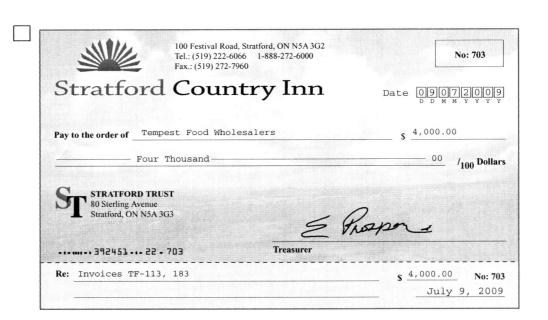

100 Festival Road, Stratford, ON N5A 3G2
Tel.: (519) 222-6066   1-888-272-6000
Fax.: (519) 272-7960

**No: 703**

**Stratford Country Inn**

Date | 0 9 0 7 2 0 0 9 |
D D M M Y Y Y Y

**Pay to the order of** Tempest Food Wholesalers    $ 4,000.00

———— Four Thousand ————    00 /100 **Dollars**

**STRATFORD TRUST**
80 Sterling Avenue
Stratford, ON N5A 3G3

*E Prosper*

⑈392451⑈ 22 · 703    **Treasurer**

**Re:** Invoices TF-113, 183    $ 4,000.00    **No: 703**

July 9, 2009

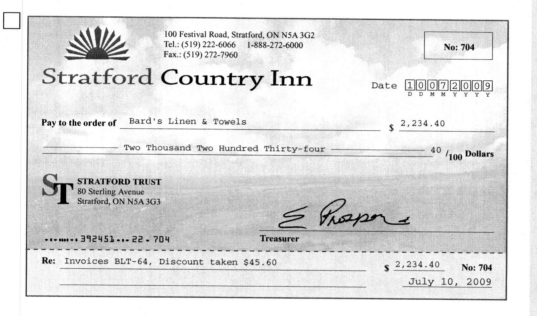

**Hamlet Holiday Agency**
60 Tibault Avenue,
STRATFORD, ON N5A 3K3

No: 349

Date  1 0  0 7  2 0 0 9
D D  M M  Y Y Y Y

Pay to the order of   Stratford Country Inn                    $ 2,342.00

——————— Two thousand, three hundred & forty-two ——————— 00 /100 Dollars

**SB** Scotia Bank
44 Welland Avenue
STRATFORD, ON N5A 3F6

Ron Doleman

Treasurer

⑆64299⑆ 168 ⑆349

Re:  Deposit #40 (Cheque #317)                                No: 349
     Invoice #701                      $2,342.00      July 10, 2009

---

100 Festival Road, Stratford, ON N5A 3G2
Tel.: (519) 222-6066    1-888-272-6000
Fax.: (519) 272-7960

No: 704

# Stratford Country Inn

Date  1 0  0 7  2 0 0 9
D D  M M  Y Y Y Y

Pay to the order of   Bard's Linen & Towels                    $ 2,234.40

——————— Two Thousand Two Hundred Thirty-four ——————— 40 /100 Dollars

**ST** STRATFORD TRUST
80 Sterling Avenue
Stratford, ON N5A 3G3

E Prospero

⑆392451⑆ 22 ⑆704     Treasurer

Re:  Invoices BLT-64, Discount taken $45.60        $ 2,234.40    No: 704
                                                   July 10, 2009

**Date:** July 11, 2009          **Invoice:** 1143

**Customer:**    Stratford Country Inn
100 Festival Road
Stratford, ON
N5A 3G2

**Phone:**      (519) 222-6066

33 MacBeth Avenue
Stratford, ON N5A 4T2
Tel: (519) 271-6679
Fax: (519) 276-8822
www.ssc.com

GST #634 214 211

| Code | Description | Price | Amount |
|------|-------------|-------|--------|
| M-114 | Lube, Oil and Filter | 40.00 | 40.00 |
| XF-1 | Fuel | 120.00 | 120.00 |
|  |  | **Sub-total** | 160.00 |

| APPROVAL | CUSTOMER COPY | | | | |
|----------|------|------|------------|------|------|
| *EP* | **Cash** | **VISA** | **On Account** | **GST** | 9.60 |
|  |  | ✓ |  | **PST** | 12.80 |
|  |  |  |  | **Owing** | 182.40 |

100 Festival Road, Stratford, ON N5A 3G2
Tel.: (519) 222-6066    1-888-272-6000
Fax.: (519) 272-7960

**No: 705**

# Stratford **Country Inn**

Date | 1 2 | 0 7 | 2 0 0 9 |
D D  M M  Y Y Y Y

**Pay to the order of**  Minister of Finance                $ 3,040.00

——— Three Thousand Forty ——————— 00 /100 **Dollars**

**STRATFORD TRUST**
80 Sterling Avenue
Stratford, ON N5A 3G3

*E Prosper*

⑈392451⑈ 22 · 705          **Treasurer**

**Re:**  PST $3,200 less 5% sales tax commission earned    $ 3,040.00  **No: 705**
for early payment ($160)                      July 12, 2009

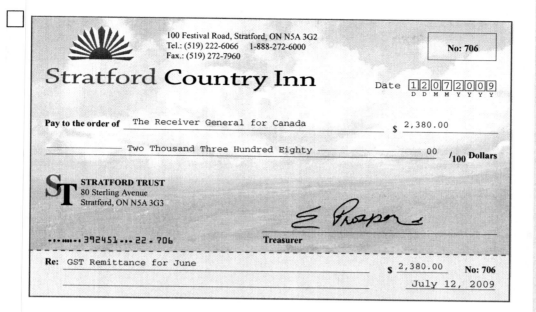

100 Festival Road, Stratford, ON N5A 3G2
Tel.: (519) 222-6066    1-888-272-6000
Fax.: (519) 272-7960

**Stratford Country Inn**

No: 706

Date | 1 2 | 0 7 | 2 0 0 9 |
D D    M M    Y Y Y Y

Pay to the order of    The Receiver General for Canada        $ 2,380.00

_____ Two Thousand Three Hundred Eighty _____ 00 /100 Dollars

**STRATFORD TRUST**
80 Sterling Avenue
Stratford, ON N5A 3G3

*E Prosper*

⑈⑆⑈⑈⑈ 392451 ⑈⑈ 22 · 706        Treasurer

Re:  GST Remittance for June                    $ 2,380.00    No: 706
                                                July 12, 2009

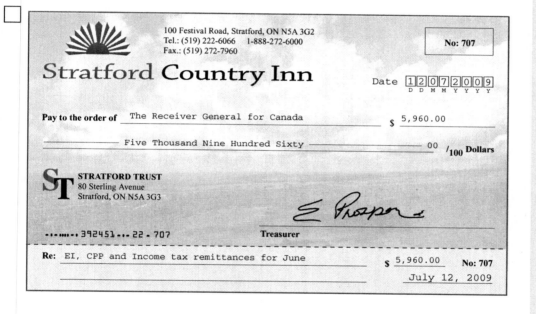

100 Festival Road, Stratford, ON N5A 3G2
Tel.: (519) 222-6066    1-888-272-6000
Fax.: (519) 272-7960

No: 707

**Stratford Country Inn**

Date | 1 2 | 0 7 | 2 0 0 9 |
D D    M M    Y Y Y Y

Pay to the order of    The Receiver General for Canada        $ 5,960.00

_____ Five Thousand Nine Hundred Sixty _____ 00 /100 Dollars

**STRATFORD TRUST**
80 Sterling Avenue
Stratford, ON N5A 3G3

*E Prosper*

⑈⑆⑈⑈⑈ 392451 ⑈⑈ 22 · 707        Treasurer

Re:  EI, CPP and Income tax remittances for June        $ 5,960.00    No: 707
                                                        July 12, 2009

100 Festival Road, Stratford, ON N5A 3G2
Tel.: (519) 222-6066    1-888-272-6000
Fax.: (519) 272-7960
prospero@stratfordinns.com

# Stratford Country Inn

*The comfort of Home*    www. stratfordinns.com

### GUEST STATEMENT

**To:** Waterloo University
Literary Club,
88 College Road,
Waterloo, ON
N2A 3F6

| | |
|---|---|
| **Check in:** | July 7/09 |
| **Check out:** | July 13/09 |
| **Room(s)** | 6 |

| Date | Transaction | Daily Rate | Price | |
|---|---|---|---|---|
| July 13/09 | Accommodation and Room Services | | 2900 | 00 |
| | Restaurant Services | | 500 | 00 |
| |    contractual prices | | | |

GST # 767 698 321

**Signature:** *J. Fornello*

| Terms: Net 5 days | | | | |
|---|---|---|---|---|
| **Clerk** CC | **Payment Method:** | CASH ☐ CHEQUE ☐ ON ACCOUNT ☑ | **GST** | 204 | 00 |
| | | | **PST 1** | 145 | 00 |
| | | | **PST 2** | 40 | 00 |
| | | | **BALANCE** | $3789 | 00 |

---

**NY Friends of Shakespeare**
33, 16th Avenue,
Buffalo, NY 13002

**No: 137**

Date | 1 | 3 | 0 | 7 | 2 | 0 | 0 | 9 |
D D M M Y Y Y Y

**Pay to the order of**   Stratford Country Inn    $ 1,000.00 (USD)

————————— One thousand ———————————————— 00/100 **Dollars**

**CB** **Chase Bank**
4, 12th Avenue
Buffalo, NY 13002

*J.Monte*

⑈⑆⑈⑆ 93937 ⑆ 301 ⑆ 137

- - - - - - - - - - - - - - - - - - - - - - - - - - - - - - - - - - - - - - -

**Re:** Deposit #42 — booking rooms in Inn. United    **No: 137**
States Currency. Currency Exchange 1.1815  $1,000.00 (USD)   July 13, 2009

100 Festival Road, Stratford, ON N5A 3G2
Tel.: (519) 222-6066    1-888-272-6000
Fax.: (519) 272-7960
prospero@stratfordinns.com

## Stratford Country Inn
*The comfort of Home*  www. stratfordinns.com

**VISA**                    | No: 28 V |

SALES SUMMARY
STATEMENT

Week __July 14, 2009__

**Accommodation**    ☑
**Restaurant**          ☑

| Transaction | Amount | |
|---|---:|---|
| Accommodation and Room Services | 4,900 | 00 |
| Restaurant Services | 2,100 | 00 |

| GST # 767 698 321 | Goods and Services Tax | 420 | 00 |
|---|---|---:|---|
| **Approved:** | Provincial Sales Tax 1 | 245 | 00 |
| | Provincial Sales Tax 2 | 168 | 00 |
| *E Prospero* | **V I S A  Receipts** | 7,833 | 00 |

---

100 Festival Road, Stratford, ON N5A 3G2
Tel.: (519) 222-6066    1-888-272-6000
Fax.: (519) 272-7960
prospero@stratford.com

| ET27 |

## Stratford Country Inn
*The comfort of Home*  www. stratfordinns.com

E M P L O Y E E   T I M E
S U M M A R Y   S H E E T

| Pay period ending: | July 14, 2009 |
|---|---|

| Name of Employee | Regular hours | Overtime hours | Sick days |
|---|:---:|:---:|:---:|
| ☐ Horatio, Hedy | 80 | 0 | 0 |
| ☐ Jones, Juliet | 80 | 0 | 1 |
| ☐ MacBeth, Mary | 80 | 2 | 0 |
| ☐ Romeo, Bud | 80 | 2 | 0 |
| ☐ Shylock, Shelley | 80 | 2 | 0 |

**Memo:**   Issue cheques #708 to #712
        Recover $100 advance from Horatio and Romeo

**Waterloo University Literary Club**
88 College Road
Waterloo, ON N2A 3F6

No: 479

Date 1 7 0 7 2 0 0 9
D D M M Y Y Y Y

Pay to the order of   Stratford Country Inn                          $ 2,789.00

———————— Two Thousand Seven Hundred & Eighty-nine ——— 00  /100 Dollars

**WT** Waterloo Trust
550 King Street
Waterloo, ON N2A 3F8

J. Fornello

Chair

⑈⑆ 60431 ⑆ 105 ⑆ 479

Re:  Deposit #41 (Cheque #413)                                    No: 479
     Invoice #702                           $2,789.00      July 17, 2009

---

100 Festival Road, Stratford, ON N5A 3G2
Tel.: (519) 222-6066   1-888-272-6000
Fax.: (519) 272-7960

No: 713

## Stratford Country Inn

Date 1 8 0 7 2 0 0 9
D D M M Y Y Y Y

Pay to the order of   Hartford Insurance Group                     $ 2,592.00

———————— Two Thousand Five Hundred Ninety-two ———————— 00  /100 Dollars

**ST** STRATFORD TRUST
80 Sterling Avenue
Stratford, ON N5A 3G3

E. Prospero

⑈⑆ 392451 ⑆ 22 ⑆ 713          Treasurer

Re:  Renewal of Insurance policy for 2 years         $ 2,592.00   No: 713
     $2,400. PST Paid $192. Total $2,592.            July 18, 2009

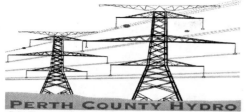

**PERTH COUNTY HYDRO**
66 Power Road, Stratford,
Ontario N5A 4P4
www.perthenergy.com

**Customer Care:**
**272-6121**

| | | | |
|---|---|---|---|
| **CUSTOMER NAME / SERVICE ADDRESS** | | | |
| Stratford Country Inn | | | |
| 100 Festival Road | | | |
| Stratford, ON | | | |
| N5A 3G2 | | | |

| | |
|---|---|
| **Date:** | July 18, 2009 |
| **Account No:** | 3921 462 513 |
| **Invoice No:** | 37232 |

| Months | Reading | Description | Net Amount |
|---|---|---|---|
| 1 | 86527 | Commercial Consumption | 300.00 |
| 1 | | Flat Rate Charge — Water Heaters | 60.00 |
| 1 | | Rental of Equipment | 40.00 |
| | | | |
| | | Total Current Charges | 400.00 |
| | | Previous Charges          385.20 | |
| | | Total Payments, Thank You   385.20 | |
| | | Balance Forward | 0.00 |
| | | Adjustments | 0.00 |

*Paid in Full with cheque #714 for $424 07/18/09  E Prosper*

| Average Daily KWh Consumption | | GST #721 431 214 | Due Date | GST 6% | 24.00 |
|---|---|---|---|---|---|
| **Same Period Last Year** | **This Bill** | **After due date, a 1.5% monthly late payment interest charge will apply.** | July 25/09 | | |
| 269 | 258 | | **Pay This Amount** | **TOTAL** | 424.00 |

**Bell**

30 Whisper Road
Stratford, ON
N5A 4N3

www.bell.ca

Account Inquiries: 273-BELL (2355)

| | |
|---|---|
| **Account Number** | |
| 519-222-6066 | |

**Account Address**

Stratford Country Inn
100 Festival Road
Stratford, ON
N5A 3G2

July 18, 2009

### ACCOUNT SUMMARY

| | |
|---|---|
| Current Charges | |
| Monthly Services (June 12 to July 12) | 240.00 |
| Equipment Rentals | 50.00 |
| Chargeable Messages | 30.00 |
| GST 634 345 373 | 19.20 |
| PST | 25.60 |
| Total Current Charges | 364.80 |
| | |
| Previous Charges | |
| Amount of Last Bill | 323.00 |
| Payment Received June 19 — Thank You | 323.00 |
| Adjustments | 0.00 |
| Balance Forward | 0.00 |

*Paid in Full — chq #715 — 07/18/09  E Prosper*

| Invoice: BC-66431 | PLEASE PAY THIS AMOUNT UPON RECEIPT | $364.80 |
|---|---|---|

**Invoice No:** AM-184

**Date:** July 19, 2009

**Sold to:** Stratford Country Inn
100 Festival Road
Stratford, ON
N5A 3G2

**Phone:** (519) 222-6066

66 Kleen Road, Stratford, ON N5A 3C3
Telephone (519) 272-4611
Fax: (519) 272-4813
www.avonservices.com

| Code | Service Description | | Price |
|------|---------------------|---|-------|
| KX-55 | Vacuum Premises<br>Floor Polishing<br>Washroom Cleaning<br>Maintenance and repairs<br><br>  Recurring bi-weekly billing<br> * new price as described<br>   in our previous notice | * | 1100.00 |

**Signature:** E Prospero

| **Terms:** Net 30 days | **GST** | 66.00 |
|---|---|---|
| **GST #631 393 461** | **Amount owing** | 1166.00 |

---

100 Festival Road, Stratford, ON N5A 3G2
Tel.: (519) 222-6066    1-888-272-6000
Fax.: (519) 272-7960
prospero@stratfordinns.com

No: 703

# Stratford Country Inn

*The comfort of Home*  www. stratfordinns.com

GUEST STATEMENT

**To:** NY Friends of Shakespeare,
33, 16th Avenue,
Buffalo, NY
13002

**Check in:** July 14/09

**Check out:** July 20/09

**Room(s):** 8

| Date | Transaction | Daily Rate | | Price | |
|------|-------------|------------|---|-------|---|
| July 20/09 | Accommodation and Room Services | | | 2600 | 00 |
| | Restaurant Services | | | 400 | 00 |
| | contractual prices | | | | |
| | | | | | |
| | All amounts billed in | | | | |
| | United States currency | | | | |
| | Exchange rate: 1.1895 CAD | | | | |
| GST # 767 698 321 | | | | | |

**Signature:** J.Monte

| **Terms:** Net 5 days | | **GST** | 180 | 00 |
|---|---|---|---|---|
| **Clerk**<br>CC | **Payment Method:** CASH ☐<br>CHEQUE ☐<br>ON ACCOUNT ☑ | **PST 1**<br>**PST 2**<br>**BALANCE** | 130<br>32<br>$3342 | 00<br>00<br>00 |

**Festival Club of Rosedale**
3 Rosedale Valley Rd.
Toronto, Ontario
M5G 3T4

No: 61

Date | 2 0 | 0 7 | 2 0 0 9
D D | M M | Y Y Y Y

Pay to the order of    Stratford Country Inn    $ 1,000.00

One Thousand    00 /100 **Dollars**

**R**  **Royal Bank**
**B**  56 Bloor Street
Toronto, ON M5N 3G7

⑈--- 34298 ⑈021 ⑈ 061

*Jane Birker*

Chairperson

Re: Deposit #43 — booking rooms in Inn

No: 61

$1,000.00    July 20, 2009

---

**Metro Arts Appreciation Group**
4400 Yonge Street,
North York, ON
M6L 3T4

No: 79

Date | 2 0 | 0 7 | 2 0 0 9
D D | M M | Y Y Y Y

Pay to the order of    Stratford Country Inn    $ 1,000.00

One Thousand    00 /100 **Dollars**

**CIBC**  CIBC
4800 Yonge Street
North York, ON M6L 3T4

⑈--- 396421 ⑈214 ⑈079

*R. Donhe*

Re: Deposit #44 — booking rooms in Inn

No: 79

$1,000.00    July 20, 2009

## STRATFORD TRUST
80 Sterling Avenue
Stratford, ON N5A 3G3

| Statement Period M D Y | Account Number | Account Enquiries | Daily Interest Rate | Annual Interest Rate |
|---|---|---|---|---|
| From 06/15/09 To 07/15/09 | 4512 6221 1384 6201 | 1-800-272-VISA | .05068% | 18.5% |

| Trans. Date | Post Date | Particulars | Amount | Bus. Exp. |
|---|---|---|---|---|
| 06 13 | 06 16 | Stratford Service Centre, Stratford, ON | 85.00 | *EP* |
| 06 18 | 06 21 | Office Supplies Unlimited, Stratford, ON | 88.00 | *EP* |
| 06 25 | 06 27 | Stratford Service Centre, Stratford, ON | 133.00 | *EP* |
| 06 28 | 06 30 | Bullrich Dept. Store #32, Stratford, ON | 113.00 | *EP* |
| 06 28 | 06 30 | Bullrich Dept. Store #32, Stratford, ON | -24.00 | *EP* |
| 07 11 | 07 13 | Stratford Service Centre, Stratford, ON | 182.40 | *EP* |
| 06 20 | 06 20 | Payment — Thank You | -422.00 | *EP* |

*Balance $577.40 paid in Full by cheque # 716*  *E Prospero*  *July 21/09*

| Credit Limit | Opening Balance | Total Credits | Total Debits | Your New Balance |
|---|---|---|---|---|
| 8500.00 | 422.00 | 446.00 | 601.40 | 577.40 |

| Available Credit | Payment Due Date Month Day Year | Overlimit or Past Due | Current Due | Minimum Payment | Payment Amount |
|---|---|---|---|---|---|
| 7922.60 | 07/24/09 | | 57.00 | 57.00 | 577.40 |

---

100 Festival Road, Stratford, ON N5A 3G2
Tel.: (519) 222-6066    1-888-272-6000
Fax.: (519) 272-7960
prospero@stratfordinns.com

## Stratford Country Inn
*The comfort of Home*   www. stratfordinns.com

**VISA**   No: 29 V

SALES SUMMARY STATEMENT

Week   July 21, 2009

Accommodation  ☑
Restaurant  ☑

| Transaction | Amount | |
|---|---|---|
| Accommodation and Room Services | 5,000 | 00 |
| Restaurant Services | 1,950 | 00 |

| GST # 767 698 321 | Goods and Services Tax | 417 | 00 |
|---|---|---|---|
| **Approved:**  | Provincial Sales Tax 1 | 250 | 00 |
| | Provincial Sales Tax 2 | 156 | 00 |
| | VISA Receipts | 7,773 | 00 |

**Sold to:** Stratford Country Inn
100 Festival Road
Stratford, ON
N5A 3G2

**TEMPEST**
*Food Wholesalers*

35 Henry Avenue
Stratford, ON N5A 3N6

**Telephone:**
**(519) 272-4464**
**Fax:**
**(519) 272-4600**
**Website:**
**www.tempest.com**

**Billing Date:** July 22, 2009
**Invoice No:** TF-344
**Customer No.:** 3423
**Customer Copy**

| Date | Description | Charges | Payments | Amount |
|------|-------------|---------|----------|--------|
| July 22 /09 | Fish and Meats | 1000.00 | | 1000.00 |
| | Fresh Fruits | 200.00 | | 200.00 |
| | Fresh Vegetables | 200.00 | | 200.00 |
| | Dry Goods | 200.00 | | 200.00 |
| | Dairy Products | 200.00 | | 200.00 |
| | Baking Goods | 200.00 | | 200.00 |
| | Recurring bi-weekly billing | | | |

| | | |
|---|---|---|
| **Terms:** Net 30 days | **Subtotal** | 2000.00 |
| GST #673 421 936 | **GST 6%** | exempt |
| **Signature:** *E Prosper* | **PST 8%** | exempt |
| Overdue accounts are subject to 16% interest per year | **Owing** | 2000.00 |

---

**Invoice No:** TL-841

**Date:** July 22, 2009

**Customer:** Stratford Country Inn
100 Festival Road
Stratford, ON
N5A 3G2

**Phone:** (519) 222-6066

**TAVISTOCK LAUNDRY** *Services*

19 Merchant Road
Stratford, ON
N5A 4C3

Phone: (519) 271-7479
Fax: (519) 271-7888
www.tavistock.com

GST #639 271 343

| Code | Description | | Price | Amount |
|------|-------------|---|-------|--------|
| C-11 | 10 Loads Sheets | * | 45.00 | 450.00 |
| C-14 | 5 Loads Pillow Covers | | 20.00 | 100.00 |
| C-20 | 15 Loads Towels | | 20.00 | 300.00 |
| | Recurring bi-weekly billing | | | |
| | * new prices | | | |

| | | |
|---|---|---|
| Overdue accounts are subject to a 2% interest penalty per month | **Sub-total** | 850.00 |
| **Terms:** Net 30 days | **GST** | 51.00 |
| **Signature:** *E Prosper* | **Total** | 901.00 |

## Zephyr Advertising Services
32 Portia Blvd.,
Stratford, ON
N5A 4T2

Telephone (519) 271-6066
Fax (519) 271-6067
www.westwinds.com
orders: contact tom@westwinds.com

Stratford Country Inn
100 Festival Road
Stratford, ON
N5A 3G2

ZA - 6998

| Date | Description | Charges | Amount |
|------|-------------|---------|--------|
| July 23, 2009 | Brochures & Flyers | 100.00 | 100.00 |
| | | GST | 6.00 |
| | | PST | 8.00 |
| **GST # 391 213 919** | **Terms:** Cash on Receipt | **Total** | 114.00 |

*Paid in full
cheque # 717
July 23/09
E. Prospero*

---

**NY Friends of Shakespeare**
33, 16th Avenue,
Buffalo, NY 13002

No: 181

Date  2 4 0 7 2 0 0 9
      D D M M Y Y Y Y

Pay to the order of   Stratford Country Inn                    $ 2,342.00 (USD)

—————————————— Two Thousand, three hundred forty-two ——— 00 /100 Dollars

**CB  Chase Bank**
4, 12th Avenue
Buffalo, NY 13002

JMonte

⑈⑈—⦂—— 93937 ⦂• 301 •• 181

**Re:** Deposit #42 — (Cheque #137) Invoice #703.                    **No: 181**
    U.S. Currency. Currency Exchange 1.181 Cdn. $2,342.00 (USD)    July 24, 2009

**33 MacBeth Avenue**
**Stratford, ON N5A 4T2**
**Tel: (519) 271-6679**
**Fax: (519) 276-8822**
**www.ssc.com**

**Date:** July 25, 2009          **Invoice:** 1207

**Customer:**   Stratford Country Inn
                100 Festival Road
                Stratford, ON
                N5A 3G2

**Phone:**      (519) 222-6066

GST #634 214 211

| Code | Description | Price | Amount |
|------|-------------|-------|--------|
| R-69 | Transmission—overhaul | 500.00 | 500.00 |
| XF-1 | Fuel | 100.00 | 100.00 |
| | | **Sub-total** | 600.00 |

| APPROVAL | CUSTOMER COPY | | | GST | 36.00 |
|----------|---------------|--|--|-----|-------|
| *EP* | Cash | VISA | On Account | PST | 48.00 |
| | | ✓ | | **Owing** | 684.00 |

---

100 Festival Road, Stratford, ON N5A 3G2
Tel.: (519) 222-6066    1-888-272-6000
Fax.: (519) 272-7960
prospero@stratfordinns.com

**No: 704**

# Stratford Country Inn
*The comfort of Home*   www. stratfordinns.com

## GUEST STATEMENT

**To:** Metro Arts Appreciation Group,
4400 Yonge Street,
North York, ON
M6L 3T4

**Check in:**   July 21/09
**Check out:**  July 26/09
**Room(s)**     5

| Date | Transaction | Daily Rate | | Price | |
|------|-------------|------------|--|-------|--|
| July 26/09 | Accommodation and Room Services | | | 2200 | 00 |
| | Restaurant Services | | | 200 | 00 |
| | contractual prices | | | | |
| GST # 767 698 321 | | | | | |

| Signature: | **Terms:** Net 5 days | | GST | 144 | 00 |
|------------|-----------------------|--|-----|-----|----|
| *R. Downes* | Clerk | Payment Method: CASH ☐ | PST 1 | 110 | 00 |
| | CC | CHEQUE ☐ | PST 2 | 16 | 00 |
| | | ON ACCOUNT ☑ | **BALANCE** | $2670 | 00 |

**Hamlet Holiday Agency**
60 Tibault Avenue,
STRATFORD, ON N5A 3K3

No: 393

Date 2 7 0 7 2 0 0 9
D D M M Y Y Y Y

Pay to the order of   Stratford Country Inn                    $ 1,000.00

———————— One thousand ————————————— 00/100 Dollars

**SB** Scotia Bank
44 Welland Avenue
STRATFORD, ON N5A 3F6

Ron Doleman
Treasurer

⑈⋯⋅⎯⎯ 64299 ⋅⋅ 168 ⋅⋅ 393

Re:  Deposit #45 — booking rooms in Inn                    **No: 393**

                                    $1,000.00    July 27, 2009

---

100 Festival Road, Stratford, ON N5A 3G2
Tel.: (519) 222-6066    1-888-272-6000
Fax.: (519) 272-7960
prospero@stratfordinns.com

**VISA**    No: 30 V

SALES SUMMARY
STATEMENT

**Stratford Country Inn**
*The comfort of Home*  www. stratfordinns.com

Week  July 28, 2009

**Accommodation** ✓
**Restaurant** ✓

| Transaction | Amount | |
|---|---|---|
| Accommodation and Room Services | 4,500 | 00 |
| Restaurant Services | 1,500 | 00 |

GST # 767 698 321

Approved: E Prospero

| | | |
|---|---|---|
| **Goods and Services Tax** | 360 | 00 |
| **Provincial Sales Tax 1** | 225 | 00 |
| **Provincial Sales Tax 2** | 120 | 00 |
| **VISA  Receipts** | 6,705 | 00 |

100 Festival Road, Stratford, ON N5A 3G2
Tel.: (519) 222-6066    1-888-272-6000
Fax.: (519) 272-7960
prospero@stratford.com

**ET28**

# Stratford Country Inn

*The comfort of Home*    www.stratfordinns.com

EMPLOYEE TIME
SUMMARY SHEET

**Pay period ending:**    July 28, 2009

| Name of Employee | Regular hours | Overtime hours | Sick days |
|---|---|---|---|
| ☐ Horatio, Hedy | 80 | 2 | 0 |
| ☐ Jones, Juliet | 76 | 4 | 0 |
| ☐ MacBeth, Mary | 80 | 0 | 0 |
| ☐ Romeo, Bud | 80 | 0 | 1 |
| ☐ Shylock, Shelley | 80 | 2 | 0 |

**Memo:**    Issue cheques #718 to #722
Recover $50 advance from Romeo

---

100 Festival Road, Stratford, ON N5A 3G2
Tel.: (519) 222-6066    1-888-272-6000
Fax.: (519) 272-7960
prospero@stratfordinns.com

**No: 705**

# Stratford Country Inn

*The comfort of Home*    www.stratfordinns.com

GUEST STATEMENT

**To:** Festival Club of Rosedale,
3 Rosedale Valley Road,
Toronto, ON
M5G 3T4

**Check in:**    July 26/09
**Check out:**   July 30/09
**Room(s)**    6

| Date | Transaction | Daily Rate | | Price | |
|---|---|---|---|---|---|
| July 30/09 | Accommodation and Room Services | | | 1800 | 00 |
|  | Restaurant Services | | | 200 | 00 |
|  | contractual prices | | | | |

GST # 767 698 321

**Signature:**    *Jane Birker*

| Terms: | | | GST | 120 | 00 |
|---|---|---|---|---|---|
| **Clerk** CC | **Payment Method:** | CASH ☐ | PST 1 | 90 | 00 |
|  |  | CHEQUE ☐ | PST 2 | 16 | 00 |
|  |  | ON ACCOUNT ☑ | **BALANCE** | $2226 | 00 |

100 Festival Road, Stratford, ON N5A 3G2
Tel.: (519) 222-6066    1-888-272-6000
Fax.: (519) 272-7960
prospero@stratfordinns.com

# Stratford Country Inn

*The comfort of Home*    www. stratfordinns.com

## M E M O

**From:** the owner's desk
**To:** Clara Claudius
July 31, 2009

1. a) Pay Owen Othello, manager, salary and sales commission for
      one month. Issue cheque #723.
   b) Pay Clara Claudius, desk attendant, salary for one month. Issue
      cheque #724.
2. Prepare adjusting entries for the following:
   a) Food Inventory on hand $1395
   b) Write off $200 of Prepaid Insurance
   c) Write off $50 of Prepaid Advertising
   d) Depreciation on assets:
      Country Inn & Dining Rooom $600
      Computers $100
      Furniture & Fixtures $600
      Vehicles $800
3. Pay quarterly balances owing as at July 1
   a) To Minister of Finance (EHT)
   b) Workplace Safety and Insurance Board (WSIB)
   c) Travellers' Life (Group Insurance)
   Issue cheques # 725, 726, 727

# R E V I E W

The Student CD-ROM with Data Files includes a
comprehensive supplementary case for this chapter.

# Appendices

# Installing Simply Accounting

The main instructions for installation refer to the regular Pro version of the program. Margin notes outline the differences for the Basic version and for the Student Pro version that accompanies this text.

**NOTES**

From the My Computer window, you can right-click D: and click Autoplay to start the autorun feature and show the Installation screens on this page.

**Start** your **computer** and the **Windows program**.

**Close** any **other programs** that you have running before beginning.

**Insert** the **program CD** in the CD-ROM drive.

Installation from the CD-ROM drive should begin immediately.

Many computers have drive D: as the CD-ROM drive, so we will use that in the keystrokes that follow.

First you must choose the language you want for the installation instructions:

**Accept English** or **choose French** from the drop-down list.

**Click OK.** The following options screen appears to begin the installation:

If you have any other programs running, click (Exit), close the other programs and start again.

**Click Install Simply Accounting**.

If installation does not begin immediately, follow the instructions in the box on page A-3.

Wait for the Setup Language selection screen to appear:

## IF INSTALLATION DOES NOT BEGIN IMMEDIATELY

You can install the program from the Windows opening screen or from the desktop. Many computers have drive D: as the CD-ROM drive, so we will use that drive in the keystrokes that follow.

**Double click** the **My Computer icon** [My Computer]. **Double click** the **Control Panel icon** [Control Panel] or **name** [Control Panel] to see the components that are installed on your computer.

If you are using the icon view for the My Computer window, you will see the Control Panel icon. If you are viewing by list or by detail, you will see the name with a small icon.

Or, **click Start** on the task bar, **choose Settings** and **click Control Panel**.

**Double click** the **Add Or Remove Programs icon** [Add or Remov...].

**Click** the **Add New Programs icon** [Add New Programs] on the left side of the window.

The installation may begin immediately at this stage. If it does not,

**Click** the **CD Or Floppy button** to proceed. Insert the CD if you have not already done so.

**Click  Next** to continue. Windows will search for the installation program.

**Click Browse**. The CD drive window should open with the Simply Accounting installation CD and the setup program shown. If it does not, locate the CD from the Browse window.

**Double click the Simply folder** to open it. The installation may begin at this stage. If not,

**Click Setup** (or **Setup.exe**).

**Click Open** to open the Run Installation Program window.

**Click Finish** to begin the installation with the Setup Language screen.

Or, you can start from the Run menu. **Choose Start** and then **click Run**. **Type d:\Simply\setup** in the Open field and **click OK**. (For drive D:, substitute the drive letter for your CD-ROM drive.)

**Click**    your **language preference** and **click Next**.

When the InstallShield setup window closes, the Welcome screen appears.  You can now choose to install the full regular or the trial version of the program:

**Accept** the **default Full Version option** and **click Next**:

You must enter the serial number exactly as it appears on the program package or CD case before you can continue.

The cursor is in the Serial Number field ready for you to enter the number.

**Type**    your **Serial Number** in the space provided.

**NOTES**

The instructions in the shaded box beside this note will begin the installation of the Simply Accounting Program directly and bypass the CD installation screens on the previous page.

**NOTES**

The serial number is printed on the Simply Accounting program CD package.

The serial number for all copies of the Student version is 24272U2-1000001

**WARNING!**

The serial number is case sensitive. You must type it exactly as it appears on the program case.

**Click**    **Next** to advance to the license agreement:

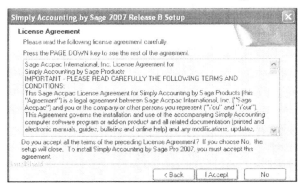

**Read**    the **agreement**, and if you accept the agreement, **click I Accept** to begin installing the program.

The next screen prompts you to enter your name and your company name:

**Enter**    the **required information**. **Press** (tab) to advance to the next field.

**Click**    **Next**. Your next decision concerns the type of installation you need:

If you are working on a network and your computer is connected to a host computer that already has the program installed, you should choose Install Workstation Components. If you are working on a stand-alone computer, or you are installing the program to a network server, you would choose Install Full Version.

**Make**    the **selection** for your system setup. **Click Next**.

Now you must choose the location of your program files:

You can accept the default location, C:\Program Files\Simply Accounting Pro 2007.

**Student Version**
In the Student version, you will not see this Company Name screen. You will register and activate the program later when you start the program.

**NOTES**
You will not see this screen for Pro single-user versions or for the Student version.

**basic Basic Version**
You will not see this screen when you install the Basic version because it applies to multi-user setups.

**basic Basic Version**
The default destination folder will be Simply Accounting Basic 2007.

To choose another folder, click Browse and choose an existing folder from the pop-up window, or type an alternative location in the Browse window. Click OK.

You will be asked if you want the program to create this folder:

**Click    Yes** to continue and select the program components to install:

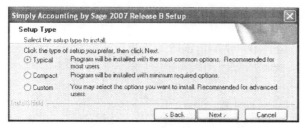

Accept the Typical installation option to include all the program elements.

**Click    Next**.

If you are updating an earlier version of Simply Accounting, you may see a message advising you that the new program will overwrite any changes you have added to customize your program. If you choose No, you should copy your customized forms to another folder before continuing with the installation. Click Yes if you do not want to keep the modifications.

Simply Accounting Pro is now available for handheld computers, so you must indicate whether you are using the program on a handheld computer:

**Make**    the **selection** for your system setup.

**Click    Next**.

The next screen asks you to enter a name for Simply Accounting in your Programs folder:

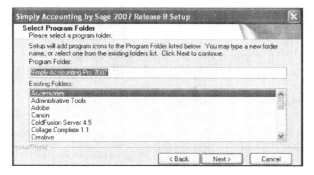

The name you enter here will be the name that appears on the Programs list. You can accept the default name, Simply Accounting Pro 2007, or type a different name such as Simply Pro 2007.

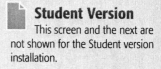
**Student Version**
This screen and the next are not shown for the Student version installation.

**Basic Version**
The Basic version is not available for handheld computers.

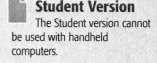
**Student Version**
The Student version cannot be used with handheld computers.

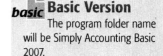
**Basic Version**
The program folder name will be Simply Accounting Basic 2007.

**Click** **Next** to see the screen about participating in the feedback program:

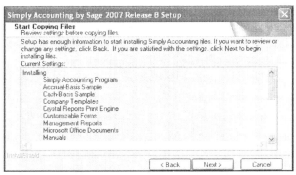

To provide feedback about the program, choose Yes. Otherwise choose No.

**Click** **Next** to proceed to the screen confirming your choice of components:

To omit any of these components, click Back to return to the previous screens and choose the Custom installation option.

By default, all components are selected for installation as follows:

- **Simply Accounting Program**: the Simply Accounting program that you will need to perform the accounting transactions for your company. It will be placed in the main Simply Accounting Pro 2007 folder under the Program Files folder or the folder location you selected.

- **Samples**: complete company records for both accrual-basis and cash-basis accounting methods for two sample companies — Universal Construction and Universal Crustacean Farm. They will be placed in the folder under Simply Accounting Pro 2007 called Samdata if you install them.

- **Templates**: predefined charts of accounts and settings for a large number of business types. These files will be stored in a folder under Simply Accounting Pro 2007 called Template. Two starter files with only charts of accounts also appear in this folder.

- **Crystal Reports Print Engine**, **Forms** and **Management Reports**: a variety of commonly used business forms and reports that you can customize to suit your own business needs and the program to access and print them. The reports and forms will be placed in a folder under Simply Accounting Pro 2007 called Forms.

- **Customizable Forms and Custom Reports**: a variety of MS Office documents designed for integrated use with Simply Accounting. They are placed in a Reports folder under Simply Accounting Pro 2007.

- **New Business Guide**: a number of checklists showing the steps to follow in setting up a new business, customized for a variety of business types in different provinces. These guides include addresses, phone numbers and Web addresses that you can contact for further information. You can access the guides from the Simply Accounting Business Assistant menu or from the Programs list.

- **Manuals**: documentation that will help you learn the program.

- **Add-in for Microsoft Outlook**: a program link that connects your data with MS Outlook. This is a Pro feature not available in Basic.

- **Upgrade Utility**: a program to convert accounting records that were created using DOS versions of the program into a Windows version of Simply Accounting. Data files in older Windows versions of the program are updated automatically.

> **Click**   **Next**.
>
> **Wait**   until the program prompts you with the Microsoft Outlook message:

***basic* BASIC VERSION**
You will not see the MS Outlook Add-in message in the Basic version.

Simply Accounting will coordinate with your Microsoft Outlook program database.

> **Click**   **OK** to continue.

You can choose to place a shortcut on your desktop to open the program.

> **Click**   **Yes** when prompted to add the desktop shortcut.

The Install program creates the folders for all the components described above. There is an additional folder, **Simply Accounting Pro 2007\Data**, that is empty initially. We will use this folder to store the data files for the applications in the workbook.

In addition, the installation procedure adds names in the Programs list for the Simply Accounting program, for Custom Reports, for the Upgrade program if it is installed and for the New Business Guide.

The next option is to view the ReadMe file, or start the program or both:

We will start the program immediately so we can register and activate the program.

> **Click**   **Yes, I Want To Start Simply Accounting**.
>
> **Click**   **Finish** to complete the installation and open the ReadMe screen.

You may be prompted to restart your computer. If so, you will see the following message:

> **Click**   **OK**.

# Registering and Activating Simply Accounting

> **Read**   the **information** about recent changes to the program that may not yet be documented elsewhere.

**⚠ WARNING!**
Wait for the Setup window to close after you close the ReadMe window. This may take awhile.

**Close** the **ReadMe screen** to see the Registration message:

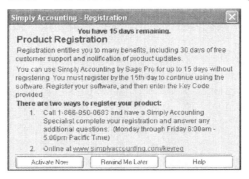

If you choose Remind Me Later, choose the Help menu and click Enter Key Code to see the screen shown above. This reminder message will also appear each time you start the program.

Until you register and activate the program, you will be allowed to use the program for a limited number of days. If you have already registered and have the activation codes, skip the next step.

Have your product serial number ready for the registration. You can register online or by telephone. The telephone number is provided. To register online, start your Internet connection. Enter the Web address given on the registration information screen or double click the Web address on this screen. Follow the instructions provided. Print a copy of the codes screen for reference.

When you register, you will provide the Serial Number from the program package or CD and receive a Client ID number, a Key Code number and a payroll ID number. These numbers will be linked to the serial number you provided and cannot be used for a different copy of the program.

**Click** **Activate Now** to start the activation procedure:

![Simply Accounting - Registration screen. You have 15 days remaining. Product Activation. Registration entitles you to many benefits, including 30 days of free customer support and notification of product updates. To continue to use the program after 15 days, you must activate your software by registering the product and entering the Key Code provided. Fields: Company Name, Serial Number (see back of CD case) 9999999 - 9999999, Client ID, Key Code. Buttons: OK, Cancel, Help.]

**Enter** your **Company Name** and the **Client ID** and **Key Code** provided by Sage Software for the program you have registered.

Enter all names and numbers exactly as they are given to you, including spaces and punctuation. The Key Code is also case sensitive, so be sure to type upper-case letters when required.

If you make a mistake, the program will warn you and you can re-enter the information.

**Click** **OK** to continue to Simply Accounting's Welcome screen:

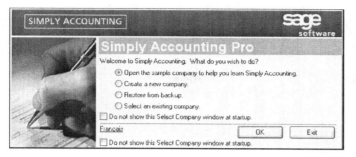

**Click    Open The Sample Company....**

You can choose accrual- or cash-basis accounting for the sample data set.

**Click    Accrual-Basis** to continue to the Session Date window:

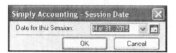

**Click    OK** to accept the default session date.

Now you may see a message about automatic program updates:

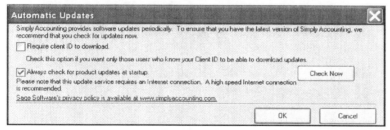

You can download updates automatically or periodically when needed. If you are working with the data files in this text, you should not update the program beyond the version we use, which is Release B. Therefore, you should turn off the automatic update option. You can get updates later from the Help menu, Check For Updates.

**Click    Always Check For Product Updates At Startup** to remove the ✓ and turn off the automatic update option.

**Click    OK** to open the sample company data file at the Daily Business Manager.

**Close    the Daily Business Manager window** to access the Home window.

## Unlocking the Payroll Features

We will unlock and activate the payroll module before proceeding. You will not need to unlock payroll in the Student version of the program.

**Choose the Help menu** and **click Unlock Auto Payroll** as shown:

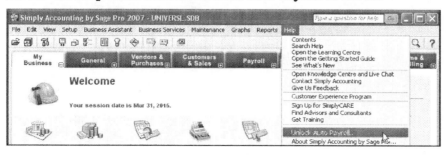

---

**Student Version**

In the Student version, you will not see the message about updates. The first time you use the program, you will receive a message about the limits of the Student version. You will be able to use the program for 14 months after activation

⚠️ **WARNING!**

If you download program updates, you may download a later version than the one we use and your payroll amounts may be different from the ones we show. Payroll tables are updated every six months and the Release indicates the payroll table dates.

**NOTES**

After working through the applications in this text, you can turn on automatic updates if you want.

**NOTES**

If you have not activated the program yet, you can activate the program from the Help menu. Choose Enter Key Code from the Help menu to open the You Have XX Days Remaining screen shown on page A-8.

An information screen about payroll services for Simply Accounting opens:

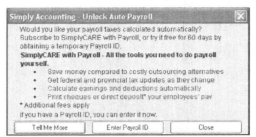

This screen advises you that you need a Payroll ID and subscription to the Simply Accounting Payroll Plan — a fee-based service — to use the payroll features in the program. To learn more about the payroll plan or to subscribe, click Tell Me More.

**Click**   **Enter Payroll ID**:

Your client ID number will be entered from the activation procedure. You must enter the Payroll ID number provided when you registered the program.

**Click**   the **Payroll ID field** and **type** the **number** provided, exactly as it is given to you.

If the activation is successful, you will see the following message:

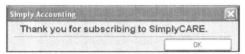

**Click**   **OK** to continue.

You can now use all features of the program.

**Click**    to close the Simply Accounting Home window.

You will see the option to make a backup copy of the data file:

Normally you would choose to back up the data but you do not need to make a copy of the sample file.

**Click**   **No**.

**Click**   **Exit** to close the Simply Accounting installation screen unless you want to install other programs or documents.

**Click**    to close the Control Panel window if it is open.

# Windows Basics, Shortcuts & Terms

## WINDOWS BASICS

This section explains the Windows terms and procedures commonly used in the text.

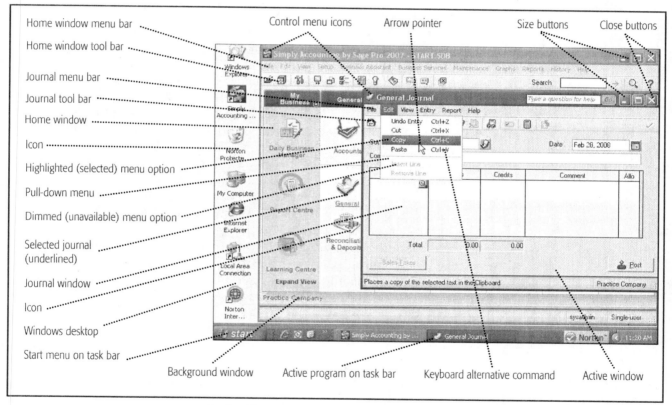

In the illustration above, the Simply Accounting program is open on the Windows XP desktop. The General Journal is open and active with the Home window in the background. The Journal's Edit menu is pulled down and Copy is selected.

The **mouse** is used to move the cursor. When you move the mouse, an **arrow** or **pointer** moves to indicate the cursor placement. If you **click** (press) the left mouse button, the cursor will move to the location of the arrow (if this is a legitimate place for the cursor to be at the time). That is, you use the mouse to **click** (point to and click) a screen location, item on a list, command or icon.

The arrow or pointer changes shape depending on what actions you may perform. When you are moving the mouse, it appears as an arrow or hand pointer.

When you are in a field that can accept text, it appears as a long **I-shaped bar**. Clicking will change it to an insertion point — a flashing vertical line in a text field. When the computer is processing information and you are unable to perform any action, you will see an **hourglass**. This is your signal to wait.

**Dragging** refers to the method of moving the mouse while holding the left button down. As you drag through the options in a menu, each one will be successively highlighted or darkened. Dragging through text will highlight it. Point to the beginning of the text to be highlighted. Then click and hold the mouse button down while moving through the entire area that you want to highlight. Release the mouse button at the end of the area you want to highlight. You can highlight a single character or the entire contents of a field. The text will remain highlighted and can be edited by typing new text. Delete text by pressing the Backspace key or (del). Clicking a different location will remove the highlighting.

To **double click** means to press the left mouse button twice quickly. This action can be used as a shortcut for opening and closing windows. Double clicking an icon or file name will open it. Double clicking the Control icon will close the window. The Simply Accounting files are set up to open journals and windows with a single click instead of a double click.

The **active window** is the one that you are currently working in. If you click an area outside the active window that is part of a background window, that window will move to the foreground. To return to a previous window, click any part of it that is showing. If the window you need is completely hidden, you can restore it by clicking its button on the task bar. Click ⬓ to reduce an active window to a task bar button.

An **icon** is a picture form of your program, file name or item. **Buttons** are icons or commands surrounded by a box frame. In Simply Accounting, clicking the Home window tool button 🏠 will bring the Home window to the front and make it active.

The **menu bar** is the line of options at the top of each window. Each menu contains one or more commands or selections (the **pull-down menu**) and can be accessed by clicking the menu name. Each window has different menu selections, and the options in the pull-down menus may differ. To choose an option from the menu, click the menu name and then click the option you want in order to **select (highlight)** it. If an option is dimmed, you will be unable to highlight or select it.

Some menus are **cascading menus**. When the menu option you want has an arrow, ▶, it has a second level of menu choices. To select from a cascading menu, click the menu bar name and point to the first-level menu option. When the next level of the menu appears, click the selection that you need.

You can **select multiple items** from a screen or list. Click the first item to select it. Then press and hold (ctrl) while you click each of the other items you want to select. The items previously selected will remain selected. If the items are in a list and you want to select several items in a row, click the first item and then press and hold (shift) while clicking the last item that you want to include. All the items between the two will also be selected. To change your selection, click somewhere else.

The **Control Menu icon** is situated in the upper left-hand corner of each window. The icon looks different for different programs and windows. It has its own pull-down menu, including the Close and Size commands. To close windows, you can double click this icon, choose Close from its pull-down menu or click the **Close button** ☒ in the upper right-hand corner of the window.

**Size buttons** are located in the upper right-hand corner of the window. Use them to make a window larger ☐ (**Maximize** to full screen size) or to reduce the window to a task bar button ⬓ (**Minimize**). If the window is full screen size or smaller than usual, restore it to its normal size with the 🗗 (**Restore**) button.

You can also change the size of a window by dragging. Point to a side. When the pointer changes to a two-sided arrow ⊞ or ⊞, drag the window frame to its new size.

---

**NOTES**

Often a program will include dialogue boxes that look like windows but do not have menu bars. Usually they require you to make a choice, such as answering a question, before you can proceed. You cannot make a dialogue box into a background window; you must click one of the options such as Yes, No, OK, Proceed, Cancel and so on to continue. Closing the dialogue box without making a choice is like choosing Cancel.

When a window contains more information than can fit on the screen at one time, the window will contain **scroll arrows** (▽, ▷, △, or ◁) in any corner or direction next to the hidden information (bottom or right sides of the window). Click the arrow and hold the mouse button down to scroll the screen in the direction of the arrow you are on.

Input fields containing data may have a **drop-down** or **pop-up list** from which to select. A **list arrow** beside the field ▽ indicates that a list is available. When you click the arrow, the list appears. Click an item on the list to add it to the input field directly.

# SHORTCUTS

## Using the Keyboard Instead of a Mouse

All Windows software applications are designed to be used with a mouse. However, there may be times when you prefer to use keyboard commands to work with a program because it is faster. There are also times when you need to know the alternatives to using a mouse, as when the mouse itself is inoperative. It is not necessary to memorize all the keyboard commands. A few basic principles will help you to understand how they work, and over time you will use the ones that help you to work most efficiently. Some commands are common to more than one Windows software program. For example, ⟮ctrl⟯ + C (press and hold the Control key while you press C) is commonly used as the copy command and ⟮ctrl⟯ + V as the paste command. Any selected text or image will be copied or pasted when you use these commands.

The menu bar and the menu choices can be accessed by pressing ⟮alt⟯. The first menu bar item will be highlighted. Use arrow keys, ⟮↑⟯ and ⟮↓⟯, to move up and down through the pull-down menu choices of a highlighted menu item or ⟮←⟯ and ⟮→⟯ to go back and forth to other menu items. Some menu choices have direct keyboard alternatives or shortcuts. If the menu item has an underlined letter, pressing ⟮alt⟯ together with the underlined letter will access that option directly. For example, ⟮alt⟯ + F (press ⟮alt⟯, and while holding down ⟮alt⟯, press F) accesses the File pull-down menu. Then pressing O (the underlined letter for Open) will give you the dialogue box for opening a new file. Some tool buttons in Simply Accounting have a direct keyboard command, and some menu choices also have a shortcut keyboard command. When available, these direct keystrokes are given with the tool button name or to the right of a menu choice. For example, ⟮alt⟯ + ⟮f4⟯ is the shortcut for closing the active window or exiting from the Simply Accounting program when the Home window is the active window.

To cancel the menu display, press ⟮esc⟯.

In the Simply Accounting Home window, you can use the arrow keys to move among the ledger and journal icons. Press ⟮alt⟯, ⟮alt⟯ and ⟮→⟯ to highlight the first icon (either the Daily Business Manager or the Accounts icon), and then use the arrow keys to change selections. Each icon is highlighted or selected as you reach it and deselected as you move to another icon.

To choose or open a highlighted or selected item, press ⟮enter⟯.

When input fields are displayed in a Simply Accounting window, you can move to the next field by pressing ⟮tab⟯ or to a previous field by pressing ⟮shift⟯ and ⟮tab⟯ together. The ⟮tab⟯ key is used frequently in this workbook as a quick way to accept input, advance the cursor to the next field and highlight field contents to prepare for immediate editing. Using the mouse while you input information requires you to remove your hands from the keyboard, while the ⟮tab⟯ key does not.

A summary of keyboard shortcuts used in Simply Accounting is included on page A-14.

## SUMMARY OF KEYBOARD SHORTCUTS

| Shortcut | Resulting Action |
|---|---|
| ctrl + A | Adjust, begin the Adjust a Posted Entry function. |
| ctrl + B | Bring the Home window to the front. |
| ctrl + C | Copy the selected text. |
| ctrl + E | Look up the Previously Posted Invoice (from a journal lookup window). |
| ctrl + F | Search, begin the search function. |
| ctrl + J | Display the journal entry report. |
| ctrl + K | Track shipment from a previously posted invoice lookup screen. |
| ctrl + L | Look up a previously posted transaction (from the journal window). |
| ctrl + N | Look up the next posted Invoice  (from a journal lookup window). |
| ctrl + N | Open a new record window (from a ledger icon or ledger record window). |
| ctrl + P | Print, open the print dialogue box. |
| ctrl + R | Recall a stored journal entry (from a journal window when an entry is stored). |
| ctrl + R | Remove the account record, or remove the quote or order (from ledger, quote or order window). |
| ctrl + S | Access the Save As function from the Home window (Home window, File menu) to save the data file under a new name. Keep the new file open. |
| ctrl + S | Save changes to a record; keep the ledger window open (from any ledger window). |
| ctrl + T | Store the current journal entry (open the Store dialogue box). |
| ctrl + V | Paste the selected text at the cursor position. |
| ctrl + X | Cut (delete) the selected text. |
| ctrl + Z | Undo the most recent change. |
| alt + C | Create another record;  saves the record you are creating and opens a new record form to create another new record. |
| alt + N | Save and close; save the new record and close the ledger. |
| alt + P | Post the journal entry or record the order or quote. |
| alt + f4 | Close the active window (if it has a close button). Closes the program if the Home window is active. |
| alt + the underlined character on a button | Select the button's action. An alternative to clicking the button and pressing enter. |
| alt | Access the first item on the menu bar. |
| alt + alt | Select the first icon in the Home window. |
| tab | Advance the cursor to the next field. |
| shift + tab | Move the cursor to the previous field. |
| Click | Move the cursor or select an item or entry. |
| shift + Click | Select all the items between the first item clicked and the last one. |
| ctrl + Click | Select this item in addition to ones previously selected. |
| enter | Choose the selected item or action. |
| Double click | Select an entire word or field contents. In fields with lists, open the selection list. |
| → | Move right to the next icon to select it or to the the next character in text. |
| ← | Move left to the next icon to select it or to the the next character in text. |
| ↓ | Move down to the next icon or entry in a list to select it. |
| ↑ | Move up to the previous icon or entry in a list to select it. |

# ACCOUNTING VS. NON-ACCOUNTING TERMS

**W**e have used accounting terms in this workbook because they are familiar to students of accounting, and because we needed to provide a consistent language for the book. The most frequently used non-accounting terms are included here for reference and comparison, in case you want to leave the non-accounting terms selected (Home window, Setup menu, User Preferences, Options screen).

## SUMMARY OF EQUIVALENT TERMS

**MAJOR TERMS**

| | ACCOUNTING TERMS | NON-ACCOUNTING TERMS |
|---|---|---|
| | General Journal | Miscellaneous Transactions |
| | Journal Entries | Transaction Details |
| | Payables | Vendors & Purchases |
| | Receivables | Customers & Sales |
| | Post | Process |

**DETAILED LIST: LOCATION**

| LOCATION | ACCOUNTING TERMS | NON-ACCOUNTING TERMS |
|---|---|---|
| Home window icon | General (Journal) | Miscellaneous Transactions |
| Setup menu – Settings screen | Payables | Vendors & Purchases |
| | Receivables | Customers & Sales |
| Setup menu, User Preferences, View screen – Modules | Payables | Vendors & Purchases |
| | Receivables | Customers & Sales |
| Graphs menu | Payables | Unpaid Purchases |
| | Receivables | Unpaid Sales |
| Reports menu and Report Centre – Financials | General Ledger | Transactions by Account |
| Report Centre – Financials | All Journal Entries | All Transactions |
| Reports menu and Report Centre | Payables | Vendors & Purchases |
| | Receivables | Customers & Sales |
| Reports menu | Journal Entries – General | Transaction Details – Miscellaneous |
| Report Centre – Accounts | General Journal Entries | Miscellaneous Transactions |
| Reports menu – Management Reports | Payables | Vendors & Purchases |
| | Receivables | Customers & Sales |
| All Icon window menus | Type | Transactions |
| Accounts window – menu | Type – General | Transactions – Miscellaneous Transactions |
| Accounts ledger window | General Ledger | Chart of Accounts Records |
| Vendors ledger window | Payables Ledger | Vendor Records |
| Customers ledger window | Receivables Ledger | Customer Records |
| All journals (button and menu) | Post | Process |

# Correcting Errors
# after Posting

**W**e all make mistakes. This appendix outlines briefly the procedures you need to follow for those rare occasions when you have posted a journal entry incorrectly and you need to reverse it manually. In most cases, you can use the Adjust Journal Entry or Reverse Entry procedures to make corrections.

Obviously, you should try to detect errors before posting. Reviewing journal entries should become routine practice. The software also has built-in safeguards that help you avoid mistakes. For example, outstanding invoices cannot be overpaid and employee wages and payroll deductions are calculated automatically. Furthermore, names of accounts, customers, vendors, employees and inventory items appear in full, so that you may check your journal information easily.

Before making a reversing entry, consider the consequences of not correcting the error. For example, misspelled customer names may not be desirable, but they will not influence the financial statements. After making the correction in the ledger, the newly printed statement will be correct (the journal will retain the original spelling). Sometimes, however, the mistake is more serious. Financial statements will be incorrect if amounts or accounts are wrong. Payroll tax deductions will be incorrect if the wage amount is incorrect. GST and PST remittances may be incorrect as a result of incorrect tax codes or sales or purchase amounts. Discounts will be incorrectly calculated if an invoice or payment date is incorrect. Some errors also originate from outside sources. For example, purchase items may be incorrectly priced by the vendor.

For audit purposes, prepare a memo explaining the error and the correction procedure. A complete reversing entry is often the simplest way to make the corrections for a straightforward audit trail. With Simply Accounting's one-step reversing entry feature from the adjust entry window, the reversing entry is made automatically. This feature is available for General Journal entries, paycheques, sales, purchases, receipts, and for most payments. Choose Adjust Invoice from the pull-down menu under the corresponding transaction menu, or click the Adjust Invoice tool in the journal. Then make the corrections if possible, or choose Reverse entry from the pull-down menu under the corresponding transaction menu, or click the Reverse tool. Under all circumstances, Generally Accepted Accounting Principles should be followed. Simply Accounting will create the reversing entry automatically and then include the correct entries if you save the changes to a journal entry.

However, this feature is not available for all journals. And when the journal entry deposit account for a receipt is not the bank account (because the deposit was made later) you need to reverse a receipt to record an NSF cheque. Therefore, we will illustrate the procedure for all journals.

Reversing entries in all journals have several common elements. In each case, you should use an appropriate source number that identifies the entry as reversing

**NOTES**

Adjusting entry procedures are shown on:

    page 45 – General Journal
    page 139 – Purchases
    page 141 – Other Payments
    page 148 – Payments
    Page 194 – Sales
    page 287 – Payroll

Reversing entry procedures are explained on:

    page 47 – General Journal
    page 149 – Purchases
    page 189 – Receipts
    page 195, note – Sales
    page 290 – Payroll

(e.g., add ADJ or REV to the original source number). You should use the original posting date and add a comment. Make the reversing entry as illustrated on the following pages. Display the journal entry, review it carefully and, when you are certain it is correct, post it. Next, you must enter the correct version of the transaction as a new journal entry with an appropriate identifying source number (e.g., add COR to the original source number).

Reversing entries are presented for each journal. Only the transaction portion of each screen is shown because the remaining parts of the journal screen do not change. The original and the reversing entry screens and most of the corresponding journal displays are included. Explanatory notes appear beside each set of entries.

## GENERAL JOURNAL: Original Entry

| Account | Debits | Credits | Comment | Allo |
|---------|--------|---------|---------|------|
| 1360 T-shirts | 432.00 | -- | T-shirts to sell at event | |
| 2670 GST Paid on Purchases | 24.00 | -- | GST paid 6% | |
| 2200 A/P - Designs U Wear | -- | 456.00 | terms: net 30 | |
| Total | 456.00 | 456.00 | | |

## Reversing Entry

| Account | Debits | Credits | Comment | Allo |
|---------|--------|---------|---------|------|
| 2200 A/P - Designs U Wear | 456.00 | -- | reversing A/P amount | |
| 1360 T-shirts | -- | 432.00 | reversing T-shirts amount | |
| 2670 GST Paid on Purchases | -- | 24.00 | reversing GST paid 6% | |
| Total | 456.00 | 456.00 | | |

## PURCHASES JOURNAL (NON-INVENTORY): Original Entry

| Item Number | Quantity | Order | Back Order | Unit | Description | Price | Tax | GST | PST | Amount | Acct | Allo |
|------|------|------|------|------|-------------|-------|-----|-----|-----|--------|------|------|
| 🔍 | | | | 🔍 | printing promotional materials | | GI🔍 | 36.00 | 48.00 | 600.00 | 5020🔍 | ✓ |

☑ Invoice Received    Freight [  ] 🔍 [       ] [       ]

GST    36.00
PST    48.00 🔍
Total   684.00

Terms: [  ] % [  ] Days, Net [20] Days

| 12/31/09 (J77) | Debits | Credits | Division |
|----------------|--------|---------|----------|
| 2670  GST Paid on Purchases | 36.00 | - | |
| 5020  Advertising & Promotion | 648.00 | - | |
|    - Sales Division | | | 388.80 |
|    - Service Division | | | 259.20 |
| 2200  Accounts Payable | - | 684.00 | |
| | 684.00 | 684.00 | |

### GENERAL JOURNAL

Use the same accounts and amounts in the reversing entry as in the original entry.

Accounts that were debited should be credited and accounts that were credited originally should be debited.

Click the Sales Taxes button if you used this screen. Choose the tax code and, if necessary, enter the Amount Subject To Tax with a minus sign.

Repeat the allocation using the original percentages.

The General Journal display is not shown because it basically looks the same as the journal input form.

You can use the Adjust Entry or Reverse Entry features instead. See page 45 and page 47.

### PURCHASES JOURNAL

The only change you must make is that positive amounts in the original entry become negative amounts in the reversing entry (place a minus sign before the amount in the Amount field).

Similarly, negative amounts, such as for GST Paid in GST remittances, must be changed to positive amounts (remove the minus sign).

If freight was charged, enter the amount of freight with a minus sign.

Use the same accounts and amounts in the reversing entry as in the original entry. Tax amounts change automatically.

Repeat the allocation with the original percentages.

You can use the Adjust Invoice and Reverse Invoice options instead (page 139 and page 149). Reversing a paid invoice will generate a credit note.

Remember to "pay" the incorrect and reversing invoices to remove them from the Payments Journal and later clear them.

### Reversing Entry

| Item Number | Quantity | Order | Back Order | Unit | Description | Price | Tax | GST | PST | Amount | Acct | Allo |
|---|---|---|---|---|---|---|---|---|---|---|---|---|
| | | | | | reverse printing invoice amt | | GI | -36.00 | -48.00 | -600.00 | 5020 | √ |

☑ Invoice Received      Freight

|  | |
|---|---|
| GST | -36.00 |
| PST | -48.00 |
| Total | -684.00 |

Terms: ___ % ___ Days, Net **20** Days

| 12/31/09 (J78) | Debits | Credits | Division |
|---|---|---|---|
| 2200   Accounts Payable | 684.00 | - | |
| 2670    GST Paid on Purchases | - | 36.00 | |
| 5020    Advertising & Promotion | - | 648.00 | |
|     - Sales Division | | | -388.80 |
|     - Service Division | | | -259.20 |
| | 684.00 | 684.00 | |

## OTHER PAYMENTS

The only change you must make is that positive amounts in the original entry become negative amounts in the reversing entry (place a minus sign before the amount in the Amount field).

Similarly, negative amounts, such as for GST Paid in GST remittances, must be changed to positive amounts (remove the minus sign).

Use the same accounts and amounts in the reversing entry as in the original entry. Tax amounts change automatically.

Repeat the allocation with the original percentages.

You can use the Adjust Invoice and Reverse Invoice options instead (page 141).

## PAYMENTS JOURNAL — OTHER PAYMENTS: Original Entry

| Acct | Description | Amount | Tax | GST | PST | Allo |
|---|---|---|---|---|---|---|
| 5150 Telephone E | telephone service | 100.00 | GP | 6.00 | 8.00 | √ |

|  | |
|---|---|
| Tax | 14.00 |
| Total | 114.00 |

| 12/31/09 (J79) | Debits | Credits | Division |
|---|---|---|---|
| 2670   GST Paid on Purchases | 6.00 | - | |
| 5150   Telephone Expense | 108.00 | - | |
|     - Service Division | | | 86.40 |
|     - Sales Division | | | 21.60 |
| 1050    Bank: Chequing CAD | - | 114.00 | |
| | 114.00 | 114.00 | |

### Reversing Entry

| Acct | Description | Amount | Tax | GST | PST | Allo |
|---|---|---|---|---|---|---|
| 5150 Telephone E | reverse telephone service charge | -100.00 | GP | -6.00 | -8.00 | √ |

|  | |
|---|---|
| Tax | -14.00 |
| Total | -114.00 |

## PAYROLL REMITTANCES

Payroll remittance entries cannot be reversed. You must make corrections in the Adjustments column of the Remittance Journal if incorrect amounts were remitted. When you enter an amount in the Adjustments column, the program warns you with the message shown here.

Positive remittance adjustment amounts create expense account entries – they do not affect the payable amounts in the ledger. You must make additional General Journal adjusting entries so that the final ledger amounts are correct.

| 12/31/09 (J81) | Debits | Credits | Division |
|---|---|---|---|
| 1050   Bank: Chequing CAD | 114.00 | - | |
| 2670    GST Paid on Purchases | - | 6.00 | |
| 5150    Telephone Expense | - | 108.00 | |
|     - Service Division | | | -86.40 |
|     - Sales Division | | | -21.60 |
| | 114.00 | 114.00 | |

## PAYROLL REMITTANCES

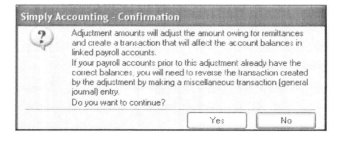

**Simply Accounting - Confirmation**

Adjustment amounts will adjust the amount owing for remittances and create a transaction that will affect the account balances in linked payroll accounts.

If your payroll accounts prior to this adjustment already have the correct balances, you will need to reverse the transaction created by the adjustment by making a miscellaneous transaction (general journal) entry.

Do you want to continue?

     [ Yes ]    [ No ]

## PAYMENTS: Original Entry

| Invoice/Pre-pmt. | Original Amount | Amount Owing | Disc. Available | Disc. Taken | Payment Amount |
|---|---|---|---|---|---|
| MT-1894 | 848.00 | 848.00 | 16.96 | 16.96 | 831.04 |
| | | | | Total | 831.04 |

| 12/31/09 (J83) | | Debits | Credits | Division |
|---|---|---|---|---|
| 2200 | Accounts Payable | 848.00 | - | |
| 1050 | Bank: Chequing CAD | - | 831.04 | |
| 5130 | Purchase Discounts | - | 16.96 | |
| | | 848.00 | 848.00 | |

## Reversing Entry

| Invoice/Pre-pmt. | Original Amount | Amount Owing | Disc. Available | Disc. Taken | Payment Amount |
|---|---|---|---|---|---|
| MT-1521 | 803.48 | 0.00 | 0.00 | | |
| MT-1894 | 848.00 | 0.00 | 0.00 | -16.96 | -831.04 |
| | | | | Total | -831.04 |

| 12/31/09 (J84) | | Debits | Credits | Division |
|---|---|---|---|---|
| 1050 | Bank: Chequing CAD | 831.04 | - | |
| 5130 | Purchase Discounts | 16.96 | - | |
| 2200 | Accounts Payable | - | 848.00 | |
| | | 848.00 | 848.00 | |

## CREDIT CARD PAYMENTS: Original Entry

| | |
|---|---|
| Credit Card Payable Account Balance: | 3,415.00 |
| Additional Fees and Interest: | 110.00 |
| Payment Amount: | 2,415.00 |

| 12/31/09 (J81) | | Debits | Credits | Division |
|---|---|---|---|---|
| 2250 | Credit Card Payable | 2,305.00 | - | |
| 5040 | Credit Card Fees | 110.00 | - | |
| 1050 | Bank: Chequing CAD | - | 2,415.00 | |
| | | 2,415.00 | 2,415.00 | |

## Reversing Entry

| | |
|---|---|
| Credit Card Payable Account Balance: | 1,110.00 |
| Additional Fees and Interest: | -110.00 |
| Payment Amount: | -2,415.00 |

| 12/31/09 (J82) | | Debits | Credits | Division |
|---|---|---|---|---|
| 1050 | Bank: Chequing CAD | 2,415.00 | - | |
| 2250 | Credit Card Payable | - | 2,305.00 | |
| 5040 | Credit Card Fees | - | 110.00 | |
| | | 2,415.00 | 2,415.00 | |

### PAYMENTS

Click the Include Fully Paid Invoices tool button.

The only change you must make is that positive amounts in the original entry become negative amounts in the reversing entry.

In the Payment Amt. field, click the invoice line for the payment being reversed.

Type a minus sign and the amount.

If a discount was taken, type the discount amount with a minus sign in the Disc. Taken field.

This will restore the original balance owing for the invoice.

If you have already cleared the paid invoice, prepare a new Purchases Journal entry for the amount of the payment (non-taxable) to restore the balance owing. Enter a positive amount in the Amount field for the amount of the cheque and the Bank account in the Account field. On the next line, enter the discount amount (positive) with the Purchase Discounts account in the Account field. This will debit the Bank and Purchase Discounts accounts and credit Accounts Payable.

You can also use the Adjust Payment tool or the Reverse Payment feature. (See page 148 and page 189.)

### CREDIT CARD PAYMENTS

Enter the same amounts as in the original entry.

Add a minus sign to the Additional Fees And Interest amount and to the Payment Amount in the reversing entry.

## INVENTORY PURCHASES

Change positive quantities in the original entry to negative ones in the reversing entry (place a minus sign before the quantity in the Quantity field).

Similarly, change negative quantities, such as for returns, to positive ones (remove the minus sign).

Add a minus sign to the freight amount if freight is charged.

Use the same accounts and amounts in the reversing entry as in the original entry. Tax amounts are corrected automatically.

Repeat the allocation using the original percentages.

You can use the Adjust Invoice and Reverse Invoice options instead (page 139 and page 149).

Remember to "pay" the incorrect and reversing invoices to remove them from the Payments Journal and later clear them.

## SALES JOURNAL

For inventory sales, change positive quantities in the original entry to negative ones in the reversing entry (place a minus sign before the quantity in the Quantity field). Similarly, change negative quantities, such as for returns, to positive ones (remove the minus sign).

For non-inventory sales, change positive amounts in the original entry to negative amounts in the reversing entry (place a minus sign before the amount in the Amount column).

Add a minus sign to the freight amount if freight is charged. Add the salesperson.

Use the same accounts and amounts in the reversing entry as in the original entry, and the same method of payment.

Repeat the allocation using the original percentages.

You can use the Adjust Invoice and Reverse Invoice options instead (page 194). Reversing a paid invoice will generate a credit note.

Remember to "pay" the incorrect and reversing invoices to remove them from the Receipts Journal and later clear them.

### INVENTORY PURCHASES: Original Entry

| Item Number | Quantity | Order | Back Order | Unit | Description | Price | Tax | GST | PST | Amount | Acct | Allo |
|---|---|---|---|---|---|---|---|---|---|---|---|---|
| W101 | 8 | | | Each | Aluminum R14 Wheels | 72.00 | G | 34.56 | | 576.00 | 1360 | |
| WN03 | 4 | | | dozen | Nickel/Chrome Wheel Nuts | 57.00 | G | 13.68 | | 228.00 | 1380 | |

☑ Invoice Received   Freight  G   3.00   50.00 ✓
GST   51.24
PST   0.00
Terms: 2.00 % 10 Days, Net 30 Days   Total   905.24

| 12/31/09 (J85) | Debits | Credits | Division |
|---|---|---|---|
| 1360  Wheels | 576.00 | - | |
| 1380  Wheel Nuts & Locks | 228.00 | - | |
| 2670  GST Paid on Purchases | 51.24 | - | |
| 5065  Freight Expense | 50.00 | - | |
|   - Sales Division | | | 50.00 |
| 2200     Accounts Payable | - | 905.24 | |
| | 905.24 | 905.24 | |

### Reversing Entry

| Item Number | Quantity | Order | Back Order | Unit | Description | Price | Tax | GST | PST | Amount | Acct | Allo |
|---|---|---|---|---|---|---|---|---|---|---|---|---|
| W101 | -8 | | | Each | Aluminum R14 Wheels | 72.00 | G | -34.56 | | -576.00 | 1360 | |
| WN03 | -4 | | | doz | Nickel/Chrome Wheel Nuts | 57.00 | G | -13.68 | | -228.00 | 1380 | |

☑ Invoice Received   Freight  G   -3.00   -50.00 ✓
GST   -51.24
PST   0.00
Terms: 2.00 % 10 Days, Net 30 Days   Total   -905.24

| 12/31/09 (J87) | Debits | Credits | Division |
|---|---|---|---|
| 2200  Accounts Payable | 905.24 | - | |
| 1360     Wheels | - | 576.00 | |
| 1380     Wheel Nuts & Locks | - | 228.00 | |
| 2670     GST Paid on Purchases | - | 51.24 | |
| 5065     Freight Expense | - | 50.00 | |
|   - Sales Division | | | -50.00 |
| | 905.24 | 905.24 | |

### SALES JOURNAL (INVENTORY AND NON-INVENTORY): Original Entry

| Item Number | Quantity | Order | Back Order | Unit | Description | Price | Amount | Tax | Acct | Allo |
|---|---|---|---|---|---|---|---|---|---|---|
| T101 | 4 | | | Each | P155/80R14 Tires | 65.00 | 260.00 | GP | 4020 Rever | ✓ |
| | | | | | repairs | | 200.00 | GI | 4040 Re | ✓ |

Comments   Freight   20.00 G ✓
GST   28.80
PST   36.80
Terms: 2.00 % 10 Days, Net 30 Days   Total   545.60

| 12/31/09 (J88) | Debits | Credits | Division |
|---|---|---|---|
| 1200  Accounts Receivable | 545.60 | - | |
| 5050  Cost of Goods Sold | 122.24 | - | |
|   - Sales Division | | | 122.24 |
| 1400     Winter Tires | - | 122.24 | |
| 2640     PST Payable | - | 36.80 | |
| 2650     GST Charged on Sales | - | 28.80 | |
| 4020     Revenue from Sales | - | 260.00 | |
|   - Sales Division | | | 260.00 |
| 4040     Revenue from Services | - | 200.00 | |
|   - Service Division | | | 200.00 |
| 4250     Freight Revenue | - | 20.00 | |
|   - Sales Division | | | 20.00 |
| | 667.84 | 667.84 | |

## Reversing Entry

| Item Number | Quantity | Order | Back Order | Unit | Description | Price | Amount | Tax | Acct | Allo | |
|---|---|---|---|---|---|---|---|---|---|---|---|
| T101 | -4 | | | Each | P155/80R14 Tires repairs | 65.00 | -260.00 | GP | 4020 Rever | ✓ | |
| | | | | | | | -200.00 | P | 4040 Re | ✓ | |

| Comments | | | | | | |
|---|---|---|---|---|---|---|
| | | | Freight | | -20.00 | G |
| Terms: 2.00 % 10 Days, Net 30 Days | | GST | | -28.80 | | |
| | | PST | | -36.80 | | |
| | | Total | | -545.60 | | |

| 12/31/09 (J90) | Debits | Credits | Division |
|---|---|---|---|
| 1400 Winter Tires | 122.24 | - | |
| 2640 PST Payable | 36.80 | - | |
| 2650 GST Charged on Sales | 28.80 | - | |
| 4020 Revenue from Sales | 260.00 | - | |
|    - Sales Division | | | -260.00 |
| 4040 Revenue from Services | 200.00 | - | |
|    - Service Division | | | -200.00 |
| 4250 Freight Revenue | 20.00 | - | |
|    - Sales Division | | | -20.00 |
| 1200   Accounts Receivable | - | 545.60 | |
| 5050   Cost of Goods Sold | - | 122.24 | |
|    - Sales Division | | | -122.24 |
| | 667.84 | 667.84 | |

## DEPOSITS or PREPAYMENTS: Original Entry

| Invoice/Deposit | Original Amount | Amount Owing | Disc. Available | Disc. Taken | Amount Received |
|---|---|---|---|---|---|
| 137 | 4,218.00 | 4,218.00 | 84.36 | | |

| Deposit Reference No. 14 | | Deposit Amount | 2,000.00 |
|---|---|---|---|
| | | Total | 2,000.00 |

| 12/31/09 (J92) | Debits | Credits | Division |
|---|---|---|---|
| 1050 Bank: Chequing CAD | 2,000.00 | - | |
| 2150   Prepaid Sales and Deposits | - | 2,000.00 | |
| | 2,000.00 | 2,000.00 | |

### DEPOSITS

You cannot enter a negative amount in the Deposit field so you must "pay" the deposit.

Click the Payment Amount field for the Deposit line and press *tab*. Deposit amounts are shown in red under the heading Deposits.

## Reversing Entry

| Invoice/Deposit | Original Amount | Amount Owing | Disc. Available | Disc. Taken | Amount Received |
|---|---|---|---|---|---|
| 137 | 4,218.00 | 4,218.00 | 84.36 | | |
| Deposits | | | | | |
| 14 | 2,000.00 | 2,000.00 | | | 2,000.00 |

| Deposit Reference No. 15 | | Deposit Amount | 0.00 |
|---|---|---|---|
| | | Total | -2,000.00 |

| 12/31/09 (J93) | Debits | Credits | Division |
|---|---|---|---|
| 2150 Prepaid Sales and Deposits | 2,000.00 | - | |
| 1050   Bank: Chequing CAD | - | 2,000.00 | |
| | 2,000.00 | 2,000.00 | |

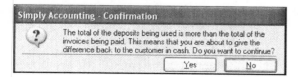

Simply Accounting - Confirmation

The total of the deposits being used is more than the total of the invoices being paid. This means that you are about to give the difference back to the customer in cash. Do you want to continue?

    Yes    No

### NOTES

When you post the transaction, you will be asked to confirm that you want to make the payment to the customer.

Click Yes to continue.

## RECEIPTS

Click the Include Fully Paid Invoices tool.

Change positive amounts in the original entry to negative amounts in the reversing entry.

In the Payment Amt. field, click the invoice or deposit line for the payment being reversed.

Type a minus sign and the amount for invoices and deposits.

If a discount was taken, type the discount amount with a minus sign in the Disc. Taken field.

This will restore the original balance owing for the invoice.

If you have already cleared the invoice, make a new Sales Journal entry for the payment amount (non-taxable) to restore the balance owing. Enter both the cheque and discount amounts as positive amounts to credit Bank and Sales Discounts.

You can use the Adjust Receipt and Reverse Receipt options instead (page 189). If the NSF cheque uses a different bank account from the deposit entry, you must reverse the receipt manually.

## RECEIPTS WITH DEPOSITS: Original Entry

| Invoice/Deposit | Original Amount | Amount Owing | Disc. Available | Disc. Taken | Amount Received |
|---|---|---|---|---|---|
| 137 | 4,218.00 | 4,218.00 | 84.36 | 84.36 | 4,133.64 |
| Deposits | | | | | |
| 15 | 1,000.00 | 1,000.00 | | | 1,000.00 |

Deposit Reference No. 15    Deposit Amount 0.00

Total 3,133.64

| 12/20/09 (J95) | Debits | Credits | Division |
|---|---|---|---|
| 1020 Undeposited Cash and Cheques | 3,133.64 | - | |
| 2150 Prepaid Sales and Deposits | 1,000.00 | - | |
| 4150 Sales Discounts | 84.36 | - | |
| 1200    Accounts Receivable | - | 4,218.00 | |
| | 4,218.00 | 4,218.00 | |

## Reversing Entry

| Invoice/Deposit | Original Amount | Amount Owing | Disc. Available | Disc. Taken | Amount Received |
|---|---|---|---|---|---|
| 120 | 1,824.00 | 0.00 | 0.00 | | |
| 137 | 4,218.00 | 0.00 | 0.00 | -84.36 | -4,133.64 |
| Deposits | | | | | |
| 15 | 1,000.00 | 0.00 | | | -1,000.00 |

Deposit Reference No. 16    Deposit Amount 0.00

Total -3,133.64

| 12/31/09 (J96) | Debits | Credits | Division |
|---|---|---|---|
| 1200 Accounts Receivable | 4,218.00 | - | |
| 1050    Bank: Chequing CAD | - | 3,133.64 | |
| 2150    Prepaid Sales and Deposits | - | 1,000.00 | |
| 4150    Sales Discounts | - | 84.36 | |
| | 4,218.00 | 4,218.00 | |

## PAYROLL JOURNAL

Redo the original incorrect entry but DO NOT POST IT!

Click the Enter Taxes Manually tool to open all the deduction fields for editing.

Type a minus sign in front of the number of hours (regular and overtime) or in front of the Salary and Commission amounts. Press (tab) to update the amounts, including vacation pay (i.e., change them to negative amounts).

For the Advance field, change the sign for the amount. Advances should have a minus sign in the reversing entry and advances recovered should be positive amounts.

Click the Deductions tab and edit each deduction amount by typing a minus sign in front of it. ▶

## PAYROLL JOURNAL: Original Entry

Income | Deductions | Taxes | User-Defined Expenses | Entitlements    Period Ending Feb 28, 2009

Earnings:

| Name | Hours | Pieces | Amount | YTD |
|---|---|---|---|---|
| Regular | 40.00 | -- | 560.00 | 5,040.00 |
| Overtime 1 | 5.00 | -- | 105.00 | 441.00 |
| Piece Rate | -- | 500.00 | 50.00 | 410.00 |
| Total | 45.00 | 500.00 | 715.00 | |

Other:

| Name | Amount | YTD |
|---|---|---|
| Advance | 100.00 | 125.00 |
| Benefits | 6.23 | 56.07 |
| Vac. Accrued | 28.60 | 302.18 |
| Vac. Paid | 0.00 | -- |
| Total | 134.83 | |

Gross Pay 721.23    Withheld -313.95    Net Pay 501.05    Post

Income | Deductions | Taxes | User-Defined Expenses | Entitlements

Deductions:

| Name | Amount | YTD |
|---|---|---|
| RRSP | 200.00 | 200.00 |
| Medical | 6.23 | 56.07 |
| Total | 206.23 | |

Income | Deductions | Taxes | User-Defined Expenses | Entitlements

| | | QPIP |
|---|---|---|
| EI | 12.87 | |
| CPP/QPP | 32.37 | |
| Tax | 62.48 | |
| Tax (Que) | | |

Income | Deductions | Taxes | User-Defined Expenses | Entitlements

Amount per pay period

| Travel Allow | |
|---|---|
| Tuition Fee | 200.00 |
| Medical | 6.23 |

Income | Deductions | Taxes | User-Defined Expenses | Entitlements

The number of hours worked in this pay period: 40.00

| | Days Earned | Days Released |
|---|---|---|
| Vacation | | |
| SickLeave | 0.25 | 1.00 |
| PersonalDays | 0.13 | |

| 02/28/09 (J69) | Debits | Credits | Project |
|---|---|---|---|
| 1240  Advances Receivable | 100.00 | - | |
| 5305  Wages: Cleaning Staff | 693.60 | - | |
| 5310  EI Expense | 18.02 | - | |
| 5320  CPP Expense | 32.37 | - | |
| 5330  WCB Expense | 21.59 | - | |
| 5350  Piece Rate Bonuses | 50.00 | - | |
| 5380  Tuition Fees Expense | 200.00 | - | |
| 5400  Medical Premium Expense | 6.23 | - | |
| 1080     Cash in Bank | - | 501.05 | |
| 2300     Vacation Payable | - | 28.60 | |
| 2310     EI Payable | - | 30.89 | |
| 2320     CPP Payable | - | 64.74 | |
| 2330     Income Tax Payable | - | 62.48 | |
| 2400     Medical Payable - Employee | - | 6.23 | |
| 2410     RRSP Payable | - | 200.00 | |
| 2430     Tuition Fees Payable | - | 200.00 | |
| 2440     Medical Payable - Employer | - | 6.23 | |
| 2460     WCB Payable | - | 21.59 | |
| | 1,121.81 | 1,121.81 | |

## Reversing Entry

Income | Deductions | Taxes | User-Defined Expenses | Entitlements          Period Ending  Feb 28, 2009

Earnings:

| Name | Hours | Pieces | Amount | YTD |
|---|---|---|---|---|
| Regular | -40.00 | -- | -560.00 | 3,920.00 |
| Overtime 1 | -5.00 | -- | -105.00 | 231.00 |
| Piece Rate | -- | -500.00 | -50.00 | 310.00 |
| Total | -45.00 | -500.00 | -715.00 | |

Other:

| Name | Amount | YTD |
|---|---|---|
| Advance | -100.00 | -75.00 |
| Benefits | -6.23 | 43.61 |
| Vac. Accrued | -28.60 | 244.98 |
| Vac. Paid | 0.00 | -- |
| Total | -134.83 | |

Gross Pay  -721.23  Withheld       313.95  Net Pay          -501.05          Post

Income | Deductions | Taxes | User-Defined Expenses | Entitlements

Deductions:

| Name | Amount | YTD |
|---|---|---|
| RRSP | -200.00 | -200.00 |
| Medical | -6.23 | 43.61 |
| Total | -206.23 | |

Income | Deductions | Taxes | User-Defined Expenses | Entitlements

| EI | -12.87 | QPIP |
|---|---|---|
| CPP/QPP | -32.37 | |
| Tax | -62.48 | |
| Tax (Que) | | |

Income | Deductions | Taxes | User-Defined Expenses | Entitlements

Amount per pay period

| Travel Allow | |
|---|---|
| Tuition Fee | -200.00 |
| Medical | -6.23 |

Income | Deductions | Taxes | User-Defined Expenses | Entitlements

The number of hours worked in this pay period:   -40.00

| | Days Earned | Days Released |
|---|---|---|
| Vacation | | |
| SickLeave | 1.00 | |
| PersonalDays | | |

| 02/28/09 (J74) | Debits | Credits | Project |
|---|---|---|---|
| 1080  Cash in Bank | 501.05 | - | |
| 2300  Vacation Payable | 28.60 | - | |
| 2310  EI Payable | 30.89 | - | |
| 2320  CPP Payable | 64.74 | - | |
| 2330  Income Tax Payable | 62.48 | - | |
| 2400  Medical Payable - Employee | 6.23 | - | |
| 2410  RRSP Payable | 200.00 | - | |
| 2430  Tuition Fees Payable | 200.00 | - | |
| 2440  Medical Payable - Employer | 6.23 | - | |
| 2460  WCB Payable | 21.59 | - | |
| 1240     Advances Receivable | - | 100.00 | |
| 5305     Wages: Cleaning Staff | - | 693.60 | |
| 5310     EI Expense | - | 18.02 | |
| 5320     CPP Expense | - | 32.37 | |
| 5330     WCB Expense | - | 21.59 | |
| 5350     Piece Rate Bonuses | - | 50.00 | |
| 5380     Tuition Fees Expense | - | 200.00 | |
| 5400     Medical Premium Expense | - | 6.23 | |
| | 1,121.81 | 1,121.81 | |

### PAYROLL JOURNAL CONTINUED

▶ Click the Taxes tab. Check the amounts for CPP, EI and Tax with the original journal entry because these amounts may be incorrect (the employee may have reached the maximum contribution since the original entry, or may have entered a different tax bracket). Change the amounts to match the original entry if necessary. The Employee Detail Report will provide the amounts entered for each paycheque.

Click the User-Defined Expenses tab. Change the original positive amounts to negative by adding a minus sign.

Click the Entitlements tab. You cannot enter a negative number for days released so you must edit the number of days earned. Click the number in the Days Earned field for the entitlements taken. Add back the number of days released from the original entry. For example, change 0.5 to 1.5 if 1 day was taken.

Repeat the allocation with the original percentages.

Remember to click the Calculate Taxes Automatically button before you make the correct payroll entry.

The year-to-date balances will be restored.

You can use the Adjust Cheque option or Reverse Cheque instead to reverse and correct the Payroll Journal entry (see page 287 and page 290). Using the reverse cheque approach may be safer, as payroll transactions are complex.

**NOTES**
When you are reversing a direct deposit entry, you must confirm that a negative amount is entered as the net deposit.
Click Yes to continue.

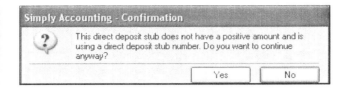

## ITEM ASSEMBLY JOURNAL

Re-enter the assembly as you did originally.

Type a minus sign in front of each quantity in the Qty field in both the Assembly Components and Assembled Items sections.

Also type a minus sign in front of the amount for Additional Costs.

## ITEM ASSEMBLY JOURNAL: Original Entry

**Assembly Components**

| Item | Qty | Unit | Description | Unit Cost | Amount |
|------|-----|------|-------------|-----------|--------|
| T110 | 20 | Each | P195/65R16 Tires | 55.00 | 1,100.00 |
| W107 | 20 | Each | Chrome-Steel R16 Wheels | 40.00 | 800.00 |
| | | | Additional Costs | | 250.00 |
| | | | Total | | 2,150.00 |

**Assembled Items**

| Item | Qty | Unit | Description | Unit Cost | Amount |
|------|-----|------|-------------|-----------|--------|
| WHP1 | 5 | pkg | Tires/Wheels/Winter Pkg | 430.00 | 2,150.00 |
| | | | Total | | 2,150.00 |

| 12/31/09 (J77) | Debits | Credits | Division |
|----------------|--------|---------|----------|
| 1420 Winter-Holiday Tire Packages | 2,150.00 | - | |
| 1360 Wheels | - | 800.00 | |
| 1400 Winter Tires | - | 1,100.00 | |
| 5045 Assembly Costs | - | 250.00 | |
| | 2,150.00 | 2,150.00 | |

## Reversing Entry

**Assembly Components**

| Item | Qty | Unit | Description | Unit Cost | Amount |
|------|-----|------|-------------|-----------|--------|
| T110 | -20 | Each | P195/65R16 Tires | 55.00 | -1,100.00 |
| W107 | -20 | Each | Chrome-Steel R16 Wheels | 40.00 | -800.00 |
| | | | Additional Costs | | -250.00 |
| | | | Total | | -2,150.00 |

**Assembled Items**

| Item | Qty | Unit | Description | Unit Cost | Amount |
|------|-----|------|-------------|-----------|--------|
| WHP1 | -5 | pkg | Tires/Wheels/Winter Pkg | 430.00 | -2,150.00 |
| | | | Total | | -2,150.00 |

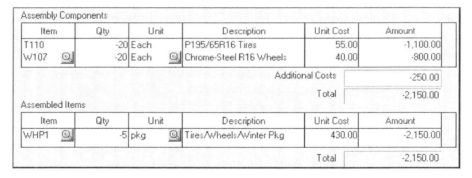

| 12/31/09 (J79) | Debits | Credits | Division |
|----------------|--------|---------|----------|
| 1360 Wheels | 800.00 | - | |
| 1400 Winter Tires | 1,100.00 | - | |
| 5045 Assembly Costs | 250.00 | - | |
| 1420 Winter-Holiday Tire Packages | - | 2,150.00 | |
| | 2,150.00 | 2,150.00 | |

## BILL OF MATERIALS JOURNAL: Original Entry

| Items to Build | | | | |
|---|---|---|---|---|
| Item | Unit | Description | Quantity to build | |
| AP100 | Package | Promotional Fitness Package | 2 | |

| 08/01/09 (J1) | Debits | Credits | Project |
|---|---|---|---|
| 1510 Promotions | 192.00 | - | |
| 1520 Accessories | - | 192.00 | |
| | 192.00 | 192.00 | |

## Reversing Entry

| Items to Build | | | | |
|---|---|---|---|---|
| Item | Unit | Description | Quantity to build | |
| AP100 | Package | Promotional Fitness Package | -2 | |

| 08/01/09 (J5) | Debits | Credits | Project |
|---|---|---|---|
| 1520 Accessories | 192.00 | - | |
| 1510 Promotions | - | 192.00 | |
| | 192.00 | 192.00 | |

## ADJUSTMENTS JOURNAL: Original Entry

| Item | Qty | Unit | Description | Unit Cost | Amount | Acct | Allo | |
|---|---|---|---|---|---|---|---|---|
| T108 🔍 | -2 | Each 🔍 | P185/60R15 Tires | 50.00 | -100.00 | 5100 Inve 🔍 | √ | |
| | | | | Total | -100.00 | | | |

| 12/31/09 (J79) | Debits | Credits | Division |
|---|---|---|---|
| 5100 Inventory Adjustment | 100.00 | - | |
|     - Sales Division | | | 100.00 |
| 1400 Winter Tires | - | 100.00 | |
| | 100.00 | 100.00 | |

## Reversing Entry

| Item | Qty | Unit | Description | Unit Cost | Amount | Acct | Allo | |
|---|---|---|---|---|---|---|---|---|
| T108 | 2 | Each | P185/60R15 Tires | 50.00 | 100.00 | 5100 Inventc | √ | |
| | | | | Total | 100.00 | | | |

| 12/31/09 (J80) | Debits | Credits | Division |
|---|---|---|---|
| 1400 Winter Tires | 100.00 | - | |
| 5100 Inventory Adjustment | - | 100.00 | |
|     - Sales Division | | | -100.00 |
| | 100.00 | 100.00 | |

---

**BILL OF MATERIALS JOURNAL**

Change the sign for the quantity in the Quantity To Build field (positive to negative or negative to positive).

Notice that the journal entries are exactly the same as those for the Item Assembly Journal transactions.

**ADJUSTMENTS JOURNAL**

Change the sign for the quantity in the Qty field (positive to negative or negative to positive).

Repeat the allocation using the original percentages.

# Working in Multi-User Mode

## WORKING IN MULTI-USER MODE

The Pro version is available in multi- and single-user versions. The Student Pro and Basic versions are both single-user versions of the program.

In multi-user mode, several people can access and work with a data file at the same time. Some features and functions are not available in multi-user mode. These restrictions are described in the text whenever they apply. Access to some aspects of the program may be restricted to the system administrator (sysadmin).

### Accessing Data Files

The Pro version allows several users to access the data files at the same time, with or without passwords. When no users and passwords are set up for a data file, access to the file is the same for multi- and single-user mode. The data file opens in single-user mode. Once the data file is open, you can switch to multi-user mode from the File menu.

If you try to open a data file that is currently used by another user in single-user mode, you will see the following error message:

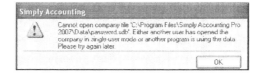

**Click** **OK** to close the message.

Only one person at a time can work with a data file in single-user mode, so you must switch the status of the open file to multi-user.

**Choose** the **File menu** and **click Switch To Multi-User Mode**.

If you have not entered users, the Add Users wizard will begin (see the instructions in Appendix G, page A-71 on the Student CD-ROM). Otherwise, you will see the following warning:

**Click** **Yes** to proceed.

**WARNING!**
Be sure to finish working with the open journals and ledgers before closing all the open windows.

No changes are apparent in the Home window, but some menu options are dimmed because they are not available in multi-user mode. All Refresh tools in the ledger and journal windows will be available and no longer dimmed.

If users and passwords have been set up for the program, you will see the following screen when you open the data file:

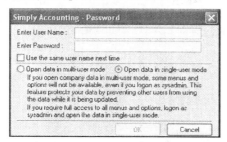

Enter your user name and password; choose whether you want to work in single-user or multi-user mode and then click OK. Passwords are case-sensitive. That is, you must type the password in upper- or lower-case letters, exactly as the password was created initially. For more information on passwords, refer to Appendix G on the Student CD-ROM.

If another user is already working with the data file when you try to access it in single-user mode, you will see the following warning:

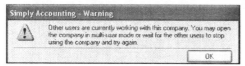

You must open the data file in multi-user mode, wait until the other users have finished or, if only one person is using the file, switch that user's file to multi-user mode.

> **Click**    **OK** to return to the Select Company window.

To switch to single-user mode at any time:

> **Choose** the **File menu** and **click Switch To Single-User Mode**.

If other users are currently using the file, you will see the following warning:

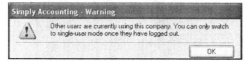

> **Click**    **OK** to return to the Home window.

If you are working in multi-user mode, your user name and "Multi-user" will appear in the status bar as shown:

When you close a data file in multi-user mode, you will see the following closing message about backups:

Before making a backup, you must switch to single-user mode. If other users are still working with the data file, close the file without making a backup.

> **Click**    **Yes** to close the file.

# Refreshing Data in Multi-User Mode

In multi-user mode, different users can work with and modify the same data file at the same time. Therefore, the program allows you to automatically refresh the data set with changes made by other users or to refresh the data set only when the Refresh option is selected. All ledger, journal and report windows include Refresh tools that allow you to update the data periodically. If you want the program to update the data continually, you can change this preference setting for individual users.

**Choose** the **Setup menu**, then **choose User Preferences** and **click Options**:

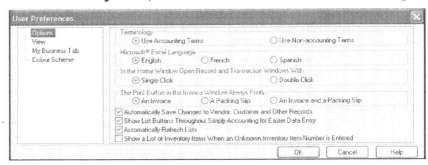

**Click** **Automatically Refresh Lists** and **click OK** to save the change.

## Refresh Tools

All journals have the **Refresh Lists** tool in the tool bar . This tool applies to the multi-user mode — different users use, access and modify the company data files simultaneously. Clicking the Refresh Lists tool ensures that you use the most recent version of the data set — the one that exists after all changes from all users have been applied.

All report windows include the **Refresh Report** tool icon . In multi-user mode, the journal entry number is omitted from the journal display (different users may be creating journal entries at the same time so the number is not known for certain until after posting).

The **Refresh Invoices** tool in the Payments and Receipts journals ensures that the list of outstanding invoices for a vendor or customer is the current one, after applying the changes made by other users.

The **Refresh Data** tool in the icon windows looks the same as the Refresh Report icon and serves the same purpose, updating accounts (vendors, customers, employees or inventory) with changes made by other users. It appears just before the Select A Report tool in all ledger icon windows. The icon is dimmed in single-user mode and when you are creating a new ledger record.

In ledger windows, the **Refresh Record tool** updates the ledger record with changes made by other users. The tool is located on the Select account line in the ledger and looks the same as the Refresh Report tool.

# "AS IS" LICENSE AGREEMENT AND LIMITED WARRANTY

READ THIS LICENSE CAREFULLY BEFORE OPENING THIS PACKAGE. BY OPENING THIS PACKAGE, YOU ARE AGREEING TO THE TERMS AND CONDITIONS OF THIS LICENSE. IF YOU DO NOT AGREE, DO NOT OPEN THE PACKAGE. PROMPTLY RETURN THE UNOPENED PACKAGE AND ALL ACCOMPANYING ITEMS TO THE PLACE YOU OBTAINED THEM. THESE TERMS APPLY TO ALL LICENSED SOFTWARE ON THE DISK EXCEPT THAT THE TERMS FOR USE OF ANY SHAREWARE OR FREEWARE ON THE DISKETTES ARE AS SET FORTH IN THE ELECTRONIC LICENSE LOCATED ON THE DISK:

1. GRANT OF LICENSE and OWNERSHIP: The enclosed computer programs and any data ("Software") are licensed, not sold, to you by Pearson Canada Inc. ("We" or the "Company") in consideration of your adoption of the accompanying Company textbooks and/or other materials, and your agreement to these terms. You own only the disk(s) but we and/or our licensors own the Software itself. This license allows instructors and students enrolled in the course using the Company textbook that accompanies this Software (the "Course") to use and display the enclosed copy of the Software for academic use only, so long as you comply with the terms of this Agreement. You may make one copy for back up only. We reserve any rights not granted to you.

2. USE RESTRICTIONS: You may not sell or license copies of the Software or the Documentation to others. You may not transfer, distribute or make available the Software or the Documentation, except to instructors and students in your school who are users of the adopted Company textbook that accompanies this Software in connection with the course for which the textbook was adopted. You may not reverse engineer, disassemble, decompile, modify, adapt, translate or create derivative works based on the Software or the Documentation. You may be held legally responsible for any copying or copyright infringement that is caused by your failure to abide by the terms of these restrictions.

3. TERMINATION: This license is effective until terminated. This license will terminate automatically without notice from the Company if you fail to comply with any provisions or limitations of this license. Upon termination, you shall destroy the Documentation and all copies of the Software. All provisions of this Agreement as to limitation and disclaimer of warranties, limitation of liability, remedies or damages, and our ownership rights shall survive termination.

4. DISCLAIMER OF WARRANTY: THE COMPANY AND ITS LICENSORS MAKE NO WARRANTIES ABOUT THE SOFTWARE, WHICH IS PROVIDED "AS-IS." IF THE DISK IS DEFECTIVE IN MATERIALS OR WORKMANSHIP, YOUR ONLY REMEDY IS TO RETURN IT TO THE COMPANY WITHIN 30 DAYS FOR REPLACEMENT UNLESS THE COMPANY DETERMINES IN GOOD FAITH THAT THE DISK HAS BEEN MISUSED OR IMPROPERLY INSTALLED, REPAIRED, ALTERED OR DAMAGED. THE COMPANY DISCLAIMS ALL WARRANTIES, EXPRESS OR IMPLIED, INCLUDING WITHOUT LIMITATION, THE IMPLIED WARRANTIES OF MERCHANTABILITY AND FITNESS FOR A PARTICULAR PURPOSE. THE COMPANY DOES NOT WARRANT, GUARANTEE OR MAKE ANY REPRESENTATION REGARDING THE ACCURACY, RELIABILITY, CURRENTNESS, USE, OR RESULTS OF USE, OF THE SOFTWARE.

5. LIMITATION OF REMEDIES AND DAMAGES:  IN NO EVENT, SHALL THE COMPANY OR ITS EMPLOYEES, AGENTS, LICENSORS OR CONTRACTORS BE LIABLE FOR ANY INCIDENTAL, INDIRECT, SPECIAL OR CONSEQUENTIAL DAMAGES ARISING OUT OF OR IN CONNECTION WITH THIS LICENSE OR THE SOFTWARE, INCLUDING, WITHOUT LIMITATION, LOSS OF USE, LOSS OF DATA, LOSS OF INCOME OR PROFIT, OR OTHER LOSSES SUSTAINED AS A RESULT OF INJURY TO ANY PERSON, OR LOSS OF OR DAMAGE TO PROPERTY, OR CLAIMS OF THIRD PARTIES, EVEN IF THE COMPANY OR AN AUTHORIZED REPRESENTATIVE OF THE COMPANY HAS BEEN ADVISED OF THE POSSIBILITY OF SUCH DAMAGES. SOME JURISDICTIONS DO NOT ALLOW THE LIMITATION OF DAMAGES IN CERTAIN CIRCUMSTANCES, SO THE ABOVE LIMITATIONS MAY NOT ALWAYS APPLY.

6. GENERAL:  THIS AGREEMENT SHALL BE CONSTRUED AND INTERPRETED ACCORDING TO THE LAWS OF THE PROVINCE OF ONTARIO. This Agreement is the complete and exclusive statement of the agreement between you and the Company and supersedes all proposals, prior agreements, oral or written, and any other communications between you and the company or any of its representatives relating to the subject matter.

Should you have any questions concerning this agreement or if you wish to contact the Company for any reason, please contact in writing: Permissions, Pearson Education Canada, a division of Pearson Canada Inc., 26 Prince Andrew Place, Toronto, Ontario M3C 2T8.